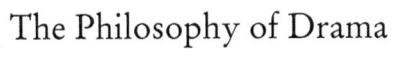

THE PHILOSOPHY OF DRAMA

JÓZEF TISCHNER

Translated by Artur Rosman

Foreword by Cyril O'Regan

University of Notre Dame Press
Notre Dame, Indiana

University of Notre Dame Press
Notre Dame, Indiana 46556
undpress.nd.edu

All Rights Reserved

Copyright © 2024 by Kazimierz Tischner & Marian Tischner

Published in the United States of America

Copyright © by Kazimierz Tischner & Marian Tischner
This translation is published by arrangement with Społeczny Instytut
Wydawniczy Znak Sp. z o.o., Kraków, Poland.

 NATIONAL PROGRAMME
FOR THE DEVELOPMENT OF HUMANITIES

This publication was supported by a grant from the National Programme
for the Development of Humanities in Poland, financed by the Polish
Ministry of Education and Science (project no. 3aH 15 0169 83), and
prepared in collaboration with The Tischner Institute (Krakow).

Library of Congress Control Number: 2024941390

ISBN: 978-0-268-20883-7 (Hardback)
ISBN: 978-0-268-20885-1 (WebPDF)
ISBN: 978-0-268-20886-8 (Epub3)

CONTENTS

Foreword, by Cyril O'Regan   vii
Translator's Preface   xv
Introduction   xix

CHAPTER 1	The Event of the Encounter	1
CHAPTER 2	The Answer to the Question, That Is, Reciprocity	46
CHAPTER 3	Going Astray	62
CHAPTER 4	Space for Being-with the Other	191
CHAPTER 5	The Last Word of the Drama	211

Notes   221
Name Index   227
Extended Table of Contents   229

FOREWORD

Cyril O'Regan

As a philosophical thinker, Józef Tischner (1931–2000) is not a household name in the West in the way that critical theorists such as Adorno and Habermas, postmodern thinkers such as Derrida, Foucault, and Marion, and phenomenologists such as Husserl, Heidegger, and Merleau Ponty are. To the extent to which Tischner's name has even marginal visibility, it tends to be in the context of the Solidarity movement, with respect to which he was the unofficial chaplain and theoretician, as well as being an independent thinker working on themes recognizable to readers of John Paul II. While this is regrettable, it is also understandable given the repression of independent thought in Eastern Europe that extended even to reflection on Marxism itself.

That Eastern intellectuals are now somewhat more visible, or at least to an extent gaining traction, is at once a reflection of the end of the Cold War era, but also perhaps the growing ennui in the West regarding the fundamental philosophical options that appear to go along three tracks: the track of praxis and critical intervention, the track of consciousness, and the track of language, all three of which seem to have run their course. While, undoubtedly, these tracks converge in a number of thinkers, the general sense is that the options are not only relatively autonomous and proceed to reproduce themselves, but also that increasingly minute differences are elevated as being philosophically significant. The problem is not simply the lack of synthesis nor the autotelic nature of the discourses, but also—and perhaps fundamentally—the lack of moral seriousness with which even critical thought is vested as indicated by the various levels of irony, sophistication, and esotericism that are essential to these discourses as productive of an intellectual elite. In any event, there is a general sense of jadedness and more than a little whiff of decadence in the virtue signalizing and intellectual posturing. In this case, Eastern European thinkers—whether writers or philosophers, whether post-Marxist or Christian—come across as more serious in that their thought is more exoteric and personally more costly and dangerous, as well as being more morally exigent in speaking to whom we are and can be and how we must act.

It can be stated with some confidence that Józef Tischner belongs among the leading group of Mitteleuropa intellectuals, inheritors equally of phenomenology—though interested in giving it both an ethical and social inflection—and the Catholic tradition of reflection on the nature of the embodied communal subject, who are constituted by the search for meaning, value, and truth and who refuse to be the children of time, power, and violence that has been the face of twentieth century Europe. For Tischner and for other East European thinkers cognizant of the failed Soviet experiment, philosophy is an urgent activity that can neither be siloed in the university nor permitted to be merely the contingent effect of a praxis.

In this respect Tischner has much in common with the Czech philosopher Jan Patočka (1907–1977), who attempted to uncover the phenomenological and classical basis of European culture distended by the Enlightenment and subverted by Marxist theory and practice. Of course, this typification of Tischner is not intended to suggest that he is self-consciously a follower of the Czech thinker. Patočka is not the Christian thinker that Tischner is—who as a priest attended to the spiritual welfare of the overwhelmingly Catholic population of the Solidarity movement. As a philosopher, Tischner can set aside his Christian convictions, but never as systematically as Patočka for whom Socrates is foundational for the search for truth and justice and for the "care of the soul" (*péče o duši*). For Tischner, Catholic social teaching is a reliable inheritance. Even more, however, there is the figure of Christ in the New Testament, and more specifically the mandate of love of "neighbor" and the parable of the Good Samaritan.

Aside from their close personal relationship, there can be no denying that Tischner and Wojtyła had similar intellectual trajectories, even if ultimately they served profoundly different cultural and institutional roles. Both have as their heritage the various Polish philosophical attempts to harmonize phenomenology and magisterial Catholic tradition. Wojtyła is an example of this tradition at a remove, appreciative of phenomenology's turn to the things themselves, though wary of Husserl's idealism, even as the most eminent Polish phenomenologist, Roman Ingarden, Tischner's former professor, was. More positively and constructively, the man who would become Pope John Paul II invested in the elaboration of a subjectivity considered to be incarnate in a community and thus already beyond the aporia of intersubjectivity that addled Husserl and preoccupied his followers, and was exercised by the notion of values that are not simply subjective preferences but are disclosures of the deep core of reality convertible with the good.

For Wojtyła, Max Scheler (1874–1928) pointed to a connecting tissue between phenomenology and the classical philosophical tradition by daring to articulate a phenomenology of value, even if he subverted the telos of such an inquiry by ruling out beforehand any and all ontological implications of the values that were phenomenologically unearthed and exposed. The two crucial texts of Wojtyła in which the synthesis between phenomenology and Catholic thought is enacted are *Love and Responsibility* (1960) and *Person and Act* (1969). In both of these texts rather than metaphysics being suspended, it is amplified respectively in accounts of conscience as the illuminating feature of selves that are tasked with the discernment of truth and goodness and corresponding action in an ambiguous world and a philosophical anthropology in which the person is ineluctable, while at the same time the community is not a secondary phenomenon constituted by free association. It is difficult to deny in the case of Wojtyła that the idea of the church influenced the more general sense of the privilege of community, even if it did not constitute it.

Tischner was a second-generation representative of a school that over the years had tended to privilege Aquinas as the main Catholic conversation partner with phenomenology. In contrast to Wojtyła, however, Tischner on the one hand had a somewhat looser and critical affiliation to Aquinas and a greater appreciation for the more existential and dramatic forms of Western thought that emphasized the relentless searching that constitutes the truly human life and is a mark of all genuine thinking, and on the other a less ecclesiastical view of solidarity. In addition to these two marks of distinction between these two major Polish thinkers, one might point to Tischner's more developed sense of responding to the signs of the time with a greater sense of philosophical elasticity and the need for conceptual improvisation beyond the reception of received philosophical categories, all the while taking steps to avoid the traps of the ideologies of historicism and Marxist views of praxis that subverted claims to truth.

This bore fruit also in developing an account of solidarity that was extra-ecclesial and that proved to be a wellspring of value independent of the institutional church. Thus, while it helps somwhat to situate Tischner as a philosophical thinker by drawing some attention to overlaps with Pope John Paul II, it would be a mistake to equate them. While Tischner's thought is similar in focus to the thought of John Paul II, it cannot be reduced to it. It has its own integrity and more nearly than the work of John Paul II occupies a kind of liminal space between magisterial Catholic thought and the searching and self-understanding of human beings in the modern world who despite the political and social circumstances have found a way to recognize themselves and others, and moreover themselves through these given others for whom they experience a profound sense of responsibility.

The text translated here, *Filozofia dramatu* (1989), is a late text by Tischner and, arguably, his most important, even if his book on solidarity has proved to be his most influential. *The Philosophy of Drama* articulates a phenomenology of values and a metaphysics of the good (*agathology*). Here we notice that Tischner combines, as John Paul II does, what Max Scheler in his articulation of axiology kept apart. Tischner's reflection on the good as objectively real represents the realization of the *telos* of a phenomenology of values that Scheler would keep hermetically sealed from the ontology of the good. If the central category in what is at once a Christian and philosophical anthropology is that of drama, Tischner supplements the category with illuminating subaltern categories such as scene, mask, and curtain.

The drama is the drama of persons in history, called to develop values in freedom and take responsibility for what is disclosed about themselves, others, and their historical community in thought and action. In short, persons—contingently but systemically—are put in situations that call for witness and testimony. This in particular is the pathos of all intellectuals in central Europe and Russia who resist doctrinaire Marxism and dare to cut against the grain of inevitable historical development. It was the fate of the Russian poet Osip Mandelstam (1891–1938) and his wife Nazezhda Mandelstam (1899–1980), of later

Russian writers such as Alexander Solzhenitsyn (1918–2004) and Joseph Brodsky (1940–1996), of the Polish-Lithuanian poet Czesław Miłosz (1911–2004), and belatedly the obligation of Polish Catholic intellectuals, who are bearers of the great tradition of a form of freedom defined by responsibility for human beings before God.

 No surprise then that in addition to retrieving, while also refiguring, Scheler's phenomenology of values in *Philosophy of Drama*, Tischner is in conversation with two other religiously disposed versions of phenomenology. The first is the ethically torqued phenomenology of Emmanuel Levinas (1906–1995) for whom the idealism of Husserl represents a betrayal of phenomenology's dedicated attention to phenomenal reality that gives itself and crucially the original givenness of other selves. The face of the other is not only always given but always given as absolute: the other is irreplaceably my responsibility in the here and now. The other influence from the heart of phenomenology is that of Paul Ricoeur, especially the Ricoeur (1913–2005) who sees that all seeing and acting occurs in an arena marked by confusion, compromise, and temptation. The self that sees and acts is everywhere marked by competing and contradictory aspirations and incentives. That Levinas, for whom the ethics of responsibility for the concrete other before me is first philosophy, and Ricoeur, who thinks of the self as being the existential tension between the affirmation of transcendent value and the codification of immanence, are privileged in Tischner's thought does not mean that other thinkers such as Husserl, Heidegger, and Hegel are cast aside. It does mean, however, that Tischner's engagement with them is far more critical than it is with respect to Levinas, Ricoeur, and even Scheler, who give Catholic thought something to build on in its efforts to articulate a Christian humanism and a humanistic Christianity that will speak to the modern age.

 If the drama of which Tischner speaks is internal in that it applies to all persons, it is also other-related in two distinct but intervolved ways. It is a drama concerning the ways in which we move toward or away from God and away from or toward other enfleshed, historically shaped, and damaged human beings whom we can aid or harm. With regard to God, while God may not be recognized as an actor in the drama of our lives, to the degree that we find hope in the most appalling of circumstances, and live in the mode of hope against hope, God in his apparent absence is at least intimated. For Tischner the good intersects history at a right angle; it interrupts its economies of untruth and violence—if only fleetingly and too occasionally. This is a view Tischner shares with Patočka, who is the mid-century Eastern European phenomenologist who articulates an agathology and who invokes the good as *epekeina tes ousias*, as beyond being, but also beyond concept and precept.

Patočka's Plato is a dynamic existential Plato of the inquiring self's search for truth and goodness and not the formalist-essentialist epistemologist of the Western philosophical tradition. Patočka's profile of Plato bears a distinct family resemblance to the Levinas of *Totality and Infinity*. And, interestingly, it also bears an elective affinity with other influential configurations of the founding philosopher of the West, for example, the Plato of Iris Murdoch in the *Sovereignty of the Good*, the Plato of Eric Voegelin in *Order and History*, and the Plato of William Desmond's *Ethics and the Between*. Yet, Tischner's transcendent Good is personal in a way that Patočka's is not and that the good of the *Republic* is not. God is the Good as God is the fullness of reality and its unstinting and sustaining giver. God is the good that as he loves human beings into existence also makes their flourishing impossible without benevolent and just relations with others and an opening to the One who creates and redeems.

Though Patočka has a sense of the situated character of human being caught in the tension between immanence and transcendence, the dramatic character of human existence is exacerbated in Tischner when he specifies further the drama of our individual and communal lives, and in particular draws attention to each person living on the razor's edge betwixt and between heaven and hell. In a sense, Tischner exceeds Patočka by essentially pressing an apocalyptic script that bespeaks the threat to humanity permanently at risk of being drowned in the blood and bile of history and its economy of lying and compromise. In *The Philosophy of Drama* Tischner avails of the novels of Dostoevsky (1821–1881) to present the moment of fundamental decision in which one either is living testimony to the good or a colluder with evil. As Tischner takes on board Dostoevsky's existential anthropology, he sees their real-life consequence in modernity and the threat to freedom and responsibility.

Again, if only in the margins, he affirms the force of Dostoevsky's anatomy of modernity as the choice between genuine freedom and its counterfeits. In one sense, Dostoevsky is a stand-alone influence in *The Philosophy of Drama*, one who gives us some hope that in modernity we can look into the abyss and come out on the other side. In another sense, Dostoevsky is the Augustine of the modern age, tasked with recharging Augustine's dramatic anthropology and exacerbating its apocalyptic charge on the level of history and politics, in the process elevating the eschatological judgment rendered by the personal God over a history that would arrogate to itself the prerogatives of the last judgment.

While *The Philosophy of Drama* is not Tischner's best known text in the West, there is general scholarly agreement that it represents the most mature statement of his personalist philosophy that soberly—if not somberly—takes the measure of the world as the hindrance to the good that human beings would do but because of circumstances, blindness, cowardice, and complicity in evil often fail to do. Still, as Michał Łuczewski argues, in his later work Tischner also shows how the fall of the Berlin Wall and the success of Solidarity could confuse and lead even such an intrinsically Augustinian thinker to entertain the view that his phenomenology of values and ontology of the Good had at that historical moment of release become unnecessary precisely because of their apparent realization in history, not recognizing (as Augustine did) the ability of power to morph and take on different forms and disguises, capitalism as well as communism, social democracy as well as socialism. Happily, Tischner's dalliance with what amounts to a view of the end of history as the end of the struggle between good and evil, à la Francis Fukuyama, was temporary. In due course, it yielded to the view that what appeared to be a kairotic moment was an object of critical analysis and moral measurement.

For the theologically literate reader it is almost impossible to read *The Philosophy of Drama* without thinking of Hans Urs von Balthasar's almost contemporary theological reflection on drama in *Theo-Drama*. Tischner does not depend in any way on the work of the great Swiss Catholic theologian, having come to know Balthasar's work only after he had written his own text. He did, however, greatly appreciate Balthasar's work and opined that an engagement with it would have made his own philosophical reflection on drama richer. Nonetheless, despite the lack of genetic dependence, their respective dramatic enterprises bear on each other. Not only in both cases is the notion of person connected with *persona* or mask, but beyond the notion of drama as aporia in need of resolution, each in his own way develops subaltern categories—in the case of Tischner the categories of scene and curtain, and in the case of Balthasar the categories of central protagonist (Christ), playwright (Father), and director (Holy Spirit). Crucially, both focus the individual person and community on the apocalyptic razor's edge of decision in which the option is made for the good God and the gift of his world or for the forces of destruction and nihilation.

Relatedly, one finds in both accounts an operative Augustinian distinction between the city of God and the city of man, even if the task for human beings is to imprint as far as possible the kingdom of God in the kingdom of man that rests on intra-worldly incentives. Another salient overlap is how both authors avail of dialogical thinkers such as Ebner, Buber, and Rosenzweig to fill out their dramatic theory and gain traction with regard to a mode of normative relationality that can function critically with respect both to the various collectivisms and to the individualisms of the modern era. Yet, the differences stand out just as prominently.

First, as is obvious from Balthasar's references to Christ, the Father, and the Holy Spirit, Balthasar's reflection on drama is explicitly theological in a way that Tischner's reflection is not, though admittedly the boundaries between the philosophical and theological in Tischner are somewhat porous, as they are also in the work of John Paul II. Indeed, Balthasar's theodramatic theory is not only theological through and through, but also enacts a form of speculative theology that in a sense pierces the veil between the world to allow a vision of the tri-personal God who creates the world and human beings in freedom and love and invites a correlative response that is enacted in our everyday dealings with the world and each other. It is also the case that in Balthasar's elaboration of theodrama the advocacy of apocalyptic rendering of drama is more self-conscious and the contrast between the city of God and city of man more self-conscious.

TRANSLATOR'S PREFACE

The labor of translation frequently feels like the lonely quest of what Charles Taylor called a "buffered self." At the end of the ordeal, the translator, like any writer, only remembers the horror of the blank page staring back mercilessly. But, unlike a conventional writer, the translator's horrors are multiplied by the mocking presence of a page filled with insights, dexterous turns of phrase, and nearly untranslatable idioms in a relatively foreign language—Polish, in the case of Józef Tischner's *Filozofia dramatu*.

Then comes the heavy lifting of learning the book's unique terminology as one translates. The process, a little like the flight of Minerva, always works in reverse. Frustratingly, you only approach a relatively adequate knowledge of the book's unique vocabulary *at the end* of the translation. Then you backtrack and correct all the things you got wrong at the end. You do this several times . . . and then you do it again, and again, and so on.

Tischner's most important contribution to twentieth-century philosophy, *The Philosophy of Drama*—an engagement with and critique of the major strands of the phenomenological tradition—demythologizes this myth of the authorial buffered self, or of a buffered self of any kind. This book—whose hard-won insights come not only from grappling with Heidegger, Levinas, Hegel, and Dostoevsky, but also from active and high-profile participation in the Solidarity movement during Poland's martial law and parish work—refuses to be yet another text about texts from the opening paragraph. It is porous to the drama of everyday life from the get-go, which, with apologies to Derrida, occurs outside the text. This porosity makes its insights useful for understanding Solidarity, the fall of Communist

Poland, the brief moment in the 90s when we thought we had left history, and whatever the present moment might be for the reader.

I also chose not to correct Tischner's apparent mix-up of murder (*morderstwo*) with homicide (*zabójstwo*). Generally, murder is intentional and interested but homicide tends not to be (there are some grey areas); Tischner reverses the intentionalities of these two concepts throughout most of the book. I should also point out the ambiguous role of "desire" in the lexicon Tischner sets up. It has a more positive valence in the first chapter on Lévinas, while it has a negative valence in the discussion of Hegel in chapter 3. I figured it would be salutary for English readers of the book to go astray with Tischner, wrestle with the text, just as Polish readers have done.

The drama of this specific translation begins with Fr. Tischner's nephew, Łukasz Tischner, who generously recommended, while I was studying with him at the Jagiellonian on a study abroad, that the Tischner Institute journal, *Thinking in Values*, consider taking me on as a translator. That's where I first cut my teeth as a translator from the Polish. Further thanks are due to him, the Tischner family, and Społeczny Instytut Wydawniczy Znak publishers for, later on in the process, giving us permission to translate this important book.

Special thanks are due to the Tischner Institute's director, Zbigniew Stawrowski, who not only applied for the generous funding for the translation from the Polish Ministry of Science and Higher Education but also successfully navigated the several changes to my and my family's lifeworld involving the home, workplace, maybe not so much the temple, but (alas!) also the cemetery.

My beloved wife, Monika, and our four kids (Dominik, Weronika, Hannah, and Joseph), are perhaps the only people who have successfully navigated more difficulties during this extended process. Monika made numerous contributions to the translation by answering my constant off-the-cuff questions about word choices, especially idiomatic expressions. She helped so much that I would not even know how to single out everything she made better (as in the rest of life).

Adam Workowski and Troy Kassien substantially contributed to the final shape of the text by reading through earlier drafts of the translation. Paweł Rojek kindly referenced large swaths of the text last-minute and adroitly resolved a crux that had been a thorn in my side for years.

I would like to thank Paweł, Cyril O'Regan (also for his foreword and unflagging support), and Gerald Beyer for being the manuscript's readers for the press. I would like to single out Professor Beyer for taking the time to compare the text with the Polish original. I adopted most of his suggestions, and he also caught a few outright errors. Ultimately, I did not go with more gender-inclusive language in order to be true to the original text, the gendering of Polish, and to not make the author seem like he was aware of important matters that came to the fore long after he wrote the text (even later in his own homeland).

All of this would not have come to fruition had I not joined the University of Notre Dame's McGrath Institute for Church Life some seven years ago at the behest of John Cavadini, Brett Robinson, and Tim O'Malley. Special thanks are due to my dear friend Jay Martin who was also part of that process and made sure that I would know what's what on campus once I arrived.

My mentors at the University of Washington's Comparative Literature department (no longer in existence; may it live again!) prepared me for this project long before it became a reality. Thank you, Cynthia Steele, for giving me another chance when you had no reason to do so; Herbert Blau, for the determination to get through it all; Doug Collins, for initiating me into the mysteries of the theological turn in French philosophy; Eugene Webb, for encouraging charitable reading; and Leroy Searle, for putting all of these things together and making sure I didn't leave ABD (the most likely outcome). My gratitude also goes out to Artur Grabowski for volunteering to teach me the history of Polish literature and thought during my study abroad in Kraków.

Last, but not least, I would like to thank the staff at the University of Notre Dame Press for all your help on this project and the many others I've undertaken with you through *Church Life Journal*. There are just too many people to list. You've been tremendous. I would like to single out Director Stephen Wrinn for being a real mensch, not just helping me navigate through this book project, but just helping me.

My apologies if I've forgotten to mention anyone. This translation was an apprenticeship in interpersonal philosophy. The collaboration goes so deep that I sometimes cannot remember where the help of Good Samaritans ends and my work begins.

INTRODUCTION

One ought to start reflecting on the philosophy of the human drama by defining the word *drama*. At any rate, this is how the literary theory of drama usually begins. It emerges from the analysis of the Greek word and slowly, through associations and distinctions, designates the scope of possible uses for the word. The main concern here is maintaining a clear boundary of meanings: the word should not blend into other words, it should not shine with their glow. However, this way of proceeding raises the suspicion that the most important goal in the philosophy of human drama is achieving conceptual clarity. However, this goal, no matter how lofty, is nonetheless a secondary goal. The main goal is giving back to the word "drama" its proper gravity. This can only be accomplished by indicating the content to which this word either directly or indirectly aims with its intention. One must use the word as a bridge to things. One must ask, Toward what reality does this word point? Whatever else one might say, it points toward human life. Understanding drama is understanding that man is a dramatic being. We shall then restore the proper meaning to the concept of drama by conducting a step-by-step elucidation of human existence as a dramatic existence.

To be a dramatic being means living through a given time surrounded by other people while having the earth under one's feet as the stage. Man would not be a dramatic being if not for these three factors: an *opening onto other people*, an opening onto the *stage* of the drama, and an opening onto the *flow of time*. Each one of these factors requires a thorough discussion. We will initially say only what is necessary, putting aside a deeper analysis for later.

Typically, attention is first given to *time*. One speaks about a specific variety of time: dramatic time. Dramatic time is not the objective time of natural science in which the physical and chemical changes of the micro- and macrocosm take place. It is also not the time of animate nature in which the life of plants and animals, from birth to death, takes place. It is also not the time of *internal time consciousness* in the sense given to it by Edmund Husserl. To put it most concisely, one ought to say that: it is the time that goes on *between us* as participants of one and the same drama. Dramatic time ties me to you, you to me, and ties us to the stage where our drama takes place. The temporal tie has some past, lasts in the present, and strives toward the future. Dramatic time is neither, strictly speaking, in me nor in you, but it is precisely between us. It has its own—proper to itself—logic that governs its continuity and irreversibility. Something must first happen so that something else can happen later. In everything that happens *later* we can know a trace of what was *before*. This logic cannot be overturned. It is possible to return to an abandoned stage, to take back a word not uttered at the right time, but it is not possible to reverse the time that flows between us. The continuity of our time is, as it were, the *substance* of drama.

The *stage* of the drama, our world, is beneath our feet. We walk upon it, see it, hear it, and touch it with our hands. The representations of the stage may vary, the ways of imagining it and conceptualizing it may vary; however, one thing will remain constant: the stage *is*. This leads to the question, In what manner does it exist? The various ontologies of the world answer this question. For Aristotle, the stage is the totality of self-sufficient existing things—*substances*; for George Berkeley, it is the shared imagination of a people—a dream, which is produced in their souls by God himself. But for people who are engaged in living through the drama, the stage of life is chiefly the plane for meetings and departures, the plane of freedom, in which man searches for a home, bread, and God, and where he finds the cemetery. The stage is located at the feet of man. The scriptures say, "Subdue the earth." Man subdues what, according to nature, is found to be *lower* than man. The fundamental act of subduing is the act of object-making, objectification. Man experiences the stage by objectifying it, by changing it into a space filled with "objects," out of which he constitutes the various wholes that serve him. Objectification is possible thanks to acts of a specific type—intentional acts. This is why we will call the relationship of man to the stage a "relationship of intentional objectification."

Around me and next to me there are *people*, especially those who are participants in the same drama in which I also take part. Against widely held views, I do not see, hear, and touch them, nor do I in any way perceive them. This is because what I can perceive is only an *externality*, and not man as man, the other as other. The other man as man can only appear when—without excluding all *externality*—he stands before me as a participant of my drama. I cannot see and hear participation in a drama—it requires a wholly different opening than the opening proper to intentional consciousness. The other man stands before me through some claim, a claim whose aftermath makes a sense of obligation arise in me. The consciousness that the other is present completes itself as a consciousness of the claim, a claim that obligates. Your question reaches my ears. It is a moment of silence, a mutual present. You await an answer. One must give an answer. This *must* is significant. Thanks to it, and within it, you are present next to me.

The opening onto the other has a dialogical character. It is substantially different from an intentional opening. Thanks to an intentional opening, the world of objects stands before us, whereas thanks to a dialogical opening, You stand by me.

What then is a drama? This concept points to man. Man lives in such a way that he participates in a drama—he is a dramatic being. He cannot live in any other way. Man's *nature* is dramatic time plus two openings—the intentional opening onto a stage and a dialogical opening onto another man. To be a dramatic being means "to exist in a specific time and opening in a specific way onto others and the world"—the stage.

Man participates in the drama differently than things found upon the stage. Man is a dramatic being in a different sense than he is a man or a woman, young or elderly. By participating in some drama, man knows, more or less clearly, metaphorically speaking, that he holds his own salvation or damnation in his hands. To be a dramatic being is to believe—rightly or wrongly—that damnation or salvation is in man's hands. Man may not be aware of upon what his salvation hinges, but despite this he can be aware that life is about something like this. Convinced that damnation and salvation are in his hands, man directs his life according to this conviction. This conviction presupposes a specific ontological structure of man: man can be the subject of a drama because he is a being-for-itself. The word "for" is key. *Appropriation* comes from it. Because man is for himself, he can *appropriate* himself. Participation in a drama is the *appropriation* of oneself, because of the hope for salvation.

All of what I have said demands a detailed discussion. What to start with? Beginnings are not at all indifferent. One ought to start from what in itself is found at the beginning. But what is found at the beginning and what beginning is at stake? In order to answer, one must identify this beginning precisely as a beginning, but it can be recognized only when one knows what the end is. So, we find ourselves in a situation with no exit: we want to know before we undertake our investigations what we can know only after we complete them. Therefore, we have to begin differently. Once more we will return to what was already sketched out, and upon this foundation we will attempt to mark out the path for how we will proceed. Will we make a mistake by doing this? This possibility is not excluded in advance. It is even possible. But this is what the practice of the philosophy of drama consists in, that it becomes a drama itself. The philosophy of drama cannot stand outside the human drama like a mirror image, but must be an integral component. When we think about the human drama of damnation and salvation, philosophy itself stands before these two possibilities—it can lose itself or it can affirm itself.

I have talked about dramatic time, about an intentional opening and about a dialogical opening. I have mentioned being-for-itself within the perspective of damnation and salvation. Let us return to the problem of the opening. This matter seems to stand at the beginning of the chain of our problems.

Consciousness of the Stage

The concept of intentionality comes from Husserl. Acts of consciousness are intentional. This means that they are essentially directed at some object. However, whenever one speaks about an object, one thinks at the same time about the subject; there can be no object without a subject, nor a subject without an object. The object and subject are closely intertwined by the principle of opposition. The subject is the necessary opposite of the object, and the object is opposed to the subject. This obviously does not exclude their belonging to each other, their unity. We can say that between the object and the subject there is a unity of opposites.

However, Husserl is not concerned with the relation between concepts. The intentional relation is the relation of the subject of consciousness to the object of consciousness. Husserl, as a result of many painstaking analyses, will finally call this relation the relation of constituting meaning. Thus, to say that intentionality belongs to the essence of the act of consciousness means, in Husserl's language, that acts of consciousness give birth to (generate) sense, both objective and subjective sense. The object that Husserl is speaking about is not an object in the sense of this, here existing, thing, but the very sense of objectivity (the sense of being an object)—an object in the sense of a correlate of a subjective act of consciousness. It is likewise with the subject. The subject is the pure subject of consciousness, the subjective condition of the possibility of all objective meaning.

This outline of the Husserlian idea of intentionality leads to two observations. We ought to accept, above all, that it can be applied toward a better clarification of the stage understood as the world, the world upon which the human drama occurs. The word "upon" is particularly significant. We are *upon the world* as upon a stage. Our relation to the stage can change during the course of the drama and can vary depending on the kinds of objects that fill out the stage. But what is essential does not undergo change. What is that which is essential? It is the open possibility of objectification. The whole world can succumb, piece by piece, to objectification. We ought to understand the meaning of this concept well. When we say that something succumbs to "objectification," we are not saying that it has gained something that it did not have before. Rather, we say that it *unveiled* what, from the very beginning, was its foundation. Everything, in order to be a thing for consciousness, must first be its object (for it). Objective meaning is the foundation upon which the meaning of things can be built. However, according to the logic marked out by its meaning, objective meaning is the opposite of subjective meaning. This means that the relation of man, as a dramatic being, to the stage is marked out by the principle of opposition. The stage is what is opposed to man at some point. This is why man must *appropriate* it for himself. Man—the dramatic being—appropriates the stage, leaving behind the opposition expressed by the subject–object opposition.

However, we must add Heidegger's point of view to Husserl's. These are ostensibly two opposed conceptions, but they essentially complement each other. It seems that one can interpret Heidegger's view in the following way: Heidegger incorporates the Husserlian theory of the genesis of objective meaning into a general theory of the history of the truth of being. He overcomes the subject–object opposition, demonstrating that it is derived from the concept of existence and the history of being. This substantially changes the image of the genesis of meaning. Objective meaning, or the meaning of being, no longer has its conditioning in the subjective conditions of possibility, but within the history of the truth of being that transcends the subject. All meaning of the object is ultimately established by the event of the meaning of being. Therefore, if objectification is something like the negative side of the process of appropriating the world, then understanding beings according to the event of the meaning of being is its positive side. Man, as a dramatic being in his relation to the stage, therefore strives to overcome the opposition in the direction of some harmony and unity with the stage. The striving toward unity is conditioned each time with the historical event of meaning, or the truth of being.

The efforts of Husserl and Heidegger belong together like two sides of the same reality. Both of them actually speak of man's relation to the stage. The matter of the relation of man to man escapes their concepts; therefore, even when they speak about it, they do so in a "scenic" manner, making man into an object, into a being. The relation to the stage is simultaneously described negatively and positively. It is negatively described by the Husserlian theory of the genesis of objective meaning in a consciousness conceived in a subjective manner, and positively through the theory of understanding a being through the meaning of being, marked out by the history of metaphysics. The concept of the object describes the negative borders of the human subject's relation toward the world, while the concept of the truth of being marks out its positive borders. The field of appropriating the stage by the dramatic being (man) stretches between these two borders. Acts of constituting meaning, such as building something—building a home, road, temple, house, workplace, and so on—have their place here.

What I say here about Husserl and Heidegger is not a textbook reconstruction of their views. I am concerned instead with an interpretation from the angle of the needs of a philosophy of drama. Despite the fact that their philosophies are not philosophies of drama in the strict sense, they nonetheless speak about drama. They talk mainly about the relation of man to the world. The emphasis on their merits is, however, at the same time a critique. This is because we would vainly search in both philosophies for what is essential to drama—a theory of the dialogical opening toward the other person. Both one and the other philosophy do not, in a decisive way, go beyond the stereotypes of monological thinking.

Let us pose one more question: What is the Husserlian *object* and what is the Heideggerian *truth of being*? Even though neither one of them says anything more detailed about this, these two concepts seem to have the following in common: they specify what can be acknowledged not only by the individual subject, or an individual existence, but also by others—by every subject and every existence. The concepts they use have a general meaning. We can say that they are abstractions—abstractions that claim for themselves pretentions to intersubjectivity. It is possible to grasp in the use of these concepts the striving toward the overcoming of subjectivism toward some agreement with others, some community with them. This means that Husserl and Heidegger build a stage. The manner of building, and the shape of what is built, varies, but there is one thing in common— the stage cannot be a stage exclusively for me, it must equally be a stage for others. In this striving, the fundamental consciousness of the presence of the other person makes itself known. The other man turns out to be close; closer than the stage. He is present before he appears on the stage as the one whom I encounter. He is present as a hidden power that demands a common plane, path, place. Since the stage is not supposed to be only for me, but also for others, is must be built from something that has a general meaning, which must be acknowledged by everyone as being real. If there were no stage, then there would not be a "where" of the place of encounter.

At this point we find a clue where to start our philosophy of drama. Out of the two openings—the intentional and the dialogical— the dialogical opening is doubtlessly more fundamental. The dialogical opening, or, strictly speaking, the other man present in us as a participant of the drama thanks to this opening, directs, as if from hiding, our reference to the stage, thereby laying down a significant condition: the scene must be in common.

Consciousness of the Other

The dialogical opening is an opening onto another human: onto a *thou*, onto *he* and *she*, onto a *we*, *you* [pl.], and *they*. The other man is present to me in it, and I am to the other. The dialogical opening substantially differs from the intentional. It does not constitute an object, nor a subject correlated to the object, and it is not "attuned" to the meaning of being. The concept of the opening is not the most fortunate. It suggests that the dialogical belongs to the same species to which the intentional also belongs. But that is not the case. Rather, it is concerned with two aspects of the same act—one presupposes the other, one penetrates the other. The other man is not my object and I am not his object. But this does not mean that we cannot *objectivize* each other, as Jean-Paul Sartre proclaimed. The dialogical relation to the stage is also not ruled out. The interpenetration of the structures of opening means that, at least within certain limits, it is possible to objectify people and to humanize dead objects.

I said at the very beginning that the other man is present within me, or present by me, through a *claim* that he awakens within me. We can see this in the consciousness of a question. The other has put a question to me. I recognize it from a voice gone quiet, from the eyes, from the expression of the face. However, the question is neither a voice that has gone quiet, nor the glow in the eyes, nor the expression on the face. The question is a claim. The one who asks, claims the right to an answer. The first answer to a question is the consciousness that one *must* answer. In this *must* we feel the presence of the other person. The other man is present by me through what I must do for him, and I am present by him through what he must do for me. The tie that comes into being between us is a tie of commitment. Commitment is a tie that ties with mutual obligation. Of what sort? We will discuss this later.

Commitments are born in encounters. The issue of the encounter is one of those issues we will return to often. Here we will cover only what seems indispensable in order to understand the dialogical relation.

In colloquial speech, we frequently hear that people, in order to meet, must have a common plane for an encounter. This does not mean only the plane of the stage, the road, the home, the workplace, and so on. Rather, it means something that we can call the "background" of the encounter. People meet each other when they have similar interests, similar tastes, a similar past, a similar hope. Even a simple question about directions assumes some common background: I ask someone for directions who seems to be as sincere as I am and who will not give a false answer to someone who is asking sincerely. The encounter seems to be a chance event: we do not know when, where, and why.... However, when it does take place, then it turns out that it was prepared by the entire past of the persons who have met. One can see, then, how significant a role in a mutual *facing each other* is played by what these people already have *behind themselves*.

What is the background of encounters? It is the widely conceived sphere of ideas lived through by people, that is, the sphere of what can be found, as if, *above* us, upon which we can never tread. It is difficult to say whether this sphere exists or not, whether it is the totality of objects, or whether it is not the totality of objects; it is also difficult to say that it does not exist, since it is the background for dialogue. We can say one thing: it ties, unveils, and commits simultaneously. It constitutes something like a new world for those encountering each other—a world of important and unimportant matters, sublime and trifling moments, sacred and ordinary times; in other words, it establishes a *hierarchy*. By undertaking a dialogue with the other, I come to him from within some hierarchy, and the other, by undertaking a dialogue with me, comes toward me from within some hierarchy. The dialogue will only be fruitful when our hierarchies are similar or when they will be able to become similar to each other.

The experience of hierarchy has a specific character: a hierarchy cannot be seen, one *participates* in a hierarchy. Participation in a hierarchy can be experienced as an attachment and a commitment. However, it is not coercion; a hierarchy does not tie us without our own consent. There are even degrees of consent, which differentiate the character of participation. My participation in the hierarchy might be deeper or shallower, closer to what is higher or to what is lower, closer to what is more connected with action or to what inclines one to restrain oneself from acting. It is similar with your participation—it can also be deeper or shallower, higher or lower, more active or passive. This is the origin of the difficulties of dialogue, but this is also the source of the need for it.

The concept of participation has a rich tradition—from Plato to variants of Thomistic participation theory. Again, it would be difficult to go into this tradition's details here. I would only like to emphasize what ideas lead astray the renewal of the participation theory today. They most frequently are, especially the Thomistic philosophy of participation, an attempt to develop an intentional theory of the object, or the theory of being, and therefore part of the philosophy of the stage. They neglect—perhaps with the exception of Platonic theory—the fact that the opening onto hierarchy, that is, onto participation, is a dialogical opening in which the primordial given is neither being nor an object, but another man—you, he, she, we, you, they. It is dialogue, not observation, which puts us at the origin of the world's hierarchy. But not like people who are staring into the water and seeing in it a reflection of what is higher and lower, but like one who steps into the stream and lets himself be carried along the current of uttered words, questions posed, answers put forward, invitations, callings, warnings, and so on. Thus, this is where the whole difficulty of talking about participation originates. As soon as we begin speaking about the background, the background stands before us, like a ladder that leads to some roof. We do not notice that we stand on a different ladder, which is our background.

It is much easier for us to talk about what is the consequence of mutual participation. The consequence is some common dramatic thread. Dialogue establishes, strengthens, and develops a spiritual reality that is either longer- or shorter-lasting, either richer or poorer—an interpersonal reality that circumscribes the essential meaning of the dialogical reciprocity of persons. This reality is made up of everything that ties people, brings them together, and embraces them, but also what divides, distances, and pushes away—what should not be talked about as if it resides in me, or you, or on the stage, but is "between us." Between us is a common dramatic thread—our drama. It is established and built up through our participation, but also vice versa—our participation is established and determined through it.

What *happens* between us—quite often what happens between us leaves its mark on the stage. A home might serve as an example.

Now we can better understand the influence of the dialogical opening onto the intentional opening. The intentional opening directs itself onto an object and always emerges from some subject, for example, the pure subject of consciousness. What is the object? It is a certain minimum—the minimum required for an opposition to come into being. What is the subject? It is the opposite of an object—nothing less and nothing more. What is a subject with regard to another man? He is the maximum of possible participation—participation that approaches identity. The shared world of objects can only be a shared world for subjects who see the same way and who, in their seeing, have the same point of observation. The striving toward an identity of subjects of consciousness is a particular type of the dramatic thread between people. The existence of such a thread is the necessary condition for objectification. Therefore, the condition for intentional objectification is the dialogical participation in the drama of identifying consciousnesses, or, more precisely, the subjects of consciousness.

The primacy of the problematics of dialogue, before all other problematics, has once again confirmed itself in this manner.

The God Question

The other issues of the philosophy of drama that I mentioned at the outset, especially the issue of time, will be left to a deeper consideration in later parts of this book. We also defer other issues for later consideration—issues of the drama with God and God's drama. The question of God is a significant question posed by man as a dramatic being. It is itself a drama. Does God exist? Where is God? Whence comes God to man? In what way can man find his God? Is the opening onto God another opening alongside the openings onto the world and the other? Perhaps the dimension of time itself is important here?

The answers can vary. For Thomistic philosophy, God makes himself known, above all, through the stage. For René Descartes, God comes to man directly, without the mediation of the world, only through an idea, which man possesses about God. For Martin Buber, God comes through the other. For some, God is distance; for others, he is close; according to some, he comes to condemn us; according to others, he comes to save us. There are even those who think that he does not come at all.

Among the many opinions and assumptions, one is especially worthy of attention: there is really only one drama—the drama with God. Every other drama and dramatic thread is only a fragment of this drama. If so, then the ideal of drama in general is religious drama. Is this for every drama of every religion? No, not every one of them—only the Judeo-Christian religion is a dramatic religion in the full sense of the word.

Without giving the last word on the matter, we will frequently reference the Judeo-Christian tradition and the metaphors that originate from it, to illustrate, maybe even support, our analyses with the material it contains. Dramatic thinking will reveal itself in this way as a "thinking from within the depths of the metaphor."

Large fragments of this introduction were already published chiefly in the monthly *Znak* and the annual *Analecta Cracoviensia*. I had the hope, when publishing them at the time, that they would contribute to my book *Controversy over the Existence of Man*, which I intended to write. But, in the meantime, the original intention has undergone, in my opinion, a favorable change: from the *Controversy over the Existence of Man*, *The Philosophy of Drama* was born. The latter name is more congruent with the things I talk about—with the concept of man as a dramatic being. So, if unforeseen obstacles do not arise, then I can expect to write more on this philosophy.

Sławomir Grotomirski was immensely helpful in preparing this publication for print. Not only did he properly prepare the manuscript and create an index of names, but he also scanned the text for redundant repetitions and stylistic ambiguities. The preparation of this publication would have been delayed greatly if not for his help. I sincerely thank him for this.

Kraków, October 1986

CHAPTER I

The Event of the Encounter

The Polish word *experience* [*doświadczenie*] is composed of two elements: "to" [*do*] and "witness" [*świadczenie*]. The first points toward striving, the second toward witnessing. Taken together they mean "going toward witnessing." When we take the concept of "experience," according to the etymology of the word, we must say that we are only given one, in the full sense of the word, properly called "experience," namely, the experience of the other person—the encounter with the other. We experience the other by going toward witnessing. All other varieties of experience—whether we experience things or ourselves—are only a diminished variety of experiencing the other.

We experience the other by encountering him. Encountering is something more than consciousness that the other is present next to me or by me. When I am tangled up in crowds on the streets, I am conscious that there are other people near me, which, however, does not mean that I am encountering them. The encounter is an event. An encounter involves a significant change in the space of being-with. The one who encounters, goes beyond—transcends—himself in the double sense of this word: toward the one to whom he can give witness (toward the other), and toward the One before whom he can submit his witness (before Him—the One who demands a witness). Therefore we ought to say that to encounter is to ex-perience Transcendence.

The issue of encountering and transcendence requires careful analysis. By undertaking the problem that is emerging, I want to refer

1

2 The Philosophy of Drama

to the views of Emmanuel Levinas—the last of the great philosophers of dialogue—who, by referring to the thought of Franz Rosenzweig, and polemicizing against Husserl and Heidegger, places the issue of witnessing right at the very core of philosophy. The experience of the other cannot be treated anymore as one of the many experiences of what can be found outside of man, but must be seen as the key experience upon which the meaning of the world depends. Exploring the meaning of that experience entails the need to undertake a critical reflection upon the European philosophical tradition. Levinas reveals an unbridgeable chasm between what I have called "the philosophy of the stage" above and what I call "the philosophy of drama." In this regard he is a faithful inheritor of Rosenzweig's thought, who in his critique of Hegel proved the impossibility of a philosophy based upon the idea of being or existence. However, referencing and using Levinas does not mean an uncritical acceptance of his views, nor the necessity of referencing them in full, rather, it means doing justice to the inspiring power of this work.

The great biblical texts are present behind Levinas's analyses, among which the story of Abraham occupies a primary place. God calls Abraham to leave the land where he settled and search for another place in the world. The calling of Abraham created a hope, and the hope created a journey. How different the journey of Abraham looks than the journey of Odysseus described from within a different cultural world. Odysseus goes toward the land that he once left, which he knows and remembers well. Abraham goes toward a promised land, which he has never seen. Odysseus guides himself by the stars as a sailor. Abraham guides himself by the signs made by people who lead him as messengers of the Infinite. From this comes the varied value of encounters with others. For Odysseus, others are more like an obstacle along the way; for Abraham, they are traces left by God. In Levinas, the other comes to us thanks to the *epiphany of the face*. The face of the other is a trace of Transcendence. Therefore, welcoming the other simultaneously means going toward God. We go toward God by giving witness to God about others. This stepping of man outside himself toward the other and toward God is transcendence in a meaningful way. It differs from the transcendence about which ontology speaks, that is, the philosophy of the stage. This is about going toward something that is *Wholly Other*, which cannot be described with the help of categories for objects (this, that) connected to the third person of the verb *to be*. This *Wholly Other* makes itself present in the face of the other, and calls man toward something that is beyond being and nonbeing.

The "face" is the key word that describes the encounter. Things have appearances; people have faces. Things appear through appearances; faces reveal themselves. Faces are traces of Transcendence. To what do these traces lead? What dramas do they open before us?

THE FACE OF THE OTHER

We read in Levinas:

> I do not know if one can speak of a "phenomenology" of the face, since phenomenology describes what appears. So, too, I wonder if one can speak of a look turned toward the face, for the look is knowledge, perception. I think rather that access to the face is straightaway ethical. . . . There is first the very uprightness of the face, its upright exposure, without defense. The skin of the face is that which stays most naked, most destitute. It is the most naked, though with a decent nudity. It is the most destitute also: there is an essential poverty in the face; the proof of this is that one tries to mask this poverty by putting on poses, by taking on a countenance. The face is exposed, menaced, as if inviting us to an act of violence. At the same time, the face is what forbids us to kill.

Further on we read: "The first word of the face is the 'Thou shalt not kill.' It is an order. There is a commandment in the appearance of the face, as if a master spoke to me."[1]

The cited passage comes from an interview Philippe Nemo conducted with Levinas. This interview had the goal of making available, to a wider public, views that are too frequently expressed in a hermetic language. Throughout his work Levinas returns repeatedly to the question of the other's face, widely modulating the accents of his answers. It is not always entirely clear what, for Levinas himself, is more, or less, significant. It is different in the text of this interview. Here he speaks straightforwardly about what is simplest and most fundamental. Let us make the text of this interview the leading thread for our analyses of Levinas's thinking.

The face of the other is certainly not a phenomenon in the classic sense of the word—it is not a phenomenon behind which some thing-in-itself hides. Despite this, the face is somehow given to us—given as a gift, as a presence, as a *consciousness* toward me, or directed at me. This does not mean that we are clearly and distinctly aware of the specificity of this gift. Totalizing philosophies striving to encompass the whole of reality with the help of the concept of being, and concepts deriving from it, have caused us to become deaf and blind to the face of the other. The responsibility of philosophy is to heal us of our narrowness. In this wider sense the philosophy of Levinas is a phenomenology—a thinking that wants to remain within a direct closeness to experience, which does not have to entail the claim that the face is the same sort of phenomenon as the phenomenon of the object.

The face of the other is given to us. We can point to a moment in time in which the epiphany of the face fulfills itself. This is because the face is given in an epiphany—an appearance or disclosure. In an epiphany the other reveals his truth. He stands before me as such, as one who is naked, destitute, commanding, and obligating. This does not mean that, in this way, we come to know something about the other that can be expressed in a judgment. The epiphany of the face does not bring any knowledge in the ordinary sense of the word. The other is what it brings—the other as such, that is, as the veracious one. This is why he is our teacher, our master. And so we read, "There is a commandment in the appearance of the face, as if a master spoke to me." Not only that, the face appears in such a manner that it elects. The epiphany of the face is not the appearance of everything to everyone, but the appearance of the veracious to the elected. What does the veracious say to the elected? He says, "Thou shalt not kill."

Further descriptions will require some ordering. Three parallel paths are drawing themselves out before us: we must describe the "face as face"; we must describe the horizon thanks to which the face can be given; and we must describe the human subject ("I") insofar as he is capable of accepting the appearance of the face. However, these three roads crisscross each other so much that we cannot demarcate a clear boundary between them. This is why we remember that by successively taking up the topics that stand before us we are involuntarily breaking up an original unity.

Face-to-Face

The French word "visage" suggests that the face is essentially visible. Does this mean the privileging of sight we know from Plato? On the contrary. The face is what is heard rather than seen. In fact, it is about neither sight nor hearing, but about the disclosure of something that goes beyond the realm of the senses. Levinas says, "I think rather that access to the face is straightaway ethical. You turn yourself toward the Other as toward an object when you see a nose, eyes, forehead, a chin, and you can describe them. The best way of encountering the Other is not even to notice the color of his eyes! When one observes the color of the eyes one is not in social relationship with the Other. The relation with the face can surely be dominated by perception, but what is specifically the face is what cannot be reduced to that."[2]

An appearance needs matter that it can utilize. But it does not dwell in this matter as a thing dwells in its manifestation. The face signifies. But not as signs, symbols, or metaphors signify. The face is a trace. What does it mean to be a trace?

Before I answer this question, I will quote a passage from the work of Stéphane Mosès about Rosenzweig and his concept of the face. Levinas wrote that Rosenzweig's thinking so deeply and comprehensively pervades his philosophy that there is no way of signaling it with quotations. Mosès's commentary sheds light on the importance and location of the problem:

> Thus divine Truth reveals itself in the human face. The highest mystical experience blends in with the face of the other man. When Rosenzweig attempts to demonstrate that the structure of the human face symbolically repeats the figure of the star, it is in order to show that this face is a summary of the ultimate meaning of being. A first triangle formed by the forehead and the two cheeks, or alternatively by the nose and the two ears—that is, the organs of pure passivity—constitutes the mask, the elementary seat of the face. A second triangle, an inverted one, drawn from

the two eyes and the mouth, is superimposed on the first and confers life and motion to the face. The eyes, organs both of vision and of gaze, through which are expressed a double relation with the visible, a relation made up at the same time of receptivity and expressivity, symbolize Creation and Revelation. The mouth, instrument of both language and silence, of living speech and the kiss, which, in biblical symbolism, stands for the ultimate encounter of man and God, in the form of the two experiences of limits, that of the mystical Revelation and that of death, is the metaphorical representation of the Redemption.[3]

Levinas's descriptions do not exactly repeat Rosenzweig's conception as outlined by Mosès. As we shall see, Levinas draws attention, above all, to the passive side of the face.

The face that appears speaks. What does it say? It says, "Thou shalt not kill." In other words, do not do what you can do with every other being—don't trample, don't cut, don't devour, don't pay back with revenge. There are many different ways of killing. The language of the face means that in the moment of encounter there also emerges the threat of murder. Where does it come from? Man lives upon the stage of the world undoubtedly thanks to the killing of plants and animals, therefore it might be easy to lose sight of the difference between animals and humans. But is this the sole basis for the threat of homicide? This would mean that a man might kill a man as if by mistake, not remembering the difference between a man and other beings. Meanwhile, things stand differently. A man can kill the other consciously, fighting him face-to-face. He can murder. If then the face establishes the prohibition of murder, then this is only possible because from the face itself there emerges some incomprehensible temptation to murder. The face, Levinas says, "as if invit[es] us to an act of violence," only to then say "thou shalt not kill."

In one of Levinas's key works, we read:

> The Other is the sole being I can wish to kill.... In the contexture of the world he is a quasi-nothing. But he can oppose to me a struggle, that is, oppose to the force that strikes him not a force of resistance, but the very *unforeseeableness* of his reaction. He thus opposes to me not a greater force, an energy assessable and

consequently presenting itself as though it were part of a whole, but the very transcendence of his being by relation to that whole; not some superlative of power, but precisely the infinity of his transcendence. This infinity, stronger than murder, already resists us in his face, is his face, is the primordial *expression*, is the first word: "you shall not commit murder." The infinite paralyses power by its infinite resistance to murder, which, firm and insurmountable, gleams in the face of the Other, in the total nudity of his defenceless eyes, in the nudity of the absolute openness of the Transcendent.[4]

The other's face puts us at the crossroads of the world. The one who has a face is *other*. It detracts the binding force of the activities, and projects for activities, that precede our movement in the world. It cannot be described using concepts that we use to describe things. It demands a language that is different from the language of ontology. The appropriate language is the language of ethics: "A relation between terms where the one and the other are united neither by a synthesis of the understanding nor by the relation of subject to object and where nevertheless the one weighs or matters or is significant to the other, where they are tied by a conspiracy that knowledge can neither exhaust or unravel."[5] The powerlessness of knowledge does not mean utter ignorance. It means the impossibility of explanation by reference to something that is more originary. The call "thou shalt not kill" has something absolute in it. It binds a relationship, which cannot be unbound by any other instance, because there is, simply put, no such instance. This does not mean that murder is physically impossible. Murders exist. They violate that which is absolute. Man is able to kill, but is unable to stop murder from being a violation.

Homicide

Since a "thou shalt not kill" exists, then this means that homicide is still possible. There is nothing easier than killing. The face itself invites one to an act of violence. The face cannot be acquired, it can only be killed. Since homicide is possible, there is also a need for a prohibition: "thou shalt not kill." We will now consider this more widely.

The death of another man is in play here. Such a death can be a homicide or murder. The difference is a matter of different motivations. Homicide is an act that can be explained, and at least partially justified, whereas murder is not justifiable; the first is the result of some "interest," whereas the second is disinterested [Throughout the book Tischner mistakenly inverts the definitions of "murder" and "homicide." See Translator's Preface.—Rosman]. We can therefore say that murder is less "animal" and more "human," only because man is capable of disinterested acts. Sigmund Freud, who searched for humanity's first crime, followed the lead of a homicide rather than a murder. The killing of the father presupposed by Freud as being committed by a horde of sons, because of their jealousy with respect to the mother, had something of the animal instinct in it and did not reach the level of a fully "human" crime. The first disinterested crime of humanity was the killing of Abel.

Cain kills his brother—this is the first hint for recognizing that murder is at issue. The basis of the murder is brotherhood. Cain does not murder in a dispute over a woman, nor in a dispute over power, nor in a dispute over bread. . . . He murders because he is guided by the very value of murder. This does not mean that no reasons hide behind this crime. It is important that they are not sufficient reasons.

It is sometimes said that Cain kills out of jealousy. Jealousy would be what explains things. But relying on jealousy is no explanation, because jealousy is an experience that is fundamentally irrational. Cain is jealous of Abel because of God's election. He kills him to become the elect . . . Is this a convincing explanation? Does a reasonable human being expect that by killing one of God's elect he would then deserve election himself? If jealousy were reasonable, then it would not be jealousy. Jealousy is all the more jealousy the fewer reasons it has. Jealousy kills without regard for the self-interest of a human being—it kills because it seems that in a meaningless world only death has meaning.

However, all this is not about semantic meaning, but about axiological meaning. Semantic meaning depends upon the functional connection of things between themselves. The hammer connects with the nail, the nail with the wall, the wall with a painting—everything is connected through the activity of driving a nail into a wall in order to hang a painting on it. Axiological meaning is concerned with values—the higher the value, the more self-sufficient is its meaning. But the opposite is also true: the more self-sufficient the meaning of a value, the higher is the value. Man is—at least for himself—a self-sufficient absolute value. Jealousy is rooted in the experience of this very value, more precisely, in its denial. The God who does not choose Cain strikes at Cain's sense of value. He destroys it. He makes it meaningless. Thence comes the jealous revenge of Cain. If he, Cain, has no value for God, then everything is without value, even Abel.

"The face is a text without context," says Levinas. The face of Abel stands before Cain—also without context. In a world without meaning, it alone desires to have meaning. In a world without values, it alone wants to be a value. In the great vale of tears, it alone is full of happiness. Precisely because it wants to have value, because it wants to be full of meaning, because it is full of happiness—precisely because of this, this face invites murder. What is at stake in this killing, in murder, is something more than death—it is about the revelation of a fundamental truth: as long as there is even one rejected person in the world, then nobody has a right to happiness.

I said above that the encounter is a going toward witness, a to-witnessing [*do-świadczenie*]. Murder appears at the end of the road that leads in the opposite direction. This is no longer about to-witnessing, but away-from-witnessing [*od-świadczenie*]. The murderer, in the last resort, is the one who refuses witnessing. When Cain is questioned by God, he answers, "Am I my brother's keeper?" To be one's brother's keeper means not only protecting him, but also witnessing for him. Cain does not witness, he refuses to witness. To refuse to witness is to go down the road of murder.

The face says, "Thou shalt not kill," "Thou shalt not murder me." This precept, or maybe calling, has something absolute about it. The word "absolute" comes from *absolvere*, "to set free." What is absolute loosens ties with this world and makes ties with the other in which this world has its justification. That which is absolute is not subject to critique and does not require a justification. It is transcendent. It says: "Thou shalt not kill." Despite everything. Despite misfortune—thou shalt not kill. That, despite everything, you have not killed, this means that something has opened for you, something that has returned the meaning you have lost. This something is Transcendence. What does it mean?

With this question we enter upon the second road that leads toward understanding the face—a road that brings us closer to its horizon.

Desire

Abraham meets wayfarers, whose faces are the traces of the Infinite, along the road to the promised land. The wanderers meet him "from the horizon of Infinity." They could only be encountered by someone who himself is open toward Infinity. An important lesson comes from this: only the one who himself is open onto Infinity can stand before the epiphany of the face. What does it mean to be opened onto Infinity? What words will render this opening? Levinas uses the word *désir*, "desire." What is desire? By posing this question we stand upon the third path of understanding the face—a path that leads us toward explaining the subjective condition for the possibility of experiencing the face. The second and third paths run parallel to each other. We will proceed in such a way that we will not lose any of them from sight. Levinas writes:

> On the other hand, the idea of the Infinite implies a thought of the Unequal. I start from the Cartesian idea of the Infinite, where the *ideatum* of this idea, that is, what this idea aims at, is infinitely greater than the very act through which one thinks it. There is a disproportion between the act and that to which the act gives access. For Descartes, this is one of the proofs of God's existence: thought cannot produce something which exceeds thought; this something had to be put into us. One must thus admit to an infinite God who has put the idea of the Infinite into us. But it is not the proof Descartes sought that interests me here.... In Descartes the idea of the Infinite remains a theoretical idea, a contemplation, a knowledge. For my part, I think that the relation to the Infinite is not a knowledge, but a Desire. I have tried to describe the difference between Desire and need by the fact that Desire cannot be satisfied: that Desire in some way nourishes itself on its own hungers and is augmented by its satisfaction: that Desire is like a thought which thinks more than it

thinks, or more than what it thinks. It is a paradoxical structure, without a doubt, but one which is no more so than this presence of the Infinite in the finite act.[6]

Desire is something like the reversal of longing ["Desire" is not consistently used by Tischner throughout the book. It later takes on a negative valence in his discussion of Hegel.—Rosman]. Longing is directed at the past, desire goes toward the future, perhaps even further, toward eternity itself. Desire and longing identically grow out of the present and are identically a protest against it. They are connected by the conviction that what is real is not present. However, longing knows well the countries it longs for, because of this it calls man to a return. Longing directed the steps of Odysseus when he was returning to Ithaca. Desire does not know its home, it never returns, it is condemned to abandon all pasts and all presents.

Nevertheless, one should not accept that desire is consciousness of some lack—the lack of something or someone—a nothingness understood as a hole in being. Ontological attempts to represent desires are meaningless. Only an ontological lack, but not a metaphysical lack, can be grasped through its surrounding context. In his imagination man compares what he does not have to what he could be when thinking ontologically—whence the striving to supplement lack might flow. But we are not concerned with supplementing a lack. Desire is not the desire for fullness, if we understand by fullness the full development of all man's capabilities and the possibilities they contain. Whoever strives toward fullness has not cured himself of egoism—he remains within himself and encloses himself within his own confines. Fullness is in the realm of need, but is not desire's goal. Desire comes to those who manage to satisfy all their needs. It is a "happy unhappiness," because it is known, above all, by those who have fully tasted happiness through satisfying their needs. Its principle is not egoism. It only knows egoism as the pain of an incompletely overcome egoism.

Desire is an opening. However, it is not an opening onto everything without distinction. If this opening did not introduce distinctions through itself, then man would not be able to encounter the other and the epiphany of the face would not have any more meaning than the rising of the sun. In desire, as an opening, there must be some sensitive point thanks to which it is possible to read the utterance proper to the face. Desire knows what it wants, even when it refuses it and does not want it.

We do not diverge from Levinas's views when we say that desire is goodness:

> The metaphysical desire tends toward something else entirely, toward the absolutely other. The customary analysis of desire can not explain away its singular pretension.... The metaphysical desire does not long to return, for it is desire for a land not of our birth, for a land foreign to every nature, which has not been our fatherland and to which we shall never betake ourselves. The metaphysical desire does not rest upon any prior kinship. It is a desire that cannot be satisfied.... The metaphysical desire has another intention; it desires beyond everything that can simply complete it. It is like goodness—the Desired does not fulfill it, but deepens it.[7]

And one more passage:

> Desire is desire for the absolutely other. Besides the hunger one satisfies, the thirst one quenches, and the senses one allays, metaphysics desires the other beyond satisfactions, where no gesture by the body to diminish the aspiration is possible, where it is not possible to sketch out any known caress nor invent any new caress. A desire without satisfaction which, precisely, understands [*entend*] the remoteness, the alterity, and the exteriority of the other. For Desire, this alterity, nonadequate to the idea, has a meaning. It is understood as the alterity of the Other and of the Most-High. The very dimension of height is opened up by metaphysical Desire. That this height is no longer the heavens but the Invisible is the very elevation of height and its nobility. To die for the invisible—this is metaphysics. This does not mean that desire can dispense with acts. But these acts are neither consumption, nor caress, nor liturgy.[8]

Three moments are tightly interwoven with each other: desire has its basis in goodness, desire directs man toward the heights of the good, desire makes man ready to die for what is invisible.

Here we can say that Levinas's thought takes on the shape of a "biblically dramatized Platonism." This is not an accusation, but an attempt to understand more deeply. Levinas owes a lot to Plato, but Plato also owes Levinas. They are united by a deep conviction that being is not the principle of the good, but that the good is the principle of being; but they are divided by their fundamental visions of the human drama. Under Levinas's pen, the good loses its abstract character, taking on the face of the orphan, widow, stranger. In the encounter with poverty, the significant question is not where and how man can find his happiness, but how it is possible to sacrifice one's happiness for the salvation of one's brother. The answer is hidden within the whole *logos* of the good. The good in action awakens and deepens the goodness of man. Man wants to be good. In wanting this, that is, in desire, there is no interest. On the contrary, to be good means to do what is good. But no good deed is capable of expressing or saturating the desire for the good. It only deepens it, leading all the way to a messianic sacrifice of life.

Levinas himself explains his relation to Plato in this way:

> But Greek metaphysics conceived the Good as separate from the totality of essences, and in this way (without any contribution from an alleged Oriental thought) it caught sight of a structure such that the totality could admit of a beyond. The Good is Good in *itself* and not by relation to the need to which it is wanting; it is a luxury with respect to needs. It is precisely in this that it is beyond being. When, above, disclosure was contrasted with revelation, in which truth is expressed and illuminates us before we sought it, the notion of the Good in itself was already being taken up anew. Plotinus [Tischner incorrectly says "Plato."—Rosman] returns to Parmenides when he represents the apparition of the essence from the One by emanation and by *descent*. Plato nowise deduces being from the Good: he posits transcendence as surpassing the totality. Alongside of needs whose satisfaction amounts to filling a void, Plato catches sight also of aspirations that are not preceded by suffering and lack, and in which we recognize the pattern of Desire: the need of him who lacks nothing, the aspiration of him who possesses his being entirely, who goes beyond his plentitude, who has the idea of Infinity. The Place of the Good

above every essence is the most profound teaching, the definitive teaching, not of theology, but of philosophy. The paradox of an Infinity admitting a being outside of itself which it does not encompass, and accomplishing its very infinitude by virtue of this proximity of a separated being—in a word, the paradox of creation—thenceforth loses something of its audacity.[9]

I will return to the matters touched upon here. I would like to highlight one thing: the logic of the good and the logic of being are two distinct logics. One needs a logic of the good in order to throw light upon the darkness of the human drama. Only it can justify the existence of concrete beings, and not vice versa. And only it can give an insight into the adventures of people who lack nothing, but who nonetheless search for another land.

Two questions arise: What is the relation of Levinasian desire to thinking, and what is its relation to freedom? Does granting desire primacy ahead of another possible opening not signify a certain sentimentality? Does the violence of desire not abolish freedom? In order to give an exhaustive answer to the first question one ought to ask it in a more fundamental way: What is thinking? This is not an easy question. Levinas does not devote any studies to it. The answer would need to be derived from his whole critique against Husserl and Heidegger, and from a general vision of the method he uses. Let us put aside these matters while emphasizing what is most important: the striving to identify thinking with desire. It seems it ought to be understood in this sense: only thanks to identifying the dimension of thinking with the dimension of desire can thinking fully become thinking. Outside of this dimension it becomes only an economic calculation exposed to the dangers of injustice and untruth. The revealing of the tie between thinking and desire is also served by such statements (among others): "The ethical relationship [constituted by the opening of desire onto the good. —Tischner] is not grafted onto an antecedent relationship of cognition; it is a foundation and not a superstructure. To distinguish it from cognition is not to reduce it to a subjective sentiment. The idea of infinity, in which being overflows the idea, in which the other overflows the same, breaks with the inward play of the soul and alone deserves the name 'experience,' a relationship with the exterior. It is then more *cognitive* than cognition itself, and all objectivity must participate in it."[10] Levinas's thesis comes down to this: desire is more "cognitive" than knowledge, but not in the sense that it is the knowing of something that knowing does not know, but in that it establishes the radical dimension of transcendence in which a transcendence proper to knowledge can find support.

Further on we read: "We separate ourselves from the letter of Cartesianism in affirming that the movement of the soul that is more cognitive than cognition could have a structure different from contemplation. Infinity is not the object of a contemplation, that is, is not proportionate to the thought that thinks it. The idea of infinity is a thought which at every moment thinks more than it thinks. A thought that thinks more than it thinks is a desire."[11] What hides behind this formulation? To "think more than it thinks" means to think something that is not thought. Let us note the difference between thinking "about something" and thinking "something." I "think about" a man—that he has gone astray. But I could not think about this if simultaneously, along with this, I did not also "think of the road"—of the road proper to the goal. Thinking is, as if, a hidden comparison of what is thought about with what, thanks to which, it is possible to think about what one is thinking about, just as one thinks—not otherwise. The one cannot be divorced from the other. Without desire there would not be thinking, and without thinking there would be no desire.

Two other passages related to the theme of truth shed some light upon this matter. If desire turns us toward the good, then thinking turns us toward the truth. The truth is here understood as tightly interwoven with the good. This interweaving, which is not explained further, allows for the following judgment: "To seek and obtain truth is to be in a relation not because one is defined by something other than oneself, but because in a certain sense one lacks nothing."[12] Therefore, the movement of knowledge can come not from the thinker but from thinking. It can cross the distances that cannot otherwise be crossed, since "truth arises where a being separated from the other is not engulfed in him, but speaks to him. Language, which does not touch the other ... reaches the other by calling upon him or by commanding him or obeying him, with all the straightforwardness of these relations. Separation and interiority, truth and language constitute the categories of the idea of infinity or metaphysics."[13] If some identification of thinking and desiring is justified, then we must acknowledge that this mysterious dimension of thinking, not fully thought through by thinking alone, is the dimension of thinking *with someone* and *for someone*. Thinking not only thinks about something or of something. Thinking thinks *with someone* and *for someone*. There are many indications that the abovementioned moment of thinking of "something" conceals in itself both of the moments highlighted here: *with someone* and *for someone*. Either way, discourse is possible thanks to it. Truth, not only as the agreement between a judgment and things but also as the plane of all possible understanding with others, is made possible along with it. This confirms the thesis that not only is it impossible to have reliable thinking without desire, but also desire without thinking.

The identification of one with the other does not mean a strict identification. This is what the drama of man depends on: the darkness sleeps within man at the very sources of the light. This is what makes ruptures possible: thinking without desire and desire without thinking.

Let us move on to the question of freedom. Am I not enslaved by the awakened desire? We are not asking about the freedom of the other toward me, but about one's own freedom toward the other. Does it not drag us into an adventure from which we cannot escape?

Standing before another person, I become aware that I am a self-willing being. The separated being is not a free being, but a self-willing one. Only the revelation of the face brings me out of my self-will and makes me truly free. Again, without going into the details, let us pause upon what is directly related to our topic.

We read in *En découvrant l'existence avec Husserl et Heidegger*:

> The other's face is the revelation not of the arbitrariness of the will, but its injustice. Consciousness of my injustice is produced when I incline myself not before facts, but before the other. In his face, the other appears to me not as an obstacle, nor as a menace I evaluate, but as what measures me. For me to feel myself to be unjust, I must measure myself against infinity. One must have the idea of infinity, which, as Descartes knows, is also the idea of the perfect, to know my own imperfection. The infinite does not stop me like a force blocking my force; it puts into question the naïve right of my powers, my glorious spontaneity as a living being, a "force on the move.". . . This way of measuring oneself

against the perfection of the infinite is not a theoretical consideration in its turn, in which freedom would spontaneously take up its rights again. It is a *shame* freedom has of itself, discovering itself to be murderous and usurpatory in its very exercise.[14]

The motif of shame, as a particular condition of freedom, appears several times in Levinas. However, shame plays a different role here than in, for example, Sartre. There shame was an expression of freedom's self-defense from another's attempts at objectification. Here it is a power that transforms self-will into freedom. Shame not only divides but it also unites. It makes one realize one's own, and the other's, separation. It makes possible the acknowledgment that there are many different freedoms in the world. It prepares a new bridge to the other—conversation, caress.

The view I put forward requires additional analyses. What is the relationship between the experience of the good and the experience of freedom? The implicitly accepted thesis that there is no freedom without the experience of the good (infinity, perfection) is deeply inspiring. But not only because the good establishes the proper measure for everything that is finite, but also, even above all, because by not being located in the orders of being, especially the causal, it can be the reason for exceeding these orders by one who himself becomes the *good incarnate*. Freedom is, after all, a liberation, and a liberation is the possibility of transcending this world's orders. Transcendence is unthinkable without support in something that is not itself transcendent.

Leaving aside further discussion of these and similar issues, let us pose the key question for us: Where in the end is the whole analysis of desire heading? The answer is this: It is heading toward explaining the origins of responsibility. What is responsibility? For Levinas it is the miracle of miracles—the basic mystery posed to philosophy: "The unsatisfiedness of conscience, the de-ception before the other, coincides with desire—this is one of the essential points of this exposition. The desire for infinity does not have the sentimental complacency of love, but the rigor of moral exigency. And the rigor of moral exigency is not bluntly imposed, but is a desire, due to the attraction and infinite height of being itself, for the benefit of which goodness is exercised. God commands only through the men for whom one must act."[15] Further on he says, "To be an I means then not to be able to escape responsibility, as though the whole edifice of creation rested on my shoulders. But the responsibility that empties the I of its imperialism and its egoism, even the egoism of salvation, does not transform it into a moment of the universal order; it confirms the uniqueness of the I. The uniqueness of the I is the fact that no one can answer for me."[16] And one more piece of this thought, "To discover such an orientation in the I is to identify the I with morality. The I before the other is infinitely responsible. The other who provokes this ethical movement in consciousness and puts out of order the good conscience of the Same coinciding with itself involves a surplus for which intentionality is not adequate. This is what desire is: to burn with another fire than need, which saturation extinguishes, to think beyond what one thinks."[17]

Responsibility for one's neighbor becomes responsibility for everything—even the world where one's neighbor exists. It coincides with the responsibility of a servant of God who believes that the fate of the world depends upon his prayer and sacrifice. One is either responsible for everything or for nothing. Only the one who is ready to die for the salvation of the other whom he encounters refrains from murder. There is no third possibility between Cain's and Abel's stances. This is the path of desire, which grows as good deeds drill down to the goodness in man.

One more passage that crowns this matter: "The I in relationship with the infinite is an impossibility of stopping its forward march, the impossibility of deserting its post . . . it is, literally, not to have time to turn back. It is to be not able to escape responsibility, to not have a hiding place of inwardness where one comes back into oneself, to march forward without concern for oneself. There is an increase of exigencies on oneself: the more I face my responsibilities the more I am responsible."[18]

THE TRACE OF THE INFINITE

Let us return to the image of Abraham again. There, in the faces of the guests who visit his tent, he discovers God's messengers. On the one hand, to discover that the other is God's messenger, he must be seen within the horizon of the Infinite. On the other hand, one cannot open oneself onto the Infinite otherwise than through the face of the other. Levinas writes, "The ways in which the other presents himself, exceeding *the idea of the other in me*, we here name the face."[19] The opening onto the Infinite—this is desire. The Idea of the Infinite has a positive sense. It does not emerge from a negation of finitude, because only nothingness could be the result of such a negation. It has to be an *a priori* presupposition, as the condition of thinking about any finitude. In order to be able to think about finitude one must implicitly perform a negation of infinity, which must appear first. Infinity conceived in this way coincides with the idea of an infinite perfection. Abraham's situation is therefore this: he sees the faces of the guests in the horizon of infinite perfection. This raises a question: What is infinite perfection? Well, according to Levinas, infinite perfection cannot be described with the help of the category of Being or being. One must use the idea of the good. In the measure that Levinas is aware of this impossibility, his metaphysics becomes increasingly the metaphysics of "something higher" than being—a metaphysics of the good.

Stephan Strasser writes that Levinas became aware of this necessity in a clear way later in his studies, which took place after *Totality and Infinity*. I do not want to argue about this here. It seems to me that already in *Totality and Infinity* the matter was clear enough to dispel all doubts. Therefore, it is something of an exaggeration to look for a philosophical turn in Levinas that is similar to Heidegger's turn.[20]

Here we will say a few clarifying words about the matter of the good and being. The scholastic theory of the so-called transcendentals said that *ens, pulchrum, verum et bonum convertuntur* [being, beauty, truth, and the good are convertible]. In light of this conception, it would be impossible to treat wholly separately the theory of being, truth, goodness, and beauty. This entailed a certain manner of understanding metaphysics: the ontology of being was at the same time a metaphysics of being, and metaphysics was an ontology of the truth and good and, if someone wanted, beauty. These assumptions were questioned neither by Hegel nor by Heidegger, even though they adopted a different conception of Being, or beings. In every instance this meant some form of ontologizing metaphysics. However, this approach had its critics. Rosenzweig reacted to it most sharply with a view to Hegel's philosophy. The biblically inspired thinking of Rosenzweig does not allow itself to be closed within a description weaved out of concepts derived from the idea of being or beings.

This thinking senses itself as called to think of the drama of man—a drama that is composed of creation, revelation (election), and salvation. Only the first of those events allows itself to be described in ontological categories, while the others—revelation or salvation—do not permit this possibility. In order to understand the significant drama of man, it is not enough to plumb the mystery of the stage alone, rather, one must reach for categories that are beyond being and nonbeing, which show something that is otherwise than being—something that is not "a manner of being." Levinas follows the tracks of the same critique, but Heidegger is more his philosophical opponent than Hegel is. He develops a thinking that he does not want to totalize.

An important corollary to this change in viewpoint is a specific dramatization of the transcendentals. Perhaps the transcendentals overlap somewhere upon the heights of abstraction and eternity, but in experience, as it appears in the worldly human drama, they are locked in a kind of *conflict*. From this come the questions, Is being truly being, or only the semblance of being? Does beauty manifest to us the truth of the world, or does it only feed us with a lie? Is that which appears as the good truly the good? Is truth *the* truth also when it makes us unhappy? Is it better to live among lies that make us happy, or among truths that bring us unhappiness? Because the transcendentals are in dispute, man discovers that his world is a fractured world and that he himself is a dramatically fractured being, substantially, and not only accidentally.

Levinas proclaims that the Infinite is a correlate of desire. From thence comes the question, What relation holds between the face of the other and the Infinite, that is—in the story about Abraham—God?

In order to answer this question, Levinas reaches for the metaphor of the trace: the face of the other is the *trace* of the Infinite:

> A trace is not a sign like any other. But it also plays the role of a sign; it can be taken for a sign. A detective examines, as revealing signs, everything in the area where a crime took place which betokens the voluntary or involuntary work of the criminal; a hunter follows the traces of the game, which reflect the activity and movement of the animal the hunter is after; a historian discovers ancient civilizations which form the horizon of our

world.... But when a trace is thus taken as a sign, it is exceptional with respect to other signs in that it signifies outside of every intention of signaling and outside of every project of which it would be the aim. When in transactions one "pays by check" so that there will be a trace of the payment, the trace is inscribed in the very order of the world. But a real trace disturbs the order of the world. It occurs by overprinting. Its original signifyingness is sketched out in, for example, the fingerprints left by someone who wanted to wipe away his traces and carry out a perfect crime. He who left traces in wiping out his traces did not mean to say or do anything by the traces he left. He disturbed the order in an irreparable way. He has passed absolutely. To be *qua leaving a trace* is to pass, to depart, to absolve oneself.[21]

Searching for God is like following his traces. This does not mean going into the past. One does not search for a paradise lost once and for all, but the land promised since time immemorial. God passes in such a way that he overpasses: "The God who passed is not the model of which the face would be an image. To be in the image of God does not mean to be an icon of God, but to find oneself in his trace. The revealed God of our Judeo-Christian spirituality maintains all the infinity of his absence, which is in the personal 'order' itself. He shows himself only by his trace, as is said in Exodus 33. To go toward Him is not to follow this trace that is not a sign; it is to go toward the others who stand in the trace of illeity."[22]

The trace is not a trace in the sand or snow. It is a trace on the face of the other. Following regular traces, we leave one behind only to find ourselves next to another, but we cannot abandon the trace that is the face of the other. This is because it is a *trace upon a trace*—we follow him who finds himself upon the traces of God.

The face of the other is the face of human destitution. Levinas lists three instances that play the role of a symbol: the widow, orphan, and stranger. Human destitution calls for rescue. Its calling does not know excuses. There is something absolute in it, even though it does not destroy freedom, but instead brings it to awareness:

> The relation with the face is not an object-cognition. The transcendence of the face is at the same time its absence from this

world into which it enters, the exiling [*depaysement*] of a being, his condition of being stranger, destitute, or proletarian. The strangeness that is freedom is also strangeness-destitution [*etrangetemisere*]. Freedom presents itself as the other to the same, who is always the autochthon of being, always privileged in his own residence. The other, the free one, is also the stranger. The nakedness of his face extends into the nakedness of the body that is cold and that is ashamed of its nakedness. Existence καθ'αυτό is, in the world, a destitution. There is here a relation between me and the other beyond rhetoric.[23]

Levinas and Others

Despite the radical critique with which Levinas protests against European philosophy, he finds allies within it to whom he willingly refers. Descartes is one of them. The concept of innate ideas, especially the concept of the idea of infinity, is supposed to be a good introduction to, even explanation of, the idea of the Infinite he is developing. Is it really? Similarities do not exclude differences.

The exceptional character of the idea of infinity depends upon, according to Descartes, its content exceeding the capacity of the act in which it is thought. Infinity cannot become the conceived content of an idea, because the act of thinking is finite, whereas its content is infinite. From this comes the conclusion: the idea of infinity does not originate in an act of the *cogito*, but must be put within it by God. Levinas takes a different path: Infinity, or the Infinite, is not given so much to thought as to desire. Our paradox is that we cannot fail to desire the Infinite and at the same time we cannot comprehend it. Our drama originates here.

However, this does not deprive the concept of the Infinite of its ambiguity. To clarify, Levinas compares his concept with the concepts of Kant and Hegel. Let us start with Kant. Levinas writes, "The Kantian notion of infinity figures as an ideal of reason, the projection of its exigencies in a beyond, the ideal completion of what is given incomplete—but without the incomplete being confronted with a privileged experience of infinity, without it drawing the limits of its finitude from such a confrontation. The finite is here no longer conceived by relation to the infinite; quite the contrary, the infinite presupposes the finite, which it amplifies infinitely.... The Kantian finitude is described positively by sensibility, as the Heideggerian finitude by the being for death."[24] Thus, Kant's infinity looms in the dark background of finitude. It is a goal toward which reason strides—gradually encompassing everything. Reason cognizing is a reason that identifies. Its ideal is the identity of everything with everything. Therefore, in the end, it is a totalizing reason—the reason of a totalization, identification, pushed into infinity. But for Levinas, the idea of the Infinite precisely signifies the impossibility of totalization.

A few words about Hegel. Levinas writes:

> Hegel returns to Descartes in maintaining the positivity of the infinite, but excluding all multiplicity from it; he posits the infinite as the exclusion of every "other" that might maintain a relation with the infinite and thereby limit it. The infinite can only encompass all relations. Like the god of Aristotle, it refers only to itself, though now at the term of a history. The relation of a particular with infinity would be equivalent to the entry of this particular into the sovereignty of a State. It becomes infinite in negating its own finitude. But this outcome does not succeed in smothering the protestation of the private individual, the apology of the separated being (though it be called empirical and animal), of the individual who experiences as a tyranny the State willed by his reason, but in whose impersonal destiny he no longer recognizes his reason.[25]

How does Levinas's conception present itself upon this background?

In opposition to Kant, and in equal measure to Hegel, this idea is an idea of desire, not reason. Reason—whether it be the pure reason of Kant or the speculative of Hegel—not only could manage without the idea of the infinite as Levinas conceives it, but in reality it does manage without it. Pure reason presupposes infinity as something negative—something that is postulated by the movement of thought itself, which continually goes beyond the finitude of that which is given here and now. Speculative reason goes in the opposite direction: it presupposes infinity as an absolute positivity in order to be able to drown and melt down all finitude within it. In both cases, infinity is merely seemingly something absolute. It essentially is, either way, relative to finitude. The matter looks different in Levinas. The Infinite is primarily given to desire, and only secondarily to thinking. Thinking about infinity is still to have it behind yourself as an object. To desire the Infinite—this is the heart of the matter. But the Infinite does not give itself to desire as the idea gives itself to thinking. The idea is a decree of thinking, contained within thinking. The Infinite is not given to desire—it is a gift that manifests itself as a calling. The Infinite comes to man in that it elects him, but not in the way that universals do—gathering by first accomplishing a blurring of differences. Electing someone means encounter, separating out from indifference, laying hold of their individuality, recognizing their value, drawing toward oneself, so that the elect can respond to election with a choice.

The Infinite conceived in this way can only be one thing: an Infinite Good. If it were otherwise, then it could not stand at the origins of freedom. Freedom is given to man as an emancipation, that is, as a path toward freedom. On the other hand, emancipation is like an answer to a question: the elect become free when they answer an election—by choosing the one who first chose them.

At this point it would be wise to return to Strasser's commentary. Levinas says that in developing the metaphysics of the good, we are moving beyond the sphere of being, beings, and all the derivative categories. However, this does not mean that we are entering into the sphere of nothingness: nothingness conceived as the negation of being is also ultimately an ontological category. In the sphere beyond being and nonbeing, the word "is" no longer has an existential character, but is purely a copula. There is no absurdity in this. The formula of beyond being signifies, as Strasser puts it, "obviously something other than *against*, or *instead*. *Beyond* in no way denies, rejects, nor substitutes. Because whoever finds oneself beyond a border does not deny the existence of a border, does not see in it anything absurd.... He only desires above it: must even pass above it to be faithful to one's philosophical message."[26] Were the ancient philosophy of light and Husserl's wholly modern philosophy of the constitutive genesis of sense not similar attempts of going beyond being?

The key to the mystery of the infinite is—as it turns out from what we have said—the question about the good. It is the good, and only the good, that is infinite in the proper sense of the word.

The Good

How can we conceive of the good? We can only conceive of it by penetrating into the depths of numerous dramatic threads interwoven between people. At the foundations of all the threads, one thing inheres: a grain of goodness awoken within man by the good.

Let us consider a textual fragment by replacing individual formulations with concrete pictures as far as possible: "Not out of weakness; no capacity corresponds to what could not be contained there. The nonpresent is incomprehensible by reason of its immensity or its 'superlative' humility or, for example, its goodness, which is the superlative itself. The nonpresent here is invisible, separated (or holy) and thus a nonorigin, anarchical. . . . The Good cannot become present or enter into representation."[27] Speaking pictorially: God appeared upon the stage of Abraham's life. Who was he? He was the one who awakened desire; nothing less, but also nothing more. Inconceivable. But not inconceivable in the way a desert one traverses is inconceivable (Kantian infinity?), nor like a starry sky that encompasses everything that is inconceivable (Hegel and his absolute?). And the good? It is inconceivable, yet engaging; invisible, yet it can see; absent, yet it makes someone present . . . it awakens goodness within man, whose expression is desire.

The entering of the Infinite Good between people constitutes something that has never existed before—a new interpersonal tie. We read further on, "No one is good voluntarily. We can see the formal structure of nonfreedom in a subjectivity which does not have time to choose the Good and thus is penetrated with its rays unbeknownst to itself. But Subjectivity sees this nonfreedom redeemed, exceptionally, by the goodness of the Good. The exception is unique. Even though no one is good voluntarily, no one is enslaved to the Good."[28] God does not enslave Abraham. But can we say that he retains his freedom? How is it possible to retain something he did not have in the first place? The Abraham who was concerned with his flocks did not have freedom. He only gained it the moment of his calling. Is freedom something to be gained? Levinas says, *racheter*, "to ransom." It seems as if Abraham first sold his freedom and then regained it thanks to a ransom. To ransom (redeem) means, above all, to acknowledge that something is a value. Thus, Abraham receives that which he has, and simultaneously that which he carelessly got rid of. He is not a slave. But the God who redeemed freedom for him has made him free.

The figure of Abraham is the beginning of religion. The essence of this religion is election: the elect chooses the one who elected him. Faithfulness flows from this. It means that the election was a lasting one. The religion of Abraham would not be a religion if it did not constitute another form of faithfulness—faithfulness toward other people, faithfulness toward a whole nation. The ex-perience [*doświadczenie*, literally, "toward witnessing"] of the face is the key to this faithfulness, because desire is essentially awakened within a man only when he encounters human destitution. A calling emerges from this destitution: thou shalt not kill. This calling finds no support in the ontological structure of the world. It disguises something absolute within itself—something that does not permit excuses. What is the face of the other? It is a trace that God has left us, therefore a sign of our election. It is a trace that cannot be abandoned in order to run after the suspect. It is a trace of a trace. One must hold fast to the human being touched by destitution, because only he can be found along the traces that God leaves as he walks the world:

> *Toward another* culminates in a *for another*, a suffering for his suffering, without light, that is, without measure, quite different from the purely negative blinding of Fortune which only seems to close her eyes so as to give her riches arbitrarily. Arising at the apex of essence, goodness is other than being. It no longer keeps accounts; it is not like negativity, which conserves what it negates, in its history. It destroys without leaving souvenirs, without transporting into museums the altars raised to the idols of the past for blood sacrifices, it burns the sacred groves in which the echoes of the past reverberate. The exceptional, extra-ordinary, transcendent character of goodness is due to just this break with being and history. To reduce the good to being, to its calculations

and its history, is to nullify goodness. The ever-possible sliding between subjectivity and being, of which subjectivity would be but a mode, the equivalence of the two languages, stops here. Goodness gives to subjectivity its irreducible signification.[29]

Agathology

The presentation of Levinas's views made here has had a selective character. It only presented the fragments that were especially dear to the author of these considerations. Specifically, they constitute a good preparation for an introduction to a concept crucial for the philosophy of drama, the concept of the *agathological horizon*, in which the idea of drama is defined more closely.

When encountering the other, I meet him within a horizon that makes an encounter possible at all, and at the same time is its product. The encountered other, and I along with him, find ourselves within a space in which something is better, something is worse, good or evil. This space is not the ordinary space of Euclidian geometry, but a hierarchical space. The good is called *agathon* in Greek. *Logos* means "that which is reasonable, wise." Let us put it this way: The encounter is the opening of the agathological horizon of interpersonal experience. The agathological horizon is such a horizon where all the manifestations of the other and myself are controlled by a specific *logos*—the *logos* of good and evil, what is better and what is worse, ascent and descent, victory and defeat, salvation and damnation. What does this depend on? When the encounter happens, I do not yet know. I only do know that something like this is at stake in every encounter.

Drama opens up the possibility of tragedy. The essence of tragedy is the victory of evil over the good. When we think about the agathological essence of tragedy, we come closer to understanding the nature of evil. Striving for self-destruction, which Heidegger mentioned,[30] flows from the nature of evil. To destroy evil means to mete out justice to evil. But in tragedy something altogether different happens. The tragic tangle of events is characterized by evil triumphing instead of being vanquished. Prometheus is punished for his merciful deed. King Oedipus becomes the victim of destiny by running away from it. The Just One dies crucified between thieves. Tragedy ends with an event in which the good demonstrates its powerlessness in the struggle with evil. We use the word *tragic* to define the possibility of tragedy. Drama conceals within itself a tragic germ, because it opens up the path to tragedy as its possibility. Whoever takes part in any drama rubs up against the possibility of tragedy, participates in tragedy in some way. This is why the perspective of the tragic is the inseparable background of every encounter, which does not mean that it is given to us clearly.

Here it is necessary to make a polemical remark directed against Max Scheler and his understanding of tragedy. First, Scheler correctly notes that "all that can be called tragic is contained within the realm of values and their relationships. In a universe free of values, such as that constructed by mechanical physics, there are no tragedies. Only where there is high and low, nobleman and peasant, is there anything like a tragic event."[31] Scheler's remark acknowledges the substantial difference between horizons: within the horizons of things (the stage) there is no possibility of tragedy, this possibility only appears within the horizon of values—human values. Further on Scheler writes, "The tragic is apparent only where the strength to destroy a higher positive value proceeds from an object possessing this positive value. The manifestation is, moreover, purest and clearest where objects of equally high value appear to undermine and ruin each other. Those tragedies most effectively portray the tragic phenomenon in which, not only is every one in the right, but where each person and power in the struggle presents and equally superior right, or appears to fulfill an equally superior duty."[32] Therefore, the tragic phenomenon has two layers: the first is the clash of positive subjects of value, spokesmen of the law and moral order; the second is the intrigue of evil which pits honest men or gods against one another and forces them into battle. Evil comes from good beings turning against each other as enemies. What makes them turn against each other? Who? Fate? Blindness? A demon? It is tragic that Prometheus offers fire to men, and the gods *have to* punish him. Pilate knows that Jesus is righteous, but *has to* wash his hands. Therefore, the good has become an adversary of another good; evil has come between them and has become the basic principle of tragedy.

There are many possible sources of tragedy, but all of them can be derived from two fundamental principles: weakness and ignorance. The tragedy of Prometheus, chained to a mountain in the Caucasus, is a tragedy of weakness—the tragic nature of fettered freedom. His own situation contains no mysteries for Prometheus. Prometheus suffers in full light, even in an excess of light; he knows why, and knows that there is no solution for him. It is different with Oedipus. The tragedy of Oedipus, as it becomes apparent, is the tragedy of ignorance. Oedipus has enough strength to escape his destiny. However, because he is surrounded everywhere by delusions, he falls victim to his fate because of them. There are also many possible tragedies resulting from combinations of weakness and ignorance. As a result, a situation can come about in which the main source of pain becomes knowledge. The wise man might die from an excess of truth. Nevertheless, these and similar types of tragedy are derivative, built on specific conceptions of the good, evil, man, and human fate. The theory of the encounter does not require of us, at least for now, a wider discussion of these concepts.

The possibility of tragedy goes hand in hand with the possibility of triumph. By opening up the first, drama simultaneously opens up the second. Triumph signifies the victory of the good against what opposes itself to the good. The *nature* of the good is unveiled to us slightly more deeply through the idea of triumph. The good is that which, by its nature, strives to come into being. To let the good be, means to render justice unto it. The good that has come into being despite evil is a heroic good. Hegel rightly notes that "the general background of a tragic action is provided in a tragedy, as it was in the epic, by that world-situation which I have previously called the 'heroic' age."[33] The heroic triumph of the good over evil can take on many forms: it can be a triumph of power that unveils the indestructibility of the good, or the triumph of the truth that demonstrates the limitation of all delusions. The ideal of triumph would be a synthesis of one and the other: the good would show itself as both indestructible and evident.

The encounter with the other is an encounter with what is really beyond me. The other is simply transcendence. The other puts me in a situation in which, even by ignoring him, I acknowledge that he exists. The presence of the other is a living consciousness of the intuition of existence. But the existence that comes along with the other is not a neutral existence, a pure existence, a perfection that manifests essence. This existence is defined agathologically. In other words, it is an existence problematized in its value by the ineffaceable perspective of tragedy. We cannot separate the experience of this existence from the experience of the evil that threatens it, from the unhappiness it threatens others with, nor from the good for which it must battle and which it must demand from others, even if it does not understand what either one or the other consists in. The existence of the other occurs in time. However, time is not the fundamental reality here, rather it is that toward which the time of the other is heading. When encountering such an existence in the other, I know that this existence is not as it should be: "the true life is absent." However, his existence is not the only one like this; mine is too, if I see it in the perspective of a mutual drama.

Prometheus suffers chained to the mountain, exposed to the pecking of the vulture, condemned to an eternal suffering without hope for death. The myth of Prometheus, Paul Ricoeur wrote, is a proposal for understanding every human existence. Why is human life like this? What is the punishment for? What is the source of our guilt? Oedipus runs away from destiny, but nonetheless falls victim to it. This is also a symbolic representation of human fate. Why is it like this? It was said of Judas that "it would be better for him if he had not been born." What about us?

In Plato we find a symbolic depiction of the man in a cave. This man is deprived of freedom and the ability to rightly judge the world. Thomistic ontology proposes to us a theory of the contingency of all encountered being, according to which the very essence of being, differing from existence in a real way, is the reason for the finitude, imperfections, and contingencies of beings. Blaise Pascal develops the thought of man enclosed between two infinities: infinite minuteness and infinite immensity; man is incapable of understanding one and the other. All these conceptions are, I think, an indirect commentary on what is given to us in the experience of the encounter. They are poetic and ontological interpretations of the basic human condition, but that condition shows itself in full light only in the encounter. These interpretations not only describe the situation but also attempt to explain it. They unveil what is by referring to being to some measure. The measure of being becomes either full freedom, or full clarity, or a pure act of being, or infinity. But before one reaches for measure, one must experience measurability. Measurability is given to us in the encounter. When facing it we ask, "How is it possible?" This is not just a question of mere curiosity, but of deep commitment.

We fall into wonder by discovering, through the encounter, that the true life is absent. This is not wonder. Wonder is joy at the sight of the good, beautiful, and true, which show themselves as even a little victorious. Nor is it really the opposite of wonder—shock at the sight of victorious evil. The one we encounter within the agathological horizon is neither the victorious good nor victorious evil. He is one in whom the good has been exposed to the working of evil. From this comes stupefaction. From stupefaction comes the question, "How is this possible?" How is it possible that Prometheus should suffer because of the good, that the retreating Oedipus should become the victim of fate, that Judas would betray, and the Righteous One should die on the cross? In such a question, rebellion is mixed with acceptance. We rebel against exposing the good to evil, we accept the good endangered by evil. The question born from such roots is concerned with the essence of existence: to be—is it good or evil? Existence is a mysterious category in which the good might unite or intertwine with evil. So, is it better to be or not to be? Scheler used to say, "The existence of a negative value is itself a negative value."[34] Is existence capable of getting rid of this negation at all? Encounter, and only the encounter, is the source of the most profound metaphysical questions.

According to Levinas, the proper horizon of the encounter is the ethical horizon: "We name this calling into question of my spontaneity by the presence of the Other 'ethics.' The strangeness of the Other, his irreducibility to the I, to my thoughts and my possessions, is precisely accomplished as a calling into question of my spontaneity, as ethics."[35] A certain ambiguity hides within this concept of ethics. By ethics we most often mean a certain *praxis* of man with man—with one or many. Ethics is both a wisdom and an art that serves action, which rebukes and praises, a way of being and of acting with others. In some instances it takes on the shape of a system, in others—aphorism, moral lesson, and confession. Yet, the agathological horizon is much more fundamental than all projects of acting. It is a horizon of light rather than power. By encountering the other, I do not yet know what I should do, or, should not do: I do not know whether I should do anything, whether anything can be done. I only know one thing: things should not be like this.

What I said above overlaps, in principle, with the concept of desire in Levinas. Abraham's desire had two aspects: the discovery of the promised land went hand in hand with discovering the land of exile. The one cannot be separated from the other.

However, let us try a distinction and guide ourselves by this distinction: the *agathological horizon* and the *axiological perspective*. The fundamental function of the agathological is unveiling and problematizing. It is similar to the light and to silence. The true life is absent. From this comes the stupefaction and the question of metaphysics, "How is it possible?" The agathological gives rise to thought. The axiological points toward action. The agathological causes existence to become a problem. The axiological points to ways of salvation. The agathological knocks man out of his present rhythm of day and night, knocks him into a limit situation, one in which freedom accepts or rejects itself, reason either wants, or does not want, to be itself, the conscience disavows itself or avows itself. The axiological is the space where freedom, reason, and conscience act. The dimensions of this space depend upon a man's sense of his power; therefore, at times it is larger, others smaller. The agathological awakens feelings of power and powerlessness. A man becomes conscious of the boundaries and limitations of humanity.

When we encounter the other, we encounter his face. What is the face? Levinas brings us closer to the answer. By referring to the terminology we have introduced, we can say that the face of the other does not come from the axiological horizon, but from the agathological horizon. Before we attempt a positive approach to the fundamental question, we will pose a helpful negative question, "What is not a face?" The face is neither a veil nor a mask. What is a veil? What is a mask?

Veil

There are many ways of veiling the face, one of the most natural and spontaneous of them is shame. We will attempt to grasp the essence of veiling's function using the example of shame. However, in order to better understand the nature of shame, there will be a couple of words about the structure of expressive emotions among which shame is numbered.

Henryk Elzenberg says about expressions that they are "the real or apparent—for some observer—disclosure through certain sensually observable objects, that is, physical (let us call them in this *manifestations* or *signs*) of certain *contents*, that is, psychic 'objects' belonging to some being, which is endowed with a psyche. Therefore, the disclosure of energy, for example, through a short and distinct command, or the happy mood of a child through smiling eyes, squeak, and leaps."[36] All expression is marked by an intentionality: it is a kind of sign, which, while being itself, points beyond itself. Shame holds a particular place among expressions: its intentionality is twofold. Shame becomes evident as shame through primary symptoms: a sudden movement of the head, blush on the cheek, and silence. At the same time, as shame, it becomes a veil, which with its manifestation attests to the nonmanifestation of something beyond it, about which, however, we can rightly say that it concerns the face. The intentionality of shame is a paradox—it is the manifestation of a certain nonmanifestation, it is a mystery given to be witnessed.

Shame would not be possible if not for the other person. Taking into consideration his point of view—the point of view of the other—we must distinguish between monological and dialogical expression. The other man is dispensable for monological expression; he is what he is even when there is no other. One can be sad both in loneliness and in the company of the other—sadness itself does not give birth to dialogue. Another person is indispensable for dialogical emotions. The very logic of their intentions requires it. These intentions shape interpersonal dialogue before words. They connect people just by existing. Such emotions are, for example, the feeling of superiority, care (*Fürsorge* in Heidegger), and shame. When we are ashamed, we are ashamed of something toward someone.

The experience of the other through shame is, as we know, Sartre's key problem. For him "being-for-others," which reveals itself in the intentional construction of shame, is the basis for "being-for-itself." To put it another way: what I am for the other person is decisive for what I am for myself—the other interrupts me into a state of shame, and shame makes me into who I am. The other is hell, but one cannot escape from this hell. I am condemned to loneliness, but my loneliness is the absence of the other whom I desire and for whom I am. Let us take a closer look at some aspects of Sartre's thinking.

Sartre begins from the analysis of a significant example. The choice of example is not by accident, it is based upon the conviction that a general thought hides in the concrete event. I am ashamed of myself toward the other, because the other has caught me red-handed peeping in on a third person through a keyhole.[37] The gaze of the other is the direct source of the shame. It throws me into a state of being accused. The other despises me. He makes an object out of me. That is when I discover that this other exists. The manner of experiencing the other is my shame toward him. This repeats itself constantly. We snoop on each other. We are accusers for each other.

What can one say about this account? Much has been written on this topic, stressing the influence of Hegel's conception of the master–slave dialectic.[38] One thing is essential for us: Sartre does not describe an encounter, but a parting, and does not point toward the moment of donning a veil, but the moment of ripping off a mask. Both parting and ripping off the mask occur where interpersonal relations develop upon the level of opposition. Whoever approaches me when I am busy peeping at another is my adversary. I can expect only contempt from him. The moment of contact with him is simultaneously the moment of parting. Much like there is no encounter between the master and the slave—this relationship is ruled by a dialectical principle of oppositions—so there is no encounter between the one held in contempt and the one holding someone in contempt. Contempt erects an impassable barrier between people. However, at the same time, just as the master is tied to the slave and the slave to the master, so the peeper and the one holding him in contempt are mutually tied together. This is how hell comes into being—a place where people are simultaneously both closest and furthest from each other. Closest, because they can touch each other, and furthest, because they cannot encounter each other.

Let us attempt to reverse Sartre's example, adapting it to the logic of encounter seen from the side of the one who encounters. How will our study of shame turn out then?

I can see that the other is ashamed of me; I know that the other is veiling himself. That which is veiled is not visible; nonetheless, the very gesture of veiling is visible. The shame of the other at my sight is a form of dialogue with me, it is a form of speech [*mowa*] whose essence is a refusal [*odmowa*]. Shame fulfills the role of a veil. The veil is not a mask: the task of a mask is to deceive me, but the task of shame is to hide. Shame indicates that there is something that the other considers a personal value, which, however, is so fragile, or even also ambiguous, that it can perish from the gaze. It is better for man to hide a value then to risk its destruction. Shame is a sign of a preference. At the same time, however, within shame one can sense the intention to manifest values, to put them under the judgment of a friendly gaze. The necessity of recognition—more or less universal—belongs to the essence of values. This is why shame is also a pain—the pain of the necessity of hiding. It pains that one must hide values. Shame is the expression of the misery of desires—the desires whose validity is not subject to doubt for the one desiring, but which can raise doubts in others. Shame does not only refuse, it also pleads. It is as if it were saying, "acknowledge the value of that which I am not revealing." The essence of the refusal and request is given by the words *because of and thanks to a fault*. The one looking is faulted for the shame. Simultaneously, however, the one who looks can receive gratitude: if you will not violate my shame, then I will believe in you.

At this point the proposed description of shame intersects with Levinas's description of the one who said, "I am ashamed of my own self-will." You be ashamed, because I am ashamed. Let your shame be the response to my being ashamed. In order for your self-will to turn into freedom by going through the purgatory of shame, your shame must first become "contaminated" with my shame. I am ashamed—it is true—but so that you feel shame and understand the meaning of respect.

The phenomenon of shame directs our attention onto the one who is ashamed, that is, the subject of shame. What is this subject? The one who is ashamed wants through his shame to protect some value. At the same time, shame is possible only in the human world. The subject concerned with value is—as I attempted to show elsewhere—the axiological-I.[39] This is not the transcendental ego in relation to the world, but the I rooted in the world, the personal-I. The personal-I, being the subject of all experiences of values in the world is also a value itself. The subject of shame—its axiological condition of possibility—is therefore a personal value, existing in the world, some, more or less defined, human dignity.

Then what is the difference between a veil and a face? It is not a quantitative difference, but a qualitative one, more precisely, the difference of subjects manifesting themselves: the veil only has meaning on an axiological level, the face on an agathological level. Nevertheless, it is as if the veil offers a passage from one sphere to the other: through reading shame I can stand at the threshold of the face's revelation.

The veil lies in the sphere of acting widely conceived and the calculations associated with it, the face does not know these types of matters. The veil is the search for an exit from a situation without exit. The face does not search for an exit. The veil is that which man *has*, while the face is that which man *is*. Dialogical emotions are what *we possess*, but simultaneously, *what possesses us*. Being *in possession* of dialogical emotion, man, in a certain way, *possesses* another man who awakens this emotion within him, but is also *possessed* by him. Man belongs to man, possesses and is possessed, abandons and is abandoned. The possessive relation disappears in the agathological horizon. We are on the plane of existence and freedom. The other is. His existence is problematic. The true life is absent. How is this possible? The other is free. I am free. Something divides us. Something unites us.

Freedom is significant here.

The freedom experienced first is not my freedom, but the freedom of the other. The veil is a manifestation of this freedom. The other may do this or that, this way or that; in light of what the other may, and how the other may, I also may. However, the word "may" is ambiguous: it functions on the level of axiology and agathology. On the level of axiology it means, "you may do so this way, or another way." On the level of agathology it means that "you cannot, you may not." Here a short fragment from Sartre's description is striking in its accuracy:

> It is for and by means of a freedom and only for and by means of it that my possibles can be limited and fixed. A material obstacle cannot fix my possibilities; it is only the occasion for my projecting myself toward other possibles and cannot confer upon them an outside. To remain at home because it is raining and to remain

at home because one has been forbidden to go out are by no means the same thing. In the first case, I myself determine to stay inside in consideration of the consequences of my acts; I surpass the obstacle "rain" toward myself and I make an instrument of it. In the second case, it is my very possibilities of going out of or staying inside that are presented to me as surpassed and fixed and that a freedom simultaneously foresees and prevents.... Thus in the look the death of my possibilities causes me to experience the Other's freedom.[40]

The freedom of the other throws me into a certain state of helplessness. I know that the other is *toward me*, but is not *for me*. I cannot possess him, I cannot comprehend him. I am shaken out of the previous plane of being-with. I cannot *have* the face of the one whom I encounter. The gods also could not *have* the face of Prometheus, and the enemies of Jesus could not have his. What am I able to do? I can — if I can read — painfully wonder. This wonder shakes me out of the "metaphysical slumber." Awakened I ask, "How is it possible that . . . ?" I go back into my depths with this question. I do no act. I do not project actions. I ask and articulate with this question the drama of the entangling of good with evil. I ask and prove my own freedom with this question.

Mask

It is neither a veil nor a face. The veil only hides the face, the mask lies. The mask, like the veil, appears only along with the appearance of another person; it loses its meaning in isolation. The mask is a mask because of the others' fault — the veil was because of them. What does it mean to say that the mask masks something? The mask's intentionality is a twisted intentionality: the mask strives to create an illusion that is the opposite of what something actually is. The dishonest person puts on a mask of honesty, the lazy person pretends to be hard-working, the unbeliever pretends to be a believer, and so on. Between the mask and the masked truth there comes into being something in the shape of an axiological opposition: the negative value wants to present itself as a positive one. It is possible to conceive of inverse-masks, when a good person pretends to be inferior, but we will leave these examples to the side.

There are times when the concept of the mask takes on a somewhat less radical meaning. We understand by the mask, then, not so much an opposition to the truth, but, rather, bringing to light some typical characteristic whose showing off, while passing over everything else, is of great import to someone. This was the meaning of masks in Greek theater, and still today in caricatures, grotesques, and even in many recognizably realist theaters. You also frequently see this concept used in this way in texts from the psychiatric field, for example, the texts of Antoni Kępiński. This does not seem to be precise. It understands the mask as a profile of a face, meaning, an expression of the truth connected with the situation.

The mask's intentions branch out widely. The mask emerges from the soul of a man as a being conscious of his own cognitive possibilities and those of others—it is his essentially free manifestation. It is concerned with others and, at the same time, it is for others and the fault of others (at least for those who are masking themselves).

When taking into account the origin of the mask—an origin that stamps its content—we can speak of a mask of a sense of dissatisfaction, an auto-ironic mask, and the mask of pained consciousness. This does not exhaust all the possibilities, but these three cases are fairly typical, besides, one can find documentation for them in the philosophical literature.

Kępiński generally speaks about a mask of a sense of dissatisfaction, tying it specifically to schizophrenia, but he admits that this phenomenon has a wider reach. Social life itself demands masks. He writes,

> When observing oneself, one accepts the viewpoint of one's milieu, and simultaneously one's own. One is an actor observed by strangers in the gallery and by friends from behind the scenes. Dissatisfaction with one's activities increases the greater the discrepancy is between a chosen role and the rejected roles, between the plan and the execution, also between the anticipated and the real reaction of the milieu. Such disparity is frequently observed in patients even before the outbreak of schizophrenia. They are bothered by dissatisfaction with themselves, because they

would like to be something other than what they are in reality. Everything turns out differently than what they planned in the role they are forced to play against their will, and so they feel its alienation all the more. They are under the impression that their mask constantly chafes them, that they are not on the outside what they truly are, that the milieu sees their bad game and can read what hides behind it.[41]

Dissatisfaction with oneself is a symptom of a growing rebellion against oneself and against those who are at fault for making one put on a mask.

Auto-irony is another type of mask. Here masking intersects with the ripping off of the mask. Auto-irony depends upon taking on a comedic stance, even mocking, toward oneself. Hegel attaches an epoch-making meaning to auto-irony. He considers it to be a symptom of a derisive consciousness whose literary exemplar is Denis Diderot's *Rameau's Cousin*. The title character is exemplary of the state of consciousness before the revolution's outbreak. Man is aware of his dependence upon the lords grinding him down, but he still derives profits from this dependence, which is why he consents to servitude. When the pressure increases, and the consciousness of debasement hits bottom, then revolution will become a necessity. A double-relation of man to others manifests itself in auto-irony: for some I have a mask of submission, for others a mask that proposes laughter at my submission—a submission that is supposed to be ostensible, because I am really concerned about "saving" values that are aesthetic, economic, political, and so on. Deception finds its extraethical justification in auto-irony. Its inseparable attribute is that of shamelessness. Hegel writes, "The content of what Spirit says about itself is thus the perversion of every Notion and reality, the universal deception of itself and others; and the shamelessness which gives utterance to this deception is just for that reason the greatest truth."[42] Auto-irony obviously does not signify a complete abandonment of the mask. It signifies a game of two masks—a mask of submissions for some and a mask mocking this submission directed at others.

One more example of a mask: the pained consciousness. This is how the matter looks close up: man knows that he wears a mask and suspects that others already know about this, or are close to having this knowledge. However, he cannot rid himself of the mask for good. His mask allows him to maintain himself on the surface of some world, even though it is a source of concerns and sufferings. Kępiński notes, "The paradox of the mask depends on the fact that, with its help, an effect is achieved that is nearly opposite of the one intended. One puts on a mask to make oneself calmer and to calm one's surroundings, but it leads to increased agitation about oneself and one's surroundings."[43] A new ambiguity arises from this: for some there is the mask, for others suffering because of the necessity of putting on a mask. The following thought is behind it: "If the mask will not give me satisfaction, if I will be pained because of it, then in this pain there is a reason for mercy; after all, we should not hit someone while he's down." Such a man believes that by revealing to others the wounds given by the mask he will thereby gain their forgiveness. And so the presence of the mask is accompanied by pained expressions, such as "I can't, but I have to." Suffering is used here as the opposite of what it is: it should stop killing, and, by awakening mercy, it should make possible maintaining oneself on the surface of the bog the world has become.

The mask also contains a reference to others. It is from the fault of others and, at the same time, it is for them. For those masking themselves, it is the flowering of alienation. In reality it attests to a reduced feeling of responsibility for oneself—it is the work of those who have not taken possession of themselves. The process of masking is paired with accusing and blaming others. The logic of the mask emerges from the feeling of guilt: a man judges, because he does not want to be judged. Masking is not only deceiving others, but is also a punishment for them: "Here I am just as you want to have me, therefore you do not really have me—you are at fault for this yourselves." The mask expresses the unrealized dream of the subjected to rule over those who rule. It achieves its goal through cunningly pushing others into a prearranged space of relationships—a space of seeming debasements, seeming exaltations, hysterical games, and so on. Anxiety is the main source of the mask (Kępiński). It pushes man into a space of being-with where the dominant structure is a structure of opposition: the other is *a priori* my enemy, and I must shelter myself in a prepared hiding place in order to protect myself from him. The mask is the look of a man through the window of a hiding place.[44]

When speaking of shame as a veil, I pointed to the subject of axiological shame: a human person existing in the world. But what is the subject of the mask? The answer is provided—more or less indirectly—by the so-called hermeneutic of suspicion. For Karl Marx, the obscure subject of the mask is the subject of class interests who in his being is concerned with the realization of the basic interests of his own class. Class egoism is the *base* of the mask, whereas the *superstructure* is culture, morality, and religion. For Friedrich Nietzsche, the subject is a subject of the resentment of the weak against the violence of the strong. The mask is an attempt to morally blame the victors for one's own loss—its contents are an ethics where losing becomes a value and winning an antivalue. Freud advances the concept of the libido suppressed by cultural demands. Gilles Deleuze—without delving into particular concepts—speaks generally of the mask's "larval subject."[45] The larval subject is a synthesis of the ability for self-debasement, self-doubt, perversity, egoism, and betrayal, it is the dark seat of lusts that provoke terror. However, above all, it is the subject of the art of lying. The mask is the main work of this art—its masterpiece.

The discovery that the other has put on a mask awakens one to asking about his truth: Who is he? Who is he truly? But also, What does the word "truth" mean?

It would seem that the truth is something that hides beyond a mask, that is, its opposite. However, it is also said that the mask masks the lack of a face. Illusions, appearances, and ornaments fall away, what remains is a man without a face, without qualities. Can the lack of a face be regarded as the truth of man? I do not think so. Unmasking does not lead to, and it cannot lead to, the lack of a face, but stretches toward the source of the masking stance, which can be, if you will, found in the vicinity of the face. Even if we accept that it is possible to lack a face, it will not be the truth of man. Lacking a face is a pure indifference to truth or falsehood, it is beyond one and the other. The one without a face is a stone.

When we encounter a mask, we cannot but ask about the face. We search for a face somewhere beyond masks. We search just as we search for the truth. What is the truth conceived as a face?

The face conceals within itself something ideal, and everything that is ideal can be given either directly (then it awakens wonder and responsibility), or through its opposite, its negation, its illusion. Lying tends toward the truth, just like the darkness toward light. It is similar with the mask and face. When we ask, Whence comes the mask? Why a mask? What is a mask for? we succumb to the call of the ideality of the face. We call this ideality the truth. This does not mean that the face is, that it lives incarnate—the heart of the matter is that, for the one masking himself, his own face exclusively can be such an ideality, which he searches for only for himself. Therefore, perhaps his mask today is only a path toward gaining a face?

Face

When encountering the other, we encounter them "in their face." Hence these questions: What is a face? The analyses we undertook were supposed to bring us closer to the face. What was the character of these analyses?

Earlier I cited Levinas's doubts as to whether a phenomenology of the face is possible. Phenomenology describes what appears, but the face does not appear, it *reveals* itself. The face does not have contents, which could possibly be isolated, compared, and compiled. The face is not an object toward which intentional acts could be directed. It is also not a bridge from me to the other and from the other to me. Therefore, methods of descriptive phenomenology have no precise application here. But we know that besides description, which depends upon an intentional pointing toward the object, there is in phenomenology a description that leads toward experience—especially toward fundamental experiences, upon which the meaning of the human world depends. Husserl calls them openings, where not only the act of opening is important, but also the horizon opened within it. The experience of the face is a fundamental experience, onto which the appropriate description should lead. The phenomenology of the face is therefore an attempt at describing an experience of the other person in such a way that it will be able to justify the witness given to him. To guide toward the face therefore means to describe the path that leads to witness. But such a description can never hit the heart of what it aims for, instead it must continually circle around it.

It is obvious for the philosophy of drama that people have faces, but things have appearances. The difference is fundamental and ineradicable. Therefore, it must be said that the revelation of the face lies at the source of all drama properly understood. Dialogue with the other can only begin from this revelation. Man's intentional-objectifying relation to the stage also has its beginning in it. Thanks to the face we can define the essence of encounter: to encounter is to encounter the other in his face.

The directing description, unlike a pointing description, directs our attention upon a horizon, that is, as if upon a background, thanks to which the face can reveal itself, and upon a subject that is able to receive such a revelation, and again upon the tie created between the one revealing himself and the one receiving the revelation. I have said very generally that the first horizon is the agathological horizon. Levinas wrote about it in more detail, stressing that it is constituted by an infinite good, which "is" beyond being and nonbeing. When it comes to the subjective aspect, I left the matter just as Levinas captured it: desire is the subjective condition of ex-periencing [*do-świadczenia*, literally, "toward witnessing"] the face as opposed to needs, and the tie between myself and the other is a tie of responsibility that contains both thinking and freedom. The face revealing itself is therefore what in the agathological horizon constitutes and justifies the tie of responsibility, and the specific experience of thinking contained within it (question: How is this possible?) and freedom (as opposed to self-will). Obviously, in applying these concepts, I did not want to develop a full theory of freedom and thinking, but—still led by the basic intention—only to guide toward the face. The analyses of the veil and the mask had the same goal in mind. Through these analyses it became apparent that human destitution is also a destitution of untruth, the necessity of hiding out and veiling, whereas the face is the human truth.

It is time to take one more step, perhaps a decisive one. This step both refers to Levinas and goes beyond him. Levinas, as I noted, stresses the passive character of the face above all: its destitution—the destitution of the widow, orphan, and the stranger. Out of the two overlapping triangles symbolizing the face mentioned by Mosès, Levinas chooses, above all, the triangle "formed by the forehead and the two cheeks, or alternatively by the nose and the two ears" as the theme of his description. But the face is not only passive, it not only speaks [*opowiada*] about experiencing destitution . . . it also responds [*odpowiada*] to poverty.

And this seems crucial: the response to destitution.

The face reveals itself as a gift of the agathological horizon—a horizon in which good and evil take on the form of a drama, while the drama announces the possibility of man's tragedy or victory. In a drama, good and evil do not stand far apart, as they do in the kingdom of concepts, instead they interweave within a common time, a common space, in one and the same man. When they are interwoven in this way they constitute a significant perspective on human history. What silence is for sound, and light is for color, that is what good and evil are for the face. The face can reveal itself thanks to them. However, the comparison with silence and light can be deceiving. We must add: this silence and this light have the shape of a cross. The symbolism of the cross is inescapable.

The face carries within itself a reflection of ideal beauty, goodness, and truth. The face is the height, concretized glory, unrepeatable sublimity, and the splendor of man. It is capable of gripping, delighting, and carrying beyond the prose of the world toward a poetics of existence. But it is also fragility, forlornness, harm, or destitution. On it are the marks of pains past and places for future ones. It is chiefly on man's face that his beauty and his life passes. Tears and dying appear here. The face is set upon the cross of existence.

However, the face does not accept the cross in a passive manner. It responds to the cross. The face's *logos* is the manner in which man overcomes the tragic perspective, which under the form of personal evil, pain, and harm has penetrated into his existence. The face is a form of human disagreement with the assertion that "the true life is absent" [Levinas. —Rosman]. The face is neither a simple manifestation of personal evil nor a manifestation of personal good—the evil that makes man unhappy and the good that makes him happy. The face is an expression of an existential movement where man strives to justify that *he is* by putting his existence under the protection of a good that brings him hope. This is because man believes that only the good is able to save.

Therefore, there is no revelation of the face without some cross in its background. But the face is not a reflection of the cross, but rather the incarnation of the glory flowing from the manner in which man responds to his cross. In the Gospel scene of the Crucifixion, this is revealed to us by three statements of Jesus: "Forgive them, for they know not what they do"; "My God, my God, why have you forsaken me?"; and "Into your hands I commend my spirit." The first reveals heroism, the second tragedy, and the third hope for salvation. This precisely is the face.

The existential response of man to his own tragedy expressed and embodied in the face we shall call the *existential pathos*. The concept of pathos points to both the pain of undergoing and the manner of overcoming of the pain, both to passivity and the most intimate activity, to both the tragedy of falling down and the effort of climbing up. By following the transformations of the existential pathos, we follow the face and its history, we follow the truth of man revealed by drama.

CHAPTER 2

The Answer to the Question, That Is, Reciprocity

A man stands before me and asks me a question. I do not know whence he came and do not know where he is going. Now he expects an answer. He clearly desires to make me a participant in some matter of his by asking, "Which one?" This I do not know. I only know as much as is in the question. A moment of tension arises. Will I answer the questioner?

What can I do? I can either answer or not; I can answer nonsensically, evasively, or falsely. One thing is certain, I do not have to answer—I can turn into a deaf stone. I cannot find any power that might force me to answer. The relationship between question and answer is not a causal relationship. In some sense, Gottfried Leibniz was right when he spoke of "monads without windows." If I do give an answer, it is only because I want to do so. If I do, how does it happen that I want to? The "wanting" was born from a question. There was no wanting before the question. What is the nature of the unique, noncausal, relationship of man to man, which makes possible the posing of questions and receiving answers?

To explain the possibility of an answer, we must abandon not only ontological categories but also logical and epistemological categories. Logic studies relations between a question and an answer only when the answer is ready. It can then decide whether the logical form of the answer matches the logical form of the question. However, logic is powerless when facing the question and answer as an event. Epistemology is similar. It is possible to investigate whether the state of things toward which the answer points fulfills the intention of the question, but it is not possible to investigate, and find a solution to, the problem of why the questioned person answers at all.

We will call the relationship that arises between the questioned and the questioner "dialogical." Inventing a name, however, does not mean grasping the essence of the problem. It means, at most, shuffling around the words in a question. So we ask, What are the roots of the dialogical relationship between man and man?

Some time passes between the moment of the question and the moment of the answer. The tension builds over this time. What will happen? The time of tension is a time that constitutes the onset of a common dramatic thread that will bind, for a shorter or longer period, the questioned with the questioner. The questioner and questioned belong to each other. What does this mean? What does it mean to say that a dramatic thread is in common? In what way does it tie people with each other? What is its manner of existing? In general, Where does it exist?

I, as the questioned, know, thanks to the question that reached me, that another man is present by me, but I also know that I am by him. The word "by" can equally mean "toward" and "next to." This has to change. It must change. The question knocks me out of the state of being "by someone," "next to someone," or even "toward someone," in order to put me in a new state—the state of being "for someone." I begin to be by responding to a question—if I answer the question—"for someone." In other words, I become responsible. The significant meaning of the question depends upon the fact that it awakens in the questioned a feeling of responsibility. For now, it does not matter how deep and stable this feeling is, its nature itself is important. Responsibility is an ethical category. To explain the genealogy of the answer to a question one must reach for the ethical element. In other words, one must abandon the spaces of ontology and logic and enter into the domain of the metaphysics of the good. However, the metaphysic of the good is closely linked with the metaphysic of evil. So we can guess that at the sources of the answer to the question posed to man there must be some kind of ethical choice—a choice between good and evil. The respondent not only gives a reply to an other, but also gives it to himself—himself as a participant in the drama of good and evil.

Question

What is a question? It is a type of request. Whoever poses a question asks for an answer. The question and answer are possible where requests are possible, therefore in a specific kind of world—in a world of destitution. If there were no world of destitution, then there would be no requests and nobody would ask anybody about anything. Every question, directly or indirectly, witnesses to some destitution.

The concept of destitution—well known to Plato's philosophy, and then forgotten—is a fundamental dramatic category that describes man's situation, even God's, in the drama of existence. Its intention points toward some pain, or "ur-pain," toward a danger that threatens creation, from which even the Creator himself cannot be entirely free, if he only ties himself to creation with a bond of participatory love. What is the destitution of the world? Levinas uses three symbols: the stranger, widow, and orphan. He writes: "The proximity of the Other, the proximity of the neighbor, is in being an ineluctable moment of the revelation of an absolute presence (that is, disengaged from every relation), which expresses itself. His very epiphany consists in soliciting us by his destitution in the face of the stranger, the widow, and the orphan."[1]

The question necessitates proximity. But it is not only about physical proximity, but, above all, about the type of spiritual proximity, which makes possible being moved by destitution—the destitution that gives birth to the request and question. Only then can the answer be a gift. According to Levinas, this gift is not a gift for the destitute and the beggar. The one answering does not answer out of pity, like a rich man who throws alms around, but rather as a pupil, who has discovered a chance for himself in the question. Levinas writes: "This gaze that supplicates and demands, that can supplicate only because it demands, deprived of everything because entitled to everything, and which one recognizes in giving (as one 'puts the things in question in giving')—this gaze is precisely the epiphany of the face as a face. The nakedness of the face is destituteness. To recognize the Other is to recognize a hunger. To recognize the Other is to give. But it is to give to the master, to the lord, to him whom one approaches as 'You' in a dimension of height."[2]

The paths drawn out here require a thorough diagnosis. The problem of destitution emerges. Does every question grow out of destitution? After all, there are questions of philosophers, questions of inquisitors, and questions of God. Are they, too, somehow related to the questions of the stranger, widow, and orphan?

Philosopher, Inquisitor, God

We have questions of the philosophers, among them questions of Husserl's transcendental ego, which talks to itself. We have questions of inquisitors who are conducting their investigations to accuse and condemn others. We have God's questions, directed at Adam who is hiding. Is not Levinas's symbolism too impoverished? Does it not require expanding?

(A) *The philosopher's question.* Can thinking work without questions posed from the outside? The myth of Gyges—the owner of a magical ring that made him invisible to other people, but he could still see them—spoke about such a possibility. Gyges incarnated the dream of rulers: to see but not be seen, to hear and not be heard, to know and not to be recognized, to derive all knowledge from himself with the aid of questions posed to himself.

The myth of Gyges found its philosophical expression in Husserl's theory of the transcendental ego. The transcendental ego emerges as the fruit of the transcendental reduction of the world. The world and the people inhabiting it become mere phenomena because of the reduction—the phenomenon of the world and the phenomenon of people. Any questions going out from the world and others toward the transcendental-I are only phenomena of questions. They are not events. They do not create obligations. The privilege of asking belongs to the same I that must also give the answer. The transcendental-I becomes, in this manner, the absolute source of meaning for all possible questions and all possible answers. Its consciousness develops within an internal dialogue with itself. It can split itself into questioning and questioned parts without losing its internal identity.

Does this mean that all the miseries of the world have become foreign to it? That they also are only phenomena of misery? Does the answer given by that I not emerge out of any obligations? Is its conversation with itself only a delightful playing with thoughts within the frame of their possibilities?

In Husserl's philosophical thinking, it is necessary to distinguish the fundamental question from the derivative questions and, as a consequence, distinguish the fundamental answer from derivative answers. The fundamental question of his philosophy is not the question of the transcendental ego, but the question emerging from the present historical moment, from the crisis of the European sciences. The crisis of the European sciences has put the truth itself in danger. Where truth is in danger, reason, science, rationality, and man himself, as a thinking being, are also in danger. Husserl's philosophy came into being as an answer to this crisis. Therefore, the whole theory of the transcendental-I does not present itself as a theory of the questioning-I, but as the theory of the I answering a previously posed historical question. Human destitution is present indirectly within it as the factor giving birth to a question, as a crisis.

The fall of truth is the misery of the questioning Husserl. The source of Husserlian philosophy's power is the experience of this misery. This is more a moral power than a power that is strictly theoretical. Theory is the answer; morality is the question. One can argue about the appropriateness of the answer, but one must acknowledge the ethos of this philosophical questioning. There is a significant difference between Gyges and the transcendental-I: the first is concerned with power, the other with truth. However, one must also acknowledge that a similar substrate of pain can be detected in every philosophy. Every philosophy grows out of concern for the truth threatened by the drama of history. In this respect, the philosopher resembles an exile who, before he can live in the world, must discern this world and help others in their discernment.

I admit that the questions and answers formulated by philosophers need not carry clear signs of human misery. However, the fundamental questions from which philosophizing begins are without a doubt a cry of pain. However, let us add: a cry and, simultaneously, a choice of a path toward an answer. Asking out of the depths of misery—Where is the truth?—the philosopher makes a choice: even though various values are endangered in the misery of the world, the threat of untruth is the most dangerous to him, and he must deal with it first. Only the fall of truth—lies, illusion, falsehood—is capable of establishing the absolute obligation of thinking, out of which all philosophy develops.

(B) *The inquisitor's question*. The questions of the inquisitor are part of a larger totality, a larger text—part of an interrogation. The dialogue of an interrogation has its own particular dramatic assumptions. It is basically a man's attack on another man, calling him names, accusing him, insulting him, throwing him into preset traps, forcing him to admit guilt. The question is an important part of the interrogation. The peak moment is the instant when the questioned must answer yes or no. But, must he really answer?

What is the relationship between the inquisitor's questions and the questions of the widow, stranger, and orphan? Is the inquisitor one of them? Does he also come from a horizon of destitution? Would it not be more appropriate to say he creates destitution?

Contrary to appearances, the power of the inquisitor over a man depends upon the inquisitor always striving to come out in the name of some destitution. He accuses in the name of destitution, calls in the name of destitution, humiliates in the name of destitution, and in the name of destitution he poses his questions. The questions of the inquisitor have a twofold purpose: he begins by leading the questioned out of his silence and only then gets him to confess his guilt. What is to be done to make the questioned stop being silent? It is necessary to awaken in him the conviction that, here and now, he has the obligation to speak, answer. He cannot be deaf to the request. He cannot be blind to misfortune. The inquisitor must present himself as a spokesman for misfortune for this purpose, and the questioned must see himself as one who by answering questions rescues someone or something. What is at stake is not yet the content of the response. The act itself is what is at stake. What is at stake is a conversation. What is at stake is planting seeds of feeling responsibility for the inquisitor who is questioning—even the smallest, like a mustard seed. The answer of the interrogated is the first sign that the inquisitor is more than dead wood in his eyes. The situation turns when the conversation begins. The interrogated shakes hands with the one who is interrogating him.

It is significant that the accused would rather lie than remain silent. It is easier to utter untruth than to say nothing. The obligation to speak is stronger than the obligations to speak the truth. Its source is the good. The responsibility to the truth turns out to be derivative.

It would be absurd to say that the inquisitor is one of the incarnations of human misery listed by Levinas. Nonetheless, he must present himself to the interrogated as a spokesman for the poverties of the one being questioned. Only in this way can he awaken in him the desire and obligation to answer. If he does not succeed, he might find himself standing accused and accounted for his intentions. The dialogue of an interrogation has something like another bottom. In essence it puts both sides in a situation of having to choose—a choice between the guilt of silence and the guilt of speaking, the guilt of speaking the truth and untruth, the guilt of punishment and merit, in other words: the choice between good and evil.

(C) *God's question.* God poses a question to man only after his fall. The question is, "Where are you?" It is like a cry of longing. Adam pushed God into the only "misery" that can touch an omnipotent and perfect being—into the destitution of love rejected. The one who elects was rejected. However, despite the rejection, he has not stopped loving. Love yearns and searches. When it does not find the beloved it calls with "where are you?" If there were no "destitution" of a God who loves, then there would be no question, calling, request. The duty of interrupting silence and giving an answer arises in Adam's soul precisely because God's calling is a request. But Adam does not give an answer. He runs, hides, and covers himself up. This is the new fault of Adam and his new, hitherto unknown, fear—the fear of answering God, of the responsibility for God besides himself, in the world. The image of the "misery" of a loving God will appear again repeatedly in the biblical texts. It will be discussed in the Song of Songs and it will take on a more realistic shape in the life and death of Christ.

The Christian religion of dialogue between man and God became possible because God himself has become like a stranger, orphan, and widow. Religion no longer relies upon the exalted feeling of wonder that raises man to heaven, nor upon rational speculation about the highest being, but upon the feeling of responsibility for the response that the questioned and called should give to the one Questioning and Calling.

Presence

The posing of a question leaves a trace in me: I know that an answer must be given. It must be given here and now. This "here and now" means that the one who asked me a question is *present*. He will be with me for as long as he does not hear an answer. There comes a moment of not talking, silence, saturated with anticipation—his anticipation of my answer. Every moment of delay is a moment of my delaying my answer to him. In this way, between myself and the other, a specific type of time constitutes itself—dialogical time, and within it its present. The questioner is present in the present. This presence is a dialogical presence. Dialogical presence is time in such a present where the questioner waits for an answer, and the questioned still does not give it. The other is present along with me, so long as the silence between the question and answer lasts. Therefore, dialogical time is not identical with Husserlian internal time consciousness—a time determined by retention, protention, and the actual present, for which the question of the other and one's answer to it are not significant, a time without presence, but also without any nonpresence of anyone. Dialogical time is a time of dramatic tension. Retention within it is a direct consciousness of the burden of the just-asked question; protention is the full-of-anticipation inclination toward an answer; and the actual present is presence—my presence for the other and his presence for me. I can know that an answer must be given precisely because the other is present. The near future is unveiled to me as a moment for the other. Something must be sacrificed in this moment. Some "yes" or "no." It becomes secondary whether you must sacrifice to get rid of the other (i.e., the inquisitor), or keep the other (i.e., brother or God) with you.

Questioner

The presence of the other—the one who in asking demands, and in demanding asks—is the presence of some destitution. Destitution in itself demands mercy. So, is the answer to a question supposed to be an act of mercy? Is it alms casually tossed to a beggar? We know from the passage quoted earlier from Levinas that this is not the case. Yet, what does this mean more closely? Levinas discovers a sign of the master in all the symbols of destitution. The stranger, widow, and orphan are not only instances of human destitution, but also signs of human greatness. Truth and wisdom flow from them toward the questioned. The true master is the one whose wisdom has its roots in the experience of destitution and awareness of tragedy. Such a master truly teaches—not when he proclaims judgments and forces others to memorize them, but when he poses questions, waiting until the one who is asked finds an answer within himself. The question is true teaching. Being a master does not mean multiplying answers, but having the ability to pose fundamental, key questions. We know this mark of mastery from Socrates and St. Augustine.

This is also why the place of the one posing questions is privileged. The questioner stands higher than the questioned. He demands an answer as the one who can lead the questioned along the paths of truth. His position is stronger. Inquisitors know this well! Therefore, going toward the truth means, above all, listening to the questions of others.

We must stress that the questioner is an ambivalent value in the eyes of the questioned. The master asks, and, in asking, promises the truth. However, he simultaneously shakes one out of the *status quo*. The master questions. To question means to promisingly negate. The master contradicts, shakes out of loneliness, from a one-sided wonder for the world, from habits, from being at peace with himself. This hurts. In the end, every master is, to some degree, an inquisitor. One must overcome oneself to answer at all. Yet, even earlier—one must overcome oneself to hear at all. Answering, one must go outside of oneself. But, what will I receive in return? How far will I have to go astray? How deeply will I have to abandon myself? I do not know. This is why I fear questioners, despite the promises they make.

Answerer

I answer a question. I answer. Why do I answer? What is my answering-I? What do I think about myself, what can I think of myself as the one who gives an answer?

I answer because the question was a request and a calling, and the request and calling constitute an ethical responsibility. I answer in order not to kill. If I remained silent, I could commit a crime against the face of the questioner. My silence would be an act of contempt—metaphysical contempt, against which no physics nor any ontology can argue. One must give an answer. It makes no difference who asks—philosopher, passerby, inquisitor. Only the face remains. All of human destitution has concentrated itself in the face to which I speak. It demands, it teaches me.

What do I know about myself as the answering-I? I know one thing: by giving an answer, that is, fulfilling the request of the questioner, I already know what it means to be good. I know through direct experience. But not in the sense that I have suddenly discovered how good I am! This would be pride and foolishness. But, rather, in the following sense: I know what it means to be good in the here and now. I give what they request. This is good. But I give so they leave me alone and stop asking. I only give this, nothing more. The rest I leave for myself. This is wrong. I respond, and in this way I prove that I am responsible. However, I would like to end my responsibility already, to distance myself and not return. I save the other. But I also save myself from the other. I give a word to hold onto myself. I hold onto myself by giving my word. To be good at the same time means to not be good, to be evil. One is always within the boundaries of finitude. The response and question are also two expressions of human finitude—like tears that flow from the eyes, blurring the vision of the world.

Reciprocity

Let our thoughts follow the path that we have gone through: the question is a request—the question of the philosopher, inquisitor, God—a demand in which the destitution of finite existence expresses itself. Thanks to the question, I know that the other is present; the questioner is a master; I, who answer, know what it means to be good here and now in this world; the dialogical bond is a bond of responsibility.

Where do these analyses lead? They lead toward a better understanding of what the word *reciprocity* means. We will have to return to the matter of reciprocity, but in the meantime let us attempt to give it a provisional definition.

There is an abyss between me and you. We are monads without windows. Neither what is happening within you is the cause of my actions, nor is what is happening in me the cause of your actions. No known causal relations tie us together. There is also no logical tie between what we think. Our experiences differ. Each one of us takes in the world differently. I do not even know whether what you call the color yellow looks the same as what I describe with this word. The metaphor of a monad without windows is not at all an exaggeration.

Yet, you ask me a question, and I do not answer. This is astounding. Great philosophy is born out of wonder for this fact—the philosophy of dialogue. We are talking. This means that you question me, and I, despite this, confirm you in your act of questioning me. This also means that, in the act of your questioning, you have questioned yourself, in order to acknowledge me in what I will say to you; leaning toward me, you await my answer. In answering your question, I affirm myself. After all, I am doing the answering. By accepting my answer, you affirm me whom you also questioned when you turned to me. After the question and answer—in general after the conversation—we are no longer the same as we were before. We owe something to each other. We can fault each other for something.

What is reciprocity?

Reciprocity means that we are, as we are, through each other. This *through* means that we can either fault each other, or we can be grateful to each other.

Nothing better expresses these structures than reciprocity.

I-Thou

The analysis of the situation between the question and answer sheds new light on the meaning of the words I-Thou. Ferdinand Ebner wrote: "Since I and Thou exclusively exist in a reciprocal reference to each other, just as there is no I absolutely stripped of a Thou, one cannot think of a Thou stripped of an I. The word is that by which not only existence is objectively constituted, 'established,' but also, above all, the relationship between the one and the other."[3]

Ebner expresses a view typical for the philosophy of dialogue. There is no, and there cannot be, an I without a Thou and no Thou without an I. What does this impossibility mean? Is the concept of the I connected to the concept of the Thou as the concept of "bigger" is connected to the concept of "smaller"? However, this would mean that these concepts have a relational meaning that does not reach the essence of what they describe. Meanwhile, however often I say "I," I am conscious that I am praising what is absolutely mine, what is me. Yet, if they are not supposed to be relational concepts, how is it possible to say that one is impossible without the other?

The best-known philosophical conceptions of the I are clearly weighed down by, implicitly or explicitly, the point of view of ontology imposed from above. The consequence of this is the application of concepts drawn from ontology to the description of the I. There are two concepts to distinguish—the concept of the subject and the concept of totality. Philosophies that are idealistically oriented strive to identify the I with the subject, which necessarily entails the identification of the world with the object. The relation between the I and non-I is reduced to the subject–object relation. Positivistically oriented philosophies discern the structure of totality within it—a totality that gathers as their component parts (elements) sense experience, data-impressions, and so on. But, neither in the first nor the second instance is the I referred to the Thou. However, this does not mean that it is granted the meaning of an independent being. The I as a subject is relative to the object; the I as a totality is relative to the parts that go into its composition. The I–Thou relation proposed by Ebner and other representatives of the philosophy of dialogue breaks with the illusions that are the consequence of the exploration of ontological concepts beyond their proper domain, and returns to the meanings of both words their proper space—the space of dialogue. But does it ultimately defend their specificity? Does saying that their meaning is relational (Ebner, Buber) not introduce in the place of one ontological form a different one?

Here is a new difficulty. The word "I" requires us to think about that which is concrete, singular, and unrepeatable. In the whole world there is not, there never was, and there never will be another I identical to me. At the same time, the I falls under the general concept of We. If something is radically individual and unique, how can it fall under general structures? If despite this it does not fall under them, it still carries the stamp of repeatability.

Let us return to the question-and-answer situation. What is the questioned I and what is the questioning Thou?

One must change the plane of inquiry to answer this question; move from the ontological level onto the axiological, from the level of a language that describes being, and exchange it for the level of values. The concept I has many meanings. Among the many meanings of this concept some are fundamental and others secondary. The most fundamental meaning is the one that points toward value—toward the axiological-I. The concept of the axiological-I touches the core of ego-experiences. These experiences are distinguished by the fact that they can be described using the word *mine*. Everything that is *mine*—my feelings, my experiences, my thoughts, my decisions point toward the I. But the I does not identify with what is *mine*, it transcends it. However, not like a substance transcending its properties, nor like the thing-in-itself transcending phenomena, but more like when in a work of art the particular value of the work transcends the qualities (matter) that underlie it, or like the logic of a melody transcending the sound of the instruments that play it. The axiological-I can be compared to a particular power of attraction that collects around itself all contents, which cannot be nobody's, precisely because they are mine. Yet, this is a different power than the power of feeling or sensation—it is the power of that which is—and this is important—the very power of "significance." The axiological-I is, because it is significant. But it is not significant (has its weight, has its own meaning) because it is. In this sense it goes beyond ontology.

Only by standing on the axiological plane of reflection can we accept the following statement by Mosès, which refers to Rosenzweig's views: "God can only say *I* to the extent that man says *thou* to him, that is, to the extent man submits his *I* to an exteriority that infuses it. But the *I* of man only constitutes itself if it has first been spoken to as a *thou*. This does not mean, tritely, that the *I* can only be defined in relation with that which it is not, but rather that the *I* is *I* only because more primordially it is a *thou* for someone else. The *I* is the response called for by the question 'Where art thou?'"[4]

The question, "Where art thou?" is full of significance. It belongs to the fundamental questions that one man can pose to another man. Other questions are only possible when the questioner already knows the answer to that question; then one can ask for directions, time, and name. When I ask for directions, I know where the questioned is. When I ask, "Where art thou?" I do not know this. I do not know his level, his reach, his path. I cannot say what counts for him. I do not know whether I count for him, whether our plane is common, whether we can hear each other. Therefore, the question, "Where art thou?" has the power of awakening one from a dream. Thanks to it, the dream passes and wakefulness begins and people begin to appear for each other. Rosenzweig writes:

> "Where are you?" This is nothing else but the question about the You. Not a question about the essence of the You: for the moment it is not even within our range of vision; and we are asking only about the "Where?" Where, then, is there a You? This question about the You is the only thing that we already know about it. But the question is enough for the I to discover itself; it does not need to see the You; by asking about it, and by testifying by means of this question that it believes in the existence of the You, even when it is not within sight, it addresses itself and expresses itself as I. The I discovers itself at the moment where it affirms the existence of the You, through the question about where it is.[5]

So what, in the end, is the questioned-I and the asking-Thou?

Bridge over an Abyss

In a certain sense, we are monads without windows. I do not know what goes on within you, nor do you know what goes on within me. Nonetheless, I know that You (Thou for me) are an I for yourself, and similarly I am I, who am an I for myself, am for you a Thou. This knowledge is a bridgehead on which it is possible to plant a bridge between you and I.

Here the word "for" is key. Something is something for someone, something has a specific sense, specific meaning, and a specific value. This means, let us say once more, that in order to reach the proper essence of the I–Thou, one must stand firmly upon the axiological plane of reflection on which we do not ask about beings, but about values. Values are characterized by the fact that they "have validity," *gelten* in German. What does this mean? It means that they can be, even should be, acknowledged by others, like a work of art. The greater the reach of a possible acknowledgment, the higher the value, and in reverse: the higher the value, the wider the reach of validity. When I say I, I am a value for myself. When I hear someone address me as Thou, I know that I am important to him, and then he becomes important for me too. When I say Him, I know that someone is important to me, but I am not important for him. This does not at all mean that "He" is only an object, as Buber suggests. When I say We, I know that you are important to me like I am for you. When I say They, I know that I am not important for them, even though they are important for me.

Validity is what joins concreteness with universality. The I does not stop existing concretely when it takes on ever-greater significance, just as every artwork does not stop being concrete, despite the fact that so many admire it. It has a universal significance: it can, and should, be acknowledged in its value always and by everyone. The I is, in the radical sense of this word, an axiological-I. In itself it is the addressee of a question, and in itself it is the giver of an answer.

The generality, or "universality," of the I is not the universality of an abstract concept under which individual designations fall. Essentially, this universality is based upon the universal claim of the value of being recognized, recognized by the sort of recognition that in a satisfactory way is fulfilled by conversation. However, we should remember that this conversation and recognition would not exist if those who are conversing with each other did not approach each other as coming from within the horizon of good and evil. Only thanks to such horizons can the I come to exist as an axiological-I, the I as a value.

To Carry a Burden and to Be a Burden

The axiological, and even more, the agathological, level of inquiry opens before us one more possibility—the possibility of understanding the following concepts: "being a burden for someone" and "to have someone as a burden." A profound meaning hides in these poetic expressions.

You asked me. Let us presuppose that you were only asking for directions. You want to go to the nearby village, and you ask, Which way? You dislodged me from my own thinking through your questions; I had to shake myself out and take a look at the world with your eyes, to take your matter upon myself, to put myself in your place, for a moment almost become you. But if you think it through well, you—to ask me at all—had to do something similar: leave your inner world, stand in my place, as if you were not yourself, but me. The monads without windows had to start talking. Here we touch upon an astounding point. There is no I without a Thou and no Thou without an I. This not only means that I and Thou reflect each other mutually like mirrors standing on opposing banks of a river, but also that You are within me, and I am within you, since we carry each other as our *burdens*. You are in me. I am in you. You are part of the history of my I, and I am part of the history of your Thou. Despite this interpenetration, we are our own selves. Ourselves to the end. We are ineradicably ourselves. I am myself when you are a burden to me, and when you are my liberation, because you truly are that too. When I met you, I felt liberated in some degree. From what? From whom? Perhaps from my own thoughts, maybe from another I that followed me like a shadow? This experience of burden-lightness is very important. But it is not a form that imprisons matter—the form Thou and the matter I. Nor does matter free itself from form—the matter I from the form Thou. This ontological language is out of place here. Here everything is a value. There is a value of the burden and the value of lightness. As a value you can be either one or the other to me. And I for you. We can lift each other up or pull each other down.

We are what we are through each other. And through each other we are where we are. This is how we develop our drama—for good or ill.

CHAPTER 3

Going Astray

Our analyses have so far revolved around the good, but we have not said much about the good itself. This is not a coincidence, but a logical consequence of the problems we are discussing. We are speaking here about the experience of encounter where we understand experience as maturing into witness: to experience an other is to give a witness about him. In order to give a witness about an other, we must become the participants of a drama. However, all drama is a drama of good and evil. The good does not reveal itself in the human drama otherwise than through witness, which it creates. A man, in order to mature into his humanity, needs the witness of others. By accepting a witness, a man simultaneously gives a witness. This exchange of witnesses is possible where the relation of reciprocity that governs it is possible. Reciprocity is reciprocity within the perspective of the good. The lack of reciprocity, especially its refusal, is accomplished within the perspective of evil.

The good is something like an axiom of drama. But it is not an axiom of reason presupposed in advance, which cannot be doubted. The good, if it is really to be the good, cannot be reasoned, but must be experienced instead. In what manner does the good give itself to be experienced? We must acknowledge, if we turn to poetical and religious metaphor, that the good is audible rather than visible. The voice of the good penetrates the noises of the world to call man to something absolute. Thinking plays solely a preparatory role in this domain: it prepares the ears to hear. It achieves its goal through a critique of the voices that drown out the voice of the good.

Let us attempt to follow the path of critical thinking and look more closely at everything that veils and drowns out the presence of the good, and what, consequently, does not allow a man to encounter another man. By following the wastelands of encounter, we can approximate the experience of the correct path. Let us look at three instances: going astray in the element of beauty, going astray in the element of the truth, and going astray in the element of the good.

A. Going Astray in the Element of Beauty

Even though we do not know precisely what constitutes the essence of beauty, it is betrayed by situations where, without any doubts and hesitations, we say that "she/he is beautiful." The seen person enchants us. The persuasive power with which she/he becomes present does not let itself be compared even with the power with which objects and landscapes impose themselves upon us. Here I will recall the description of the meeting between Levin and Kitty in Leo Tolstoy's *Anna Karenina*:

> He knew she was there by the joy and fear that overwhelmed his heart. She stood at the other end of the rink, talking to a lady. There seemed to be nothing very special in her dress, nor in her pose; but for Levin she was as easy to recognize in that crowd as a rose among nettles. Everything was lit up by her. She was the smile that brightened everything around. "Can I really step down there on the ice and go over to her?" he thought. The place where she stood seemed to him unapproachably holy, and there was a moment when he almost went away—he was so filled with awe. Making an effort, he reasoned that all sorts of people were walking near her and that he might have come to skate there himself. He stepped down, trying not to look long at her, as if she were the sun, yet he saw her, like the sun, even without looking.... When she finished the turn, she pushed herself off with a springy little foot and glided right up to Shcherbatsky. Holding onto him and smiling, she nodded to Levin. She was more beautiful than he had imagined her.[1]

The task we put before ourselves here is grasping the relations that take place between the experiencing of the beauty of another human being (enchantment) and the encounter with him in the element of the good, that is, the existential experience of his face. Our assumption is not a theory of beauty. The experience of beauty itself must suffice—the certainty that the person I see and hear is beautiful. This is how Levin experiences beauty. However, before we take a closer look at that experience, we will turn our attention to a few general matters.

Beauty as Light and Justification

Contact with the beauty of another person, surrendering to his or her charms, enchantment with the other—all of this is so difficult for reflection to grasp, and simultaneously so deeply moves the one whom it meets that it must be recognized not as one of the facts of human everydayness, but as an *event*, in the meaning close to the one given this word by Heidegger. Events are always events of meaning. Thanks to them, and starting from them, the life of man and his surrounding world change their value, their meaning. The word "event" [wy*darzenie*] brings to mind the gift [*dar*]. "New" meaning is what is "gifted" in the event, a new order of the world encompassing man, a new sense to words uttered. Thanks to the event of beauty, man touches, with the core of his person, something that has the power of justification, or the rejection of justification, of his presence on the world's stage.

Literary descriptions of human beauty, for example, the passage from Tolstoy above, willingly use the metaphor of light. Light is a painterly description of meaning. It symbolizes meaning. What light is for the eye, the meaning of things is for reason. The light of beauty can blind, but only thanks to light is it possible to see something. The situation is similar with the sense of things. Things become comprehensible thanks to the senses that serve them. I understand what the piece of paper lying before me is, because it is located in a semantic field determined by the ability to read and write. Meaning is a hidden beginning that highlights, out of concealment, the manner of my understanding things. Something similar is affected by encountering human beauty. From that moment, whatever I think, feel, and see, I see, feel, and think because the other is beautiful.

Plato already reached for symbolism of light: "But turning to beauty, it shone out, as I said, among its companions there, and once here on earth we found, by means of the clearest of our senses, that it sparkles with particular clarity."[2] Levin feels that the sun has shone next to him: "Everything was lit up by her. She was the smile that brightened everything around.... He stepped down, trying not to look long at her, as if she were the sun, yet he saw her, like the sun, even without looking."[3] The other appears to us as the source of light, whereas the things that surround them shine with their light. But the light does not only radiate outside a man, but also from within his interior, unveiling his sensations and feelings that are invisible in the everyday. Note the beautiful fragment describing the meeting of Johannes with Cordelia in Kierkegaard's *Seducer's Diary*:

> A transfiguring ceremoniousness sweeps over the scene, a soft morning light. She is silent; nothing breaks in upon the stillness. My eyes glide softly over her, not desiringly—that would truly be brazen. A delicate fleeting blush, like a cloud over the meadow, fades away, heightening and fading. What does this blush signify? Is it love, is it longing, hope, fear, for is not red the color of the heart? By no means ... she is amazed—not at herself but within herself. She is being transformed within herself. This moment craves stillness; therefore no reflection is to disturb it, no noise of passion is to disrupt it. It is as if I were not present, and yet it is my very presence that is the condition for this contemplative wonder of hers. My being is in harmony with hers. In a state such as this, a girl is adored and worshiped, just as some deities are, by silence.[4]

The light brings forth the otherwise elusive turn of man toward himself, felt as wonder at oneself, toward a previously unknown wealth whose existence is made conscious to man by another man. However, there would not be such discoveries if not for beauty. Beauty unveils communion and beauty establishes communion.

Light makes vision possible, even though it remains invisible. This vision is specific. It is not a simple reflection of things and events according to the order proper to them, but a preferential reflection, according to some hierarchy of values. For Levin the world lit by the presence of Kitty is not a visible world, so much as a momentous, important, and almost holy world. Similarly in Kierkegaard: Johannes sees and guesses at not only that which simply is, but that which is valuable and important. His lively empathy for the depths of the other's soul takes place alongside the conjuncture that this is love, this is longing, hope and fear, to stop at the moment of wondering at oneself in which the intimate tie between him and Cordelia will take root. The light illuminates and brings out of the shadows that which is most precious at a given moment: that the other is such as they are thanks to me, so that the price of this wonder ought to be some sort of gratitude.

The ascent symbolism Plato used carries similar connotations. Beauty grasps man and carries him upward along invisible degrees of the value hierarchy. To ascend upward means not only seeing wider and deeper, but, above all, to see what is most important. The ascent upward grants participation in the wisdom that knows the place of phenomena. Whoever approaches the sun will see his wings scorched. The symbolism of light includes the symbolism of sacrifice. To see the true order of things one must participate in the light, but to participate in the light one must sacrifice something of oneself.

Standing before the beauty of another human being, we face something that is not, and cannot be, foretold. Beauty cannot be foretold, it is other—other than the surrounding world, other than people we have known so far, even different than the remembrances written in memory. Levin knew Kitty, carried within himself an image of her in his memory, despite this reality . . . reality surprised him. This means that beauty is transcendent: it goes not only beyond everything that is not it, but also differs from other varieties of beauty. It is unrepeatable. The encountered person is only once beautiful in this way, as they are now. Tomorrow she will be beautiful differently. The unrepeatability of beauty's every instance increases its value all the more. It introduces an alternative: now or never. It awakens a painful desire to make what is being experienced now into eternity. To eternalize beauty means to make eternal one's wonder, one's enchantment, one's happiness.

The gratuity of beauty is also an important feature of the experience. Beauty stands before us as a gift, as a grace freely given. It is not only that nothing foretells beauty, but also nothing is able to arrest beauty at the side of the one who has become enchanted. Beauty cannot be purchased, possessed, taken into slavery. It has no price. Its right is the right of whim. Nobody is the owner of beauty. When it appears, it appears—because it wants to; it also leaves, because it wants to. Kant wrote, "The beautiful prepares us to love something, even nature, without interest."[5] Therefore, we can speak of a specific kind of *disinterestedness* in beauty. The word "interest" comes from *interesse*, "between being." Beauty is not between objects and between beings. It is above them. It is important to distinguish what in being is the condition *sine qua non* for the appearance of beauty from beauty itself. Beauty is neither harmony, nor proportion, nor rhythm—it is something else and something more. Beauty reveals to us a new and uncommon level of being and carries us there; sometimes it is said that it enraptures. We leave behind the whole of life's prose. Only the poetry of being stands before us. Beauty marks out a new center for our spiritual life. This can be seen especially clearly in the instance of being enchanted by someone. Only starting from the experience of beauty does a deeper interest in the whole facticity of the other begin, if only what the other's name is, where they live, and what they do.

One more thing: whoever has encountered the beauty of the other, who has been touched by this beauty to the quick, knows from the start that this beauty is a human beauty. The human being, not a thing or object, appears to us in his or her beauty. It is not the case that we first encounter a beautiful body, but only later, later, as a result of the next step, we become aware that this is the body of a human being. The beauty of the human is from the start a human beauty, not the beauty of an artwork. The human being whom I see is a beautiful gaze, grace of movement, sensitivity to the world, speech, sadness, joy, thoughtfulness, weeping, inner wonder, sublimity, haughtiness, modesty, and contempt. Beauty, by unveiling, unveils the soul of man from the start. Kierkegaard says, "The basic concept of man is spirit, and one should not be confused by the fact that he is also able to walk on two feet."[6] The beauty of man is characterized by a particular dramatic depth, thanks to which all gestures, words, and acts of man come to the fore and are given utterance. The beauty of man demands thinking about drama. What is more, it participates in the drama itself and has within it a task marked out. At any moment it can become a tragic beauty, or a victorious beauty, awaken despair or joy, it can save or condemn. It is sometimes said that beauty leads to madness. There is no exaggeration in this. Madness always appears where experience is more expansive and deeper than the capacity of the human spirit. And beauty, precisely the beauty of an encountered human being, is sometimes greater than the possibilities of human perception.

Justification

Beauty is the beauty of a man, beauty enables one to know some kind of human mystery, it is a grace, which allows one to live differently and die differently. Is that all? What meaning does beauty have for one who is beautiful? What relationship is there between beauty and its subject?

First, one thing must be repeated: no being, as a being, carries the justification of its existence and of what it is within itself. What is does not derive from itself the right to existence. Existence in itself does not exclude absurdity. Some value is always what is capable of justifying the existence of an object. Only in the presence of values—absolute values—do we not ask, "Why?" Beauty belongs to such values. The beauty incarnate in a man, therefore, reveals itself from the beginning as a value, which justifies his existence. When we see the other in his beauty, we not only know that the other is, but also why he is. He is, because he is beautiful; he exists so that beauty can exist within him. The answer to the question is given right there. So we ask instead: What should be done so that the other remains close, so that his beauty does not pass by? We can say that beauty includes a reference to existence. Beauty includes a reference to existence in such a sense that it itself justifies the object's existence, which it envelops. It is only existence, and only such an existence, which is existence justified. In other words, such a being should truly exist.

We will touch upon the key questions of aesthetics here in passing. For example, in Roman Ingarden's aesthetics, the following question appears: What is the relationship between beauty and the beautiful? Ingarden, following Kant in this instance, thinks that beauty and the world constituted by beauty are indifferent to existence or nonexistence. The literary work is built from quasi-judgments that refer the reader not so much toward the real world, but toward the represented world, merely intentional. Beauty completes an as-if derealization of the object (or the subject), puts it outside of real existence. Kant wrote, "But if the question is whether something is beautiful, one does not want to know whether there is anything that is or that could be at stake, for us or for someone else, in the existence of the thing, but rather how we judge it in mere contemplation (intuition or reflection)."[7] Artistic creativity would therefore be the art of creating illusions. Raymond Polin writes in the same spirit, "The aesthetic universe is not the universe in which one lives, but a universe in which one dreams."[8]

The intention of all values is the justification, or the refusal to justify, what either is or can be. Positive values justify being, while negative values refuse to justify beings. Existence, being, thing, and object are the center of gravity for values. The operating of art is an operation consistent with the laws of value-gravitation. The point here is to constitute a justified existence in light of which the whole, so-called real world could present itself as only the appearance of real being, a partial truth, a metaphor of the truth. This is why, in the literary work of art, there are no quasi-judgments, but true judgments—judgments that define how the world should be. Obviously, they need not do this directly. It is not the represented world that then becomes an appearance of a real world, but the real world—the world of a partial justification—that simulates true reality. The literary work of art strips sociology, science, and history of their truth, all of which absolutize existing reality and raise it to the level of final truth. This is especially evident in the case of the beauty of another. The power of persuasion of this experience is precisely that it shows not only what something or someone is, but also that this something, or that someone, contains within themselves their being's justification.

All of these experiences—the experience of light, ascent, justified existence—make the matter of being-with the beauty of a person acquire an existential meaning. When enthralled by the spell of another, man feels that this opens up, before him, the perspective of living out the one-of-a-kind adventure of participating in the very source of being's meaning. Seemingly, nothing after the encounter with beauty changes; however, everything changes—the world, and the man himself. His life becomes as if purer, innocent, holy. Even if the existence of the enchanted is not beautiful at all, it can find, in the beauty of another, some justification. Existential hope awakens. But how is it that the beauty of the other can justify my existence? What intimate bond of man with man is built by enchantment? It is certainly a human bond, therefore different from one between a viewer and a masterpiece of art. What is the human character of this bond, but also, what is its nonhuman character? I said above that it is possible to go mad from beauty. Where might one find this moment of cruelty in the experience of beauty, which makes you enchanted with madness?

The enchanted person gains a specific self-knowledge. Beauty surpasses man, reveals before him a different, unreachable world, therefore, as if in passing, it casts him off, and holds him at a distance. All approaches to beauty would mean its profanation. Beauty does not allow itself to be touched, even when it gives itself, and then it always demands some sacrifice. Rather, by associating with beauty, one is further from it than closer to it. What can the discoverer of beauty say about himself except that he feels unworthy of it? It is in this unworthiness that the grandeur of the enchanted hides. He has the right to say about himself, "I am the one who discovered your beauty." There is a deep meaning in this. For beauty is not beauty for itself, but also for someone's gaze, admiration, wonder. It requires recognition by its very nature. It cannot be a light shining for nobody, a call in the waste, speech for nobody. The discovery of beauty, and enchantment by it, is the fulfillment of its sense. What would beauty be without such a discovery? It would be beauty gone to waste. However, things are different thanks to the discoverer. Thus, I am a discoverer. I am the one who is enchanted, who has fallen silent full of wonder, who "prays with the eyes" (Plato, *Symposium*). You were surrounded by a crowd of barbarians so far, but I do not belong to this crowd. Thanks to this I am worth more. I am the one who knows well about the tragedy of beauty. I am the genius of this discovery. I hope that the other will notice it. Beauty only achieves the fullness of its joy when it finds a genius who discovers it. Kierkegaard writes that in order to become a discoverer, one needs a geniality of the senses. Only sensuality brought to perfection can touch the spell of the other. However, when the senses achieve genius, they are only a step away from madness. The possibility of a precise description ends at this point. The generalizable disappears. The one enchanted is tied to uniqueness, unrepeatability, exceptionality. His speech is the speech of poetry. Kierkegaard speaks of a "musical lyricality." The grace of the beautiful flowing down upon the one enchanted is at the same time lyrical and musical: "If I were to describe this lyricism with a single predicate, I would have to say: it sounds."[9] It is light, it flows, it builds a bright space around me, it squeezes out tears, bends the knees. But also, it should last forever! But it only sounds. Since it sounds, therefore it flows away, passes, and is in jeopardy. Beauty is immeasurably fragile. This very fragility foreshadows a tragedy. Beauty is simultaneously absolute and fragile, justifying being and needing being . . . to be able to reveal itself.

I cannot now go into the details of the theory of sensory perception, which modern philosophy has been developing since at least the time of Descartes. I will pay attention to one of its aspects. The development of this theory, as we know, went in the direction of searching for what is most elementary in perception, in the direction of dividing up the whole into its parts, first leading to the separation of particular senses from the others (i.e., in John Locke the separation of the spatial sense from the sense of sight, hearing, or taste); then within individual sensory data, the separating out of elementary sensory datums, which had to be correlates of sensory qualities. Even the Husserlian theory of perception went, to a certain degree, in this direction. One restores the whole only from the elementary components of perception. But attempts to build a whole from the parts, as Gestalt psychology indicated, do not reach that goal. Nothing more could be found in the reconstructed whole than what was found in the elementary data. At the same time, even the simplest perception of things goes far beyond what is hidden in the elementary data.

The theory of the senses outlined here and there by Kierkegaard heads in a different direction. The whole sensuality of man strives toward synthesis. The synthesis is supposed to be fulfilled in one unique discovery—the discovery that the other is beautiful. Only in this discovery is the destiny of the senses fulfilled. But the unrepeatable beauty of a human being can be deduced neither from the data of individual senses, nor from the combination of sensory data from all the senses taken together. Beauty transcends all the sense qualities, even though it does not break away from them. This is its paradox, that it acknowledges the discoverer's sensuality, but it simultaneously forces him to transcend it.

The discovery of another's beauty, enchantment with it, and the dignity of the one-of-a-kind discoverer flowing from it are only one aspect of the matter, if you will, the joyful aspect of enchantment. But, enchantment has another side. The discovery of beauty must be paid for—paid for with suffering. The specificity of this suffering decides about the quality of the nascent bond formed with the other. "True sublimity is the value of all," says Kierkegaard.[10] This means that to discover beauty as beauty is to, at the same time, renounce possessing beauty, because beauty, just like light, cannot be possessed exclusively for oneself. It is turned toward universality. We know stories of knights-errant of the Middle Ages, who traveled from city to city proclaiming the glory of their most beautiful ladies, calling to duel other "geniuses of the senses" similar to themselves if they dared to have a different opinion about this topic. Whatever else one might say, such action grows out of the logic proper to beauty. Beauty lets itself be discovered, but it cannot be grasped, taken as a possession. Kierkegaard senses this well. Beauty for him is not a dead gaze at an object, but a light that gives and takes life, a flame that warms but also burns, it is a value from which the true drama of man starts. What is at stake in this drama is not about being, or not being, charmed, but about saving oneself or perishing. In light of Kierkegaard's texts, all purely esthetic treatments of beauty, which are discussed in textbooks of esthetics, are pathetic oversimplifications.

The adventure with the beauty of another begins in Kierkegaard from taking up the stance of the page (the author develops his reflections as a commentary upon Mozart's *Marriage of Figaro* and *Don Giovanni*). Beauty makes a page out of the enchanted person. The page admires and serves, the page remains silent, because he lacks the words: "The sensuous awakens, yet not to motion but to a still quiescence, not to delight and joy but to deep melancholy."[11] Enchantment is first a "still quiescence" alongside beauty. Beauty does not let you have a word. Words turn out to be too impoverished. Beauty ought to be revered with silence. Beauty also promises, and in this way does not allow you to leave it. A paradox arises, because beauty also does not allow you to approach, it is too great, too unattainable, too fiery. Beauty demands sacrifices. The first sacrifice offered to beauty is the sacrifice of the freedom of movement. One must remain nearby. This is how beauty increasingly takes its discoverer into possession: "Desire possesses what will become the object of its desire but possesses it without having desired it and thus does not possess it. This is the painful but also in its sweetness the fascinating and enchanting contradiction, which with its sadness, its melancholy resonates through this [first] stage."[12] Possesses without possessing ... Beauty has already taken its discoverer into possession, but the discoverer knows that he has no right to take beauty into possession. He must remain only a discoverer. This contradiction hurts. The pain of this contradiction finds its expression in . . . a sigh. The desire of the page is "altogether vague about its object, it nevertheless has one qualification—it is [an] infinitely deep [sigh]."[13] The sigh expresses the pain of an unconsummated possessing, but expresses it *for somebody*. Somebody should hear it. But who? Obviously, the one causing pain—the beautiful, other, person. The sigh asks for mercy, because beauty, even though it enchants, is capable of being cruel—it possesses, but itself is free. Let us take a step further in tracking the pains born of beauty. Beauty possesses but does not let itself be possessed. Beauty is not obligated by any fidelity. It can both look and not look, listen and not listen, take into account and not take into account, come and go. Should the one who makes the discovery be faithful to beauty? Yes, of course. Nonetheless only until the moment he discovers a greater beauty and an even sweeter slavery. This is why "desire aims at discoveries. This urge to discover is the pulsation in it, its liveliness. It does not find the proper object of this exploration, but it discovers the multiplicity in seeking therein the object that it wants to discover."[14] Kierkegaard is a great witness to these matters, but let us call another witness, Plato: "A person who would set out on this path in the right way," says Diotima, "must begin in youth by directing his attention to beautiful bodies, and first of all, if his guide is leading him aright, he should fall in love with the body of one individual only, and there procreate beautiful discourse. Then he will realize for himself that the beauty of any one body is closely akin to that of any other body, and that if what is beautiful in form is to be pursued, it is folly not to regard the beauty in all bodies as one and the same."[15] Enchantment does not create fidelity. The possessing of the enchanted is relative, but so is the power of the beautiful over the enchanted.

At this point we turn to the tragic nature of beauty.

Tragic Nature of Beauty

The meaning of tragedy is marked out by the experience of encounter. Possession by itself—possession not fulfilled and unfulfillable—tends toward tragedy. The beauty of another person is a perfection given evidently. Beauty is simultaneously familiar and hostile, beauty attracts and distances, promises and refuses, makes happy and miserable, is cruel and gracious. The desire to have beauty for oneself is taken all the way to the summit. At the same time, it is subject to an absolute contradiction. Beauty is precisely what one would want to have, but cannot have. Enchantment becomes the misfortune of the enchanted. And yet it is also their happiness. Misfortune hides in happiness, and in misfortune hides happiness. The enchanted are happy, but happy in the wrong way.

You could call this a disease of the senses, or, more pointedly, madness. Madness depends upon a disturbance in the structure of intentionality. Sensuality—when it exceeds the boundaries of its genius—does not direct itself toward the external world, but searches more for experience of itself, focuses on its own experience, the experience of longing, recollecting, dreaming, desiring, representing, and imagining in which every "you are mine" shows itself to be one more illusion. The pain of possession, present mainly in longing, is the core of self-knowledge for the one whom beauty has enchanted. The enchanted one fully becomes one painful sigh, an attempt to grasp something ungraspable, to grasp the world in the palm of the hand. The pain of self-knowledge does not allow one to know the truth about the other. Who is this other? For the self-knowledge paralyzed by madness, it is only beauty, nothing else, nothing more. Whom does beauty need? Nobody! What does the enchanted do in its rays? He does not know himself. This is why he exists on the boundary of the encounter.

Does a possibility of moving beyond these contradictions exist?

Crossroads

I said above that beauty is a promise in which only the presence of the promise-maker does not fall under doubt, whereas the contents of the promise cannot cross the threshold of ambiguity. Ambiguity is the key to the problem. What does that mean? Kant says that "the beautiful is the symbol of the morally good."[16] The full meaning of these words will disclose itself only when we refer it to the situation of enchantment.

We are right in the middle of the drama with the other. We are constantly at the crossroads. The other's beauty, which showed itself to us among the byways, hides something absolute in itself. The other man truly is. He is in his beauty. Beauty justifies his being—his, not mine. He comes closer. He is a promise for me—an absolute promise. He takes me into possession. If he possesses me, my being gains some justification. But there is anxiety: a promise is not unambiguous. What does beauty promise to me? It promises some good. But what kind? Beauty is only a symbol. Perhaps the whole meaning exhausts itself in promising? Maybe only the promising itself is the good here?

Two possibilities open up here.

The first possibility relies upon passing from the plane of beauty to the plane of the ethical good, as Kant suggests. Beauty promises good, but the good is the domain of ethics. Beauty does not disappear, but constantly refers to the good. Aesthetics turns out to be a preface to ethics, enchantment is the first step before an encounter. The role of beauty is fulfilled. The meaning of the adventure with beauty would depend upon opening before man a more substantial horizon, the horizon of good and evil.

The second possibility seems more complex. It relies upon the identification of beauty with the good. Beauty as beauty becomes the same thing as the good. Beauty is the only absolute. It also subordinates the truth to itself. The good would be the good only insofar as it would be beautiful. Also, the truth would be the truth only as much as it would be beautiful. What does not let itself be identified with beauty would have to be evil and false.

Charles Baudelaire's *Flowers of Evil* are a poetic expression of such an experience of beauty—an experience that absolutizes:

> But is it not enough that your appearance can
> Restore to joy a heart that flees from what is true?
> What if you are inane, what if indifferent!
> Mask, decoration, hail! Beauty, I worship you![17]

In this perspective, all "evil" created by beauty, or which beauty needs, is not an evil. It is justified, since it serves beauty. Suffering is not killing, betrayal is not betrayal, contempt is not contempt. Beauty is the only thing that counts, and all the things thanks to which it becomes more beautiful. The beautiful who serve beauty, raised to the dignity of an absolute, are free of faults.

Mystery of the Face

Both the page and the discoverer are enlivened by one desire: that beauty take them under its wings. To be under the protection of beauty is to be possessed by beauty. To be possessed by beauty is to find in beauty justification and salvation. However far the rays of beauty reach, that far its warmth radiates. This creates hope for saving one's life: my existence gains meaning in proximity to what is meaning through itself. Beauty is acknowledged as an axiological absolute, which justifies and itself does not need justification. The desire of the enchanted to remain in the proximity of beauty, to have it and to be possessed by it, emerges from here. As we can see, the game is not about trifles. Beauty creates a boundary situation for man. A big problem arises: In what way is it possible to be possessed by beauty and to possess that beauty at the same time?

At this point we touch upon the difference between human beauty and the beauty of objects. Beyond the beauty of the other man, one feels freedom. The other man is free. This is why he can do something, should do something, wishes something for himself, and does not wish something for himself. From this comes the sigh of the page, the pain of the discoverer, the sufferings of the enchanted; a constant cry for others to deign to recognize their beauty as their true face, and with this recognition also acknowledge their recognition of their beauty. Therefore, the matter of the other's beauty does not end at enchantment only. Reciprocity is at stake. It is about the other discovering and acknowledging in himself what I found and acknowledged. In this way my enchantment will become his interior reality. He will know my trace on his face. He or she will become my *work of art*. But it will not be a visual work of art, but a dramatic work of art. The other will become an artist in a drama that I suggested to him. His freedom will take a step down the path that I devised. And in this way, only in this way, I will be someone else's property—his property, and he will be my property. We will accompany each other like shadows, "aesthetically entangled with each other."

What then does "my" beautiful other become for me? He is a work of dramatic art. What am I for him? I am an artist who brought his beauty to its fullness. We take up our fate together, like one picks up a plot on stage. We have one hope: that the finale of the play be more beautiful than its beginning.

Kierkegaard speaks of *seduction*, but seduction here is conceived exclusively in the aesthetic sense, as the art of artistic creation. The pain of creating is a pain that goes both ways—both of the creator and the created. Pain should not be feared, because from pain art is born: "Now, Don Giovanni not only is a success with the girls, but he makes the girls happy—and unhappy—yet strangely enough in such a way that that is what they want, and it would be a poor sort of girl who would not wish to become unhappy in order to have been happy once with Don Giovanni."[18] But before unhappiness comes (who knows anyway, maybe it will not come?), there is the hour of experiencing beauty, sating oneself with it—seeing what is uncovered. What should the one sating himself do? "She is rich, but she does not realize that she possesses anything; she is rich—she is a treasure."[19] Thus she must be made aware of who she is for her to make of her beauty her face. Beauty will purify her of all faults.

What does the artist expect from such a work of art? He expects it to be a full, that is, a self-sufficient work of art. The artist acts according to the logic of beauty. Beauty should not need anyone, not even the artist. True artists know this well.

> She must be strengthened within herself before I let her find support from me. Now and then it may seem as if I were seeking to make her my confidante in my freemasonry, but that is only momentary. She herself must be developed within herself; she must feel the resilience of her soul; she must come to grips with the world and lift it. . . . She must owe me nothing, for she must be free. Only in freedom is there love; only in freedom are there diversion and everlasting amusement. Although I am making arrangements so that she will sink into my arms as if by a necessity of nature and am striving to make her gravitate toward me, the point nevertheless is that she should not fall like a heavy body but as mind should gravitate toward mind. Although she will belong to me, yet it must not be in the unbeautiful way of resting upon me as a burden. She must be neither an appendage in the physical sense nor an obligation in the moral sense. Between us

two, only freedom's own game will prevail. She must be so light to me that I can carry her on my arm.[20]

This text from Kierkegaard proposes one thing: the aesthetic justification of infidelity. This is understandable. Faithfulness is an ethical value. The situation described is aesthetic.

The artist cannot but strive for the work of art to tear itself away from him. He does not incur any moral obligations toward it, especially any obligation to faithfulness. The perfect artwork is self-sufficient. If creation is a magnanimous act, then there should be no gratitude. To create means to get rid of, to possess less. But this is what the artist cannot do. He needs justifications from his own work. Thus, something must exist between him and his work, even if it were to be only called "free play." From this the demand that the work acknowledges in him its artist. This is why the artist simultaneously desires to possess and not possess. He wants to embrace something, which he cannot embrace. He gives freedom to what he cannot abandon. His magnanimity is a great jealousy at the same time.

Cordelia is a work of art. She suffers, but it is not an ordinary suffering. She is uncommonly beautiful, therefore she must endure an uncommon suffering. Her uncommon suffering is uncommonly beautiful thanks to Johannes, who does not admire Cordelia's experiences: "Never will I call you 'my Johannes,' for I certainly realize you never have been that, and I am punished harshly enough for having once been gladdened in my soul by this thought, and yet I do call you 'mine': my seducer, my deceiver, my enemy, my murderer, the source of my unhappiness, the tomb of my joy, the abyss of my unhappiness. I call you 'mine' and call myself 'yours.'"[21]

That passage contains the essence of aesthetic tragedy. It points to a contradiction in the soul that recognizes that her face is wholly hidden in her beauty. The human being believes that she has become an artwork. To believe that one is an artwork is to embroil oneself in the opposition of being and simultaneously not being someone's. This can be called "the tragedy of appearances." One seemingly has the freedom to determine oneself, but one in actuality does not have such a freedom. The artist is seemingly faithful to his work, but in reality the very nature of creation frees him from faithfulness. There is seemingly no loneliness, but in reality there is loneliness and it is doubled—the work and artist separately, the work and artist together. The sole consolation is admiration in the eyes of the artist—the ingenious discoverer. But this admiration contains an insensitivity to someone else's pain. That is why the aesthetic of experiencing the other becomes the source of a hell—a hell that is no better by being an aesthetic hell.

Kierkegaard does not give Johannes the last word, but instead describes the whole matter with a laconic objectivism. He makes an allusion to the conscience: "Conscience takes shape in him merely as a higher consciousness that manifests itself as a restlessness that does not indict him even in the profounder sense but keeps him awake."[22] Therefore, the artist has no feeling of fault: his watchfulness is not so much the voice of conscience as it is fear of revenge.

It sometimes happens that the figures created by artists visit them in their dreams to conduct a final judgment. Johannes is armored. He does not believe in the truth of Cordelia's accusations. The artist divinized Cordelia because of her beauty, recognizing at the same time that in beauty the opposition between good and evil, truth and illusion, disappears. Cordelia's naïveté also is beautiful, because it is the naïveté of a girl who at first did not know what adventure she was getting into, and now she does not know what, and for what, she is accusing. Her final judgment only makes the drama more beautiful. We can take away from it only its beauty. Even if the judgment gives Johannes some pain, it is only aesthetic pain, rooted in the destructive power that marks all great beauty.

B. Going Astray in the Element of Truth

Two examples illustrate man's relation to the truth: the defense of Socrates and the defense of Raskolnikov from Dostoevsky's *Crime and Punishment*. Socrates defends himself against a false accusation, while Raskolnikov defends himself against an accusation that is true. For Socrates the truth is the path toward saving his life, whereas for Raskolnikov lying is the path toward saving his life. This is how ambivalent man's relation to the truth can be.

Nietzsche wrote:

> We do not consider the falsity of a judgment as itself an objection to a judgment; this is perhaps where our new language will sound most foreign. The question is how far the judgment promotes and preserves life, how well it preserves, and perhaps even cultivates, the type. And we are fundamentally inclined to claim that the falsest judgments (which include synthetic judgments *a priori*) are the most indispensable to us, and that without accepting the fictions of logic, without measuring reality against the wholly invented world of the unconditioned and self-identical, without a constant falsification of the world through numbers, people could not live—that a renunciation of false judgments would be a renunciation of life, a negation of life. To acknowledge untruth as a condition of life: this clearly means resisting the usual value feelings in a dangerous manner; and a philosophy that risks such a thing would by that gesture alone place itself beyond good and evil.[23]

Nietzsche states that the falsehood that serves life is a higher value than a truth that opposes life. But what is life? Life expresses itself chiefly through the need for power, "because every drive craves mastery."[24] The lust for power emerges from the will to power, which is directed in three directions: in the direction of self-control, controlling others, controlling the world of nature. This threefold controlling is supposed to be served by thinking liberated from the commandment to serve the truth. Raskolnikov's thinking falls within these three dimensions. However, one moment is particularly pronounced in him: the ethical moment. The condition of living in modern society is an ethical life—ethics justifies and denies justification to human life. But preserving ethical purity is almost impossible in life. Therefore, the full justification of man by ethics is impossible. At best it is possible to maintain appearances of justification and appearances of being ethical. The creation of such appearances is the special task of lying and living in the element of the lie.

In what ways is it possible to convince others about the validity of such thinking? Nietzsche again: "A new breed of philosophers is approaching. I will risk christening them with a name not lacking in dangers. From what I can guess about them, from what they allow to be guessed (since it is typical of them to want to remain riddles in some respect), these philosophers of the future might have the right (and perhaps also the wrong) to be described as those who attempt. Ultimately, this name is itself only an attempt, and, if you will, a temptation."[25]

Thinking whose mode of persuasion is not pointing toward the truth but tempting with promises is characterized by two features. First, it puts its stamp upon the meaning of the I–Thou relation: it is significant and decisive that the other recognize me, my promises, and my speech. In no other instance is the relation to the other so important and so strong. Second, the reference of thinking toward the world is ruled by one basic intention: the intention to create illusions, delusions, and appearances. No other thinking shows us the ambiguity of the world as does thinking in the element of the lie. Both moments intertwine with each other and make it so that lying speech becomes speech of particular emphasis, which can go from fear right up to the highest degrees of enchantment. How much knowledge about man is in this speech—about his weaknesses and dreams, about what man flees from and strives toward! At times it seems that one must know more to be able to lie than to say the truth.

To clarify the mystery of thinking, especially thinking in the element of truth, one usually accepts Socrates's (the defender of truth) point of view. Here there is Plato—a philosopher who loves the truth—surrounded in his cave by the delusions of the world. Here is Descartes, arguing with the evil demon, who is bent on deceiving him even about what seems obvious. The philosopher grants himself the right to defend the truth against the untruth and makes himself the representative of the rest of us, who, he thinks, also desire to be saved through the truth. The philosopher does not feel any fault in himself. He has not killed anyone—it is the others who are lurking to take his life. When the philosopher thinks, he always thinks from the depths of his innocence. With this the philosopher feeds the hope that from his position he will see better and understand deeper the work of the spirit over the construction of the house of truth. But is this conviction correct? Maybe on the contrary? Maybe the ethical position of the philosopher is his illusion? Perhaps the fundamental situation of man is Raskolnikov's situation—lying in order to save his life? Maybe the right human ideal is the evil demon who must deceive to have power and must have power to live. Is not more intellectual effort needed to build a home of lies than a home of truth? This would be interesting: to spy upon the mind's work on building such a home. Who knows whether then we might not better unveil the power of the truth and the powerlessness of lying—when we look at it not through the eyes of its lovers, but through the eyes of those who hate the truth?

Let us recall the situation in which Raskolnikov found himself. He committed a crime—he killed a woman. He is being interrogated. Raskolnikov lies. To lie means to present the untruth to other as the truth. When Raskolnikov is asked whether he killed, he answers that he did not kill. He then interprets the circumstances of the murder according to this lie: "A man with even a bit of development and experience will certainly try to admit as far as possible all the external and unavoidable facts; only he'll seek other reasons for them, he'll work in some feature of his own, a special and unexpected one, that will give them an entirely different meaning and present them in a different light."[26] By presenting the untruth as the truth, the liar strives to perpetuate the untruth in the system of delusions created in this way. Delusion does not stand at the source of untruthful speech, rather, it is untruthful speech, lying, which stands at the source of the delusion.

Knowledge of the truth is the premise of lying: the liar knows how things really are, but says something else—that is why he lies. The situation is different in delusion—the speaker does not know how things really are, it seems to him that things are as he sees and hears, therefore he is convinced that he is speaking the truth. It is similar with errors. But the matter of delusions and errors is not the point of our considerations at this moment. We are looking at lying— its essence and the conditions it depends upon.

Value of Lying

Lying is a special case of the I–Thou relation—it consists in giving the untruth to the other as the truth. It presupposes that the truth is known to the liar—in any case he is convinced of that—but for some reason he does not pass the truth to others. Moreover, lying presupposes that the one being lied to either does not know the truth or, at least, is not certain about it. If things were otherwise, then lying would not make sense. One more presupposition: the liar recognizes the value of the truth and the value of truthfulness, and therefore knows that in lying he does evil, but is convinced that he has to proceed this way. This last presupposition—an axiological presupposition—requires further explanation.

The act of lying is not the result of an absolute rejection of the truth as a value. One can imagine a radical overturning of the order of values whose result would be putting the untruth in the place of the truth, and the truth in the place of untruth. What has been the good so far would become evil, and what was evil would become good. We would no longer proclaim that everyone has a right to the truth, but that everyone has the right to untruth. Such an absolute overturning of values turns out to be impossible. The famous "liar's paradox" already demonstrates this. When proclaiming that the untruth stands higher than the truth, I proclaim a new truth in whose name I call for the recognition of a perverse principle. In this way, I negate the initial intention of an absolute rejection of the truth. The liar does not deny that truth and truthfulness are positive values. The liar even confirms the validity of this view. What does he do? He offers untruth as truth, that is, he pretends, feigns, the truth. In feigning the truth, the liar pays homage to the value he renounces.

Simulating a value that one rejects is called *hypocrisy*. "Hypocrisy is," says de la Rochefoucauld, "the homage vice pays to virtue." The liar's homage to the truth hides in every lie. This homage is even necessary, because it enhances the credibility of the liar. This is why every act of lying usually turns into the beginning of a whole series of appearances whose goal is to make the one being lied to understand that the lying subject recognizes, without reservation, the binding power of the truth. The system of such appearances must be logically coherent. It cannot deviate from the rules of coherent truth. The preservation of these rules turns out to be indispensable for the addressee of the lie to acknowledge the untruth given to him.

In this way the lying act presupposes truth's value from at least three different sides: it recognizes that the other expects truthfulness and rightly expects that the lie the liar gives him cannot present itself as a lie, but must instead simulate the truth, and that he, as a subject of a lie, must respect the rules of coherent truth, according to which I must build a system of hypocritical illusions. This way I, as the liar, cannot help but be aware that the truth rubs up against me on all sides.

Two Conceptions of the Truth

There are also dialogical conditions besides the axiological conditions for the lie. The lie, one can say, is the introduction of misunderstanding into the interior of understanding. The lie is only possible in a space constituted by a common language in which the basic role is played by the identical (for the liar and the one being lied to) understanding of the concept of the truth. A difference in the understanding of truth's essence negates the possibility of the lie as a dialogical act. But it does not negate the lying intention, from one side, and the suspicion of the lie, from the other side.

In the dialogue between Raskolnikov and Porfiry, we come across a certain ambiguity. Fundamentally, an understanding close to the classical one is in force: the truth is the agreement of knowledge with the reality knowledge is concerned with, and truthfulness is the agreement of speech with the interior conviction of the speaker. The key question of dialogue is, Who killed? Raskolnikov says, I did not kill. Therefore, he is lying. Let us agree that we will call such an understanding of the truth and truthfulness *common sense*.

But the dialogue under discussion has another side. The killing of the pawnbroker—a social parasite—is for Raskolnikov not the same kind of act as killing an innocent. Raskolnikov freed society from an intolerable burden by killing. Besides this he also professes the view that outstanding individuals have the right to extraordinary deeds, if these deeds benefit the future of humanity. From this comes the question, What is the reality that the judgments of reason are supposed to adapt to? After all, this reality does not yet exist. It must be created first. Therefore, instead of saying that reason through cognition agrees with reality, we must say that it creates it, and it creates the truth in creating reality. Raskolnikov's murderous act changes meaning. It is no longer a crime, but a necessary intervention of the artist who is preparing material for a future edifice. Since society is the object of the treatment here and the goal is achieving power, then let us call the conception of truth corresponding to this situation *political truth*. Common sense with its truth stands in opposition to political reason and its truth, just as political reason stands in opposition to common sense and its truth.

Let us first deal with the lie on the level of common sense, and then we will move onto problems connected to the political conception of truth.

The reader must forgive me: the nature of the issues under discussion is such that it is impossible to carry out a strict delimitation—from this comes the necessity of intertwining one thread with the other.

Common Sense

The basic assumption of the common understanding of the truth is the assumption of an objective reality to which all cognition relates. Raskolnikov really exists. The pawnbroker exists. There is an ax, room, the pledge. . . . Above all, there is the homicide. From this comes the question, Did you kill or not kill? Raskolnikov lies. With this lie he attempts to *hide* "objective reality."

Let us look closer at the drama drawing itself out.

Game upon a Double Stage

Every lie is a lie about something—it has an intentional dimension. In virtue of the intentional dimension, the lie touches the stage of the human drama. This stage takes on a double meaning—different for the liar and different for the one lied to. For Raskolnikov, there was "I killed." For others something contradictory holds true, "I did not kill." From this emerges the key task of the liar: how to present a picture of the stage, and the course of events happening on the stage, in order to hide the homicide.

The double meaning of the stage has its organizational basis in the crime. The homicide is an event that surpasses all other events with its reality. It clearly divides the course of the life of the killer into the part before and the part after the homicide. It organizes about itself, like around an axis, the life-space of the killer. Its presence is strong, stronger than the booming of thunder, the cry of the city, the roar of the biggest waterfalls.... And yet it needs to be hidden, as if it did not exist. The more strongly it makes itself known, the more it has to be hidden, but the more carefully it is hidden, the more it emerges from behind the curtains.

The liar strives to constitute around himself, then pass onto others, a second world by pushing into the subconscious the recurring remembrances of the homicide. Work on this second world requires a particular kind of effort. The liar must distinguish between the more or less significant circumstances—the ones whose meaning can be changed and those that cannot be changed and thus must be hidden. The change of meanings cannot proceed totally arbitrarily, but must be in accord with the rules of semantic coherence. In turn, every denial of the event must be something more than only a denial of fact—it will be best if the conditions of their possibility will also be denied. It is not enough to say, "I did not kill." One must rather say, "I could not have killed."

Hence the concern for destroying traces. Traces speak by themselves. The construction of a world for others can be successful only under the condition of erasing traces. We read in Dostoevsky:

> By the time Raskolnikov reached his house, his temples were damp with sweat and he was breathing heavily. He hastily climbed the stairs, walked into his unlocked apartment, and immediately put the door on the hook. Then he rushed fearfully and madly to the corner, to the same hole in the wallpaper where the things had lain, thrust his hand into it, and for several minutes felt around in it carefully, going over every cranny and every crease in the wallpaper. Finding nothing, he stood up and drew a deep breath. Just as he was coming to Bakaleev's steps, he had suddenly imagined that something, some chain, a cufflink, or even a scrap of the paper they had been wrapped in, with a mark on it in the old woman's hand, might somehow have slipped down and lost itself in a crack, afterward to confront him suddenly as unexpected and irrefutable evidence. He stood as if pensively, and a strange, humiliated, half-senseless smile wandered over his lips. Finally he took his cap and walked quietly out of the room. His thoughts were confused. Pensively, he went down to the gateway.[27]

Yet, the more Raskolnikov erases traces, the more they multiply, becoming ever closer. Before there was only a forgotten piece of paper, now already sweat on the brow.... Is it even possible to completely erase all traces?

Double Dialogue

A lie is always a lie for someone, is directed at someone. Who is this *someone* who is lied to? Above all, he is not a bodiless and bloodless object; lying is not the same thing as objectifying. It also does not mean recognizing in the other an equal Thou. There can be no equality without reciprocity, and in lying, reciprocity is precisely violated: by lying to my neighbor I give him untruth as truth, demanding in exchange truth, not untruth.

There remains only one possibility: the other is a "He." However, this word must be understood in a specific sense, because it appears inseparably with "You [Thou]." The pretending to truthfulness contained in lying entails in it a need for a constant movement, within the dialogue with the other, from a relation of I–Thou reciprocity to refusing reciprocity on the I–He level. This movement leaves a mark both on the concept of the I and on the concept of the Thou. The fruit of this constant change in meaning is the word "That One." Who is That One? "That One" is the lasting addressee of the lie who, depending on the circumstances, becomes at some point an equal Thou, and then at some other point an unequal He ("Mister").

Such movement requires a particular sensitivity from the liar. It is related to the game on the double stage: a different stage belongs to him understood as a Thou, and still a different one understood as a He. Hence the tensed attention and ceaseless insecurity of the liar—an insecurity that must be hidden as the trace of a trace. Raskolnikov again:

> "You seemed to be saying yesterday that you wished to ask me ... formally ... about my acquaintance with this ... murdered woman?" Raskolnikov tried to begin again. "Why did I put in that *seemed*?" flashed in him like lightning. "And why am I so worried about having put in that *seemed*?" a second thought immediately flashed in him like lightning. And he suddenly felt that his insecurity, from the mere contact with Porfiry, from two

words only, from two glances only, had bushed out to monstrous proportions in a moment . . . and that it was terribly dangerous — frayed nerves, mounting agitation. "It's bad! It's bad! . . . I'll betray myself again."[28]

The insecurity of the liar is the expression of the suspicion that he is the object of constant observation from That One. The one lied to looks and listens. Who knows what he is thinking? He observes me with watchful suspicion. Who am I for him? I am what he is for me, that is, I am Thou and non-Thou, I am He and Non-He, I am That One. That One, who is both within him and in me, is not the participant of a dialogue. He does not speak. He only looks and listens. When I talk, I only talk with You. That One exists outside of conversation. But not like a tree trunk, but as an attentive and suspicious observer. It would be a great victory of lying if it were possible to destroy That One. Let him disappear absorbed by You. In essence, the whole of lying is a struggle against his existence. But He has a strange ability for rising from his own ashes.

The paradox of a dialogue of lies is that it is not possible without a simultaneous truthfulness. The external lie must be accompanied by an internal truthfulness. In order to lie to the other, I must tell myself the truth; otherwise the lie would not be possible. To know how to hide the truth, you must constantly keep an eye on it.

The internal dialogue of truthfulness circles around the key task of self-defense. It is saturated by the anxiety of the liar about himself. Anxiety leads to a cleavage of ego-consciousness into I-for-myself and I-for-others. The first I is the subject of the dialogue of truthfulness, and the second I is the subject of the dialogue of the lie.

The metaphor of a cleft consciousness forces us to think about the force that penetrates into the interior of consciousness and makes a painful division there. Whence flows this force? The sources of the cleaving force is That One. That One observes, suspects, and is always ready to step forward with an accusation that cannot be overthrown. That One — is an investigating judge. Every lie has its investigating judge who cleaves the consciousness of the liar into two separate parts with his suspicion.

I and Thou, I and He, I and That One — this is the framework of the space in which the dialogue of the lie develops along with all of its contiguities. The double stage is the projection of the double dialogue, and the double dialogue is the projection of the double stage. The stage-for-me is the correlate of the I-for-myself; the correlate of I-for-others is the stage-for-others. My drama for me unfolds upon the first stage, and upon the second stage my drama for others unfolds. Lying skillfully means to be able to change dialogical relations, and, at the same time, to be able to move from one stage to the next without multiplying traces of the crime.

Experience of Existence

The painstaking building of a double stage and the leading of a double dialogue serves one fundamental goal—masking what is. What is? There is a crime. What does this mean? Is the crime the way things are? Is it the same way as people are? Or, maybe just like I am? Besides that, is it now or did it take place in the past? Is it in perception, in remembrance, or in an intrusive imagining? When saying that a crime is, we point to a particular way of living through reality: what is has a *criminal meaning.* The crime colors everything, even the world that lies far from the crime. The power of its presence is unequaled. But what really exists here? I or the world? the world or another person?

Let us recall a passage from Dostoevsky's *Crime and Punishment*:

"But why do you . . . come asking . . . and say nothing . . . what does it mean?" Raskolnikov's voice was faltering, and the words somehow did not want to come out clearly. This time the tradesman raised his eyes and gave Raskolnikov an ominous, gloomy look. "Murderer!" he said suddenly, in a soft but clear and distinct voice. Raskolnikov was walking beside him. His legs suddenly became terribly weak, a chill ran down his spine, and it was as if his heart stood still for a moment; then all at once it began pounding as if it had jumped off the hook. They walked on thus for about a hundred steps, side by side, and again in complete silence. The tradesman did not look at him. "What do you . . . what . . . who is a murderer?" Raskolnikov muttered, barely audibly. "*You* are a murderer," the man replied even more distinctly and imposingly, smiling as if with some hateful triumph, and again he looked straight into Raskolnikov's pale face and deadened eyes. Just then they came to an intersection. The tradesman turned down the street to the left and walked on without looking back. Raskolnikov remained on the spot and gazed after him for a long time. He saw him turn around, after he had gone fifty steps or so, and looked at him standing there motionlessly on the same spot. It was impossible to see, but Raskolnikov fancied that the man once again smiled his coldly hateful and triumphant smile. With slow, weakened steps, with trembling knees and as if terribly cold, Raskolnikov returned and went upstairs to his closet. He took off his cap, put it on the table, and stood motionlessly beside it for about ten minutes. Then, powerless, he lay down on the sofa and painfully, with a weak moan, stretched out on it; his eyes were closed. He lay that way for about half an hour. He was not thinking of anything. There were just some thoughts, or scraps of thoughts, images without order or connection—the faces of people he had seen as a child, or had met only once somewhere, and whom he would never even have remembered; the belfry of the V—y Church; the billiard table in some tavern, an officer by the billiard table, the smell of cigars in a basement tobacco shop, a pothouse, a back stairway, completely dark, all slopped with swill and strewn with eggshells, and from somewhere the sound of Sunday bells ringing.... One thing followed another, spinning like a whirlwind. Some he even liked, and he clung to them, but they would die out, and generally something weighed on him inside, but not very much. At times he even felt good.... The slight chill would not go away, but that, too, felt almost good.[29]

What is is neither perceived nor experienced, but lived through. What is that which is? It is a criminal existence. A criminal existence is given to us in the manner of living through. This living through is based upon turning away from existence. Therefore, we do not reach it through the mediation of intentional acts as we do with objects existing in this world. The crime is present within the dark sphere of consciousness, at the sources of intention, which turn away from it. Consciousness of the crime is neither clear nor distinct, like the Cartesian *cogito*. It is also not the result of an existential judgment with whose help existential Thomism hunts for real beings. And yet the power of its presence exceeds all others. Its consciousness penetrates deeper than the consciousness of one's own body, it takes feelings and reason into its possession and fills the heart with fear. In the end, it makes an obedient servant out of the one who desires to be the ruler of men.

Criminal existence continually makes ever-new circles. The beginning of the crime is in me—in my soul, in my hand. Later the crime goes beyond me, it includes an object, which will be the tool of the crime. Finally, there appears what is decisive: the victim. If there were no victim, there would be no crime. But there is a victim. Traces remain after the crime is committed. Then the problem of witnesses emerges. There is also the investigating judge. How to convince the investigating judge that I did not kill? One must build a double stage and develop a double dialogue. One must take up a double game. Suddenly somebody comes up and says, "You are a murderer." The circle of criminal existence closes. I am its axis.

Living through what I am comes to completion only when I hear from the outside, "You are a murderer." Suddenly the illusions vanish. The world as I know it so far crumbles. There is no stage—everything falls apart. What actually has happened? After all, Raskolnikov knows full well what he did. Did he think that a man becomes a murderer not when he kills but when others find out about it? And maybe until then he was just a killer? The difference is quite substantial: homicide can be justified somehow, but not murder. Raskolnikov justified his act before himself, trusting that a justification before himself is a justification before the whole world. Suddenly it becomes apparent that this is not how it is. What is he to do, should he kill the witness? Yet, how many others must perish on the road toward a happy world? Dostoevsky reveals the spiritual state of the criminal after a sudden unmasking. This state can only be described with one word: falling apart. Raskolnikov now knows who he is, but he does not know in what world he exists. But without knowing in what world he exists, Raskolnikov does not ultimately know who he is.

Since Hegel's time, much has been written about the mediated self-consciousness. The subject of consciousness, in order to become himself, needs recognition from another consciousness. The famous relation between the master and slave is an example. Does a similar relation hold in the case of murder?

It seems that here one should pay attention to one particular moment—the moment of interior admission. No external recognitions of self-knowledge by self-knowledge have the power to constitute its core—its *ipseity*—if they are not recognized as appropriate by its own interior instantiation. You cannot impose the consciousness of the murderer upon anyone without his permission. This permission is not possible without interior verification. Verification depends upon encountering the truth. Raskolnikov does not recognize himself as a murderer because someone else told him, but because he really is one. The liar succumbs to the truth that was in him. But to know that such a truth was in him, it was necessary that someone come from the outside and say, "You are a murderer."

Common World

Let us recall the words of Raskolnikov once more: "A man with even a bit of development and experience will certainly try to admit as far as possible all the external and unavoidable facts."[30] This returning of what is essential to the one lied to originates in two assumptions: from the assumption of a common world, in which there is no need to distort, and from the assumption of reciprocity in lying, that is, the possibility of putting a lying I in the place of the Thou asking about the truth.

What is the common world? The idea of a common environment possesses several layers of meaning. Most commonly, it is passed over in silence, assumed that it is the common world of many equally truthful subjects of experience. The world of the environment includes all that can be carved out as common, and this also takes on the meaning of an objectively existing reality. An objectively existing tree is a tree-object that remains after rejecting the differences introduced by the individual perception of a particular human being. The differences between concrete perceptions are easily grasped without even asking others about their appearance—it is enough when one and the same subject changes the vantage point of their observation of the world. Such an altering of the point of view upon the world became an integral ingredient of Husserl's phenomenological method. It was supposed to help in reaching the essence of phenomena; this essence should appear as what is unchangeable upon the background of change in nonessential moments.

However, the meaning of the world will change considerably when we accept that the subject observing the world is not the transcendental ego—the impartial observer of the genesis that constitutes sense—but an evil demon, who desires to constitute a world under his rule. The condition of ruling is undoubtedly some "common world" of the ruler and his subjects. The ruler must give his subjects a semblance of truth, must "admit as far as possible all the external and unavoidable facts," and in this way establish some boundaries for his lies. Yet, it must be admitted that the shadow of the initial lie will be cast even upon this truth—upon the space common to the liar and the one lied to. The truth that must serve the lie bears the weight of this servitude. The "common world" is not free from this weight.

A philosopher in dispute with the evil demon fights for some minimum of truth free from suspicion. He utters the famous "I think, therefore I am." The evil demon does not need to deny this discovery. He even needs it. The subjected should know his existence well, care about it, and in the name of this care subject himself to the demon. The dispute with the demon begins only when the philosopher puts forward a hypothesis contrary to the hypothesis of the demon: a good God exists, who always says the truth. Man carries within himself the God of truthfulness. This God is closer to man than man is to himself. The idea of such as God is the condition of thinking about the world. Do not the arguments that result from the idea of God, including the ontological argument, show this? One must accept the existence of the God of truthfulness. Only later does lying become possible. Lying is a deviation from truthfulness, but it pretends to be truthful. Integrity must initially reign for there to be a deviation. In the common world of the liar and the one lied to there appear gleams of this righteousness. They shine even through the shadow cast upon the world by the need to serve the liar.

The evil demon, who knows this well, suffers deeply. The common world shared with those lied to is a source of pain and fear. Footprints appear in this world—somebody can come along and read their meaning. The ax, which in the world of truth serves to cut wood, can have bloodstains on it. The pawnbroker's pledges might stick in the wallpaper cracks. Even the smallest trace of a lie is enough for a trust built up with great difficulty to fall into ruins. Brows become wet with sweat.

The fear of the truth being revealed forces the liar to maintain a special relationship with the one lied to. Of what sort? Let us assume that I lie. I must present my lie as the truth. To achieve this goal I must stand in the place of the one lied to, to see as he sees, to hear as he hears, to think as he thinks. Substitution, the interchangeability of places, is the condition of the lie. I continue to ask, What would I do in your place and what would you do in my place? In this way the lying-I continually calls into being a truthful-I in itself. The more I want to lie to it [the truthful-I], the more intensely I must acknowledge it. But, in the final analysis, who is this truthful Opponent? Is it not the truthful God, whom I battle within myself? By lying I carry Him in myself as an inalienable idea.

In the end, what is the common world of the liar and the one being lied to? It is not only a piece of space like a battlefield full of signs and traces—a bloody ax, a mark on the stairs, a receipt of debt... The deepest semantic layer of the common world is constituted by the perspective opened by the ideal of an absolute truthfulness in which the absolute truth can appear—one that can only be revealed to the eyes of God. This ideal is the hope of those lied to. It is also the despair of liars, because they must assume it, so that they can deviate from it.

Emotions of the Liar

I already spoke about the fear of the truth. Out of our fear of it we seek help in a lie. Lying is the killer's hope. Lying is directed externally, toward others. A lie directed externally is accompanied by an interior truth. The greater the need for a lie, the clearer the consciousness of the truth. I am a murderer. Can this be somehow justified? Thus, justification should be universally valid, and therefore real. The pressure of the truth lets itself be known again! Therefore, it is better to cover up a homicide. Whatever else might be said, it is better to lie.

This is the axiological situation of the liar: when he fears the truth, he feels that this fear demeans him. In the end, he must defend himself, and the need for a defense is always something demeaning. But to feel demeaned is at the same time to feel that the opponent is someone higher than I am. This is how the axiological axis of superiority–inferiority, around which the dialogue of the interrogation revolve, comes into being. This axis is as if an essential *a priori* of this dialogue.

But the liar—we remain on the side of the liar—cannot admit that his place is to be found at the bottom of the axis. It would mean admitting he is a liar. Therefore, he must protest, at first internally, later also externally. This protest expresses itself in an increased demand for respect. Liars demand respect with such obsessiveness from those they lie to that this in itself awakens suspicions . . .

Raskolnikov says: "'Porfiry Petrovich!' he said loudly and distinctly, though he could barely stand on his trembling legs, 'at last I see clearly that you do definitely suspect me of murdering that old woman and her sister Lizaveta. For my own part I declare to you that I have long been sick of it all. If you believe you have the right to prosecute me legally, then prosecute me; or to arrest me, then arrest me. But to torment me and laugh in my face, that I will not allow!'"[31]

In turn, excessive care about respect results in an exaggerated respect for the investigating judge, in whom one can notice a tone of ridicule. The investigating judge replicates the hypocrisy. But this hypocrisy is different than Raskolnikov's hypocrisy. When it does not hide that it is hypocrisy, then hypocrisy becomes an allusion to the truth. The situation is dangerous. The truth is approaching. Porfiry says: "'Ah, my esteemed sir! Here you are . . . in our parts . . .' Porfiry began, reaching out both hands to him. 'Well, do sit down, my dear! Or perhaps you don't like being called esteemed and . . . dear—so, *tout court*? Please don't regard it as familiarity. . . . Over here, sir, on the sofa.'"[32]

But such overt hypocrisy evokes an even greater anxiety. Raskolnikov is sensitive: "'He reached out both hands to me, and yet he didn't give me either, he drew them back in time,' flashed in him suspiciously."[33]

The dialogue-interrogation is a dialogue of suspicion. Who suspects? Above all, the investigating judge. Let us momentarily shift our attention to this figure. The investigating judge makes the preliminary assumption that the other (Raskolnikov) is lying. However, this assumption should not come to light, so as not to arouse the sensitivity of the liar. Revealing the suspicion makes getting to the truth much more difficult. On the other hand, the very fact of hiding suspicions knocks the investigating judge from his position of sincerity. And so the answer to Raskolnikov's untruth becomes Porfiry's untruth. Lies beget lies, suspicion begets suspicion. The initial axis of axiological superiority–inferiority is displaced: the one who was at the bottom migrates to the top, and the one who was at the top migrates to the bottom. It may even lead to the breaking of the axis, and then both of them will find themselves at the bottom, not only as identical criminals, but as liars who are similar.

It can therefore be said that the interrogation dialogue is a constant voyage through fragile, breaking, and changing axiological axes. On the shaky ground of dialogue, words change their usual meaning. Questions become accusations and answers become indictments. Jumping from axis to axis, it is as if the speakers lose the main thread. However, it only appears that way. In place of the fundamental question, "Who killed?" there appears another one, for example, Who respects whom more, and who less? By expressing respect or refusing respect, the speakers move from one stage to another. Will they not stumble when passing? Will not one of them slip and fall from a crowded and busy axis? Departing from the main thread has a specific purpose: it is about pulling a liar into a trap. But what is a trap?

Trap

There are, generally speaking, two kinds of traps—accidental traps and traps with bait. Taking into account the type of bait, we could further extend our distinctions, but this is not necessary. We know that man used to set traps for animals to satisfy his hunger. By setting a trap for another human being, he extends the old tradition. Whoever senses in himself the soul of a hunter will hunt people with pleasure.

The accidental trap is relatively the least effective.

The hunter digs a hole along the path usually trod by animals, and he appropriately masks it and waits until one of them carelessly puts a leg there. Something similar happens with man. The investigating judge suddenly asks about a detail, seemingly unconnected to the matter, and waits for a careless word.

"So, passing by on the stairs before eight o'clock, did you at least notice two workers in the open apartment—remember?—on the second floor? Or at least one of them? They were painting, didn't you see? This is very, very important for them! . . . "

"Painters? No, I didn't see . . ." Raskolnikov answered slowly, as if rummaging through his memories, at the same time straining his whole being and frozen with anguish trying to guess where precisely the trap lay, and how not to overlook something. "No, I didn't see, and I didn't notice any open apartment either . . . but on the fourth floor" (he was now in full possession of the trap and was triumphant). "I do remember there was an official moving out of the apartment . . . opposite Alyona Ivanovna's . . . yes . . . that I remember clearly . . . soldiers carrying out some sofa and pressing me against the wall . . . but painters—no, I don't remember any painters being there . . . and I don't think there was any open apartment anywhere. No, there wasn't . . ."

"But what's the matter with you!" Razumikhin exclaimed suddenly, as if coming to his senses and figuring things out. "The painters were working on the day of the crime itself, and he was there two days earlier! Why ask him?"[34]

A trap with bait has a different construction. We assume that the lie of the liar is the means to some lofty goal. The liar has a soul, and his soul is full of fears, but also hopes. The fear of death is in it. There is also the hope of some exaltation. One and the other can be the bait in a trap: confess to it and you will save your life; confess the truth and you will attain honors. However, the most subtle form of bait—the bait for connoisseurs—looks completely different.

Here is the investigating judge. He is That One—the man without a face. A conversation with someone like that is not even a conversation. Can it be a lie? The investigating judge knows well: so long as the liar does not discover a human face in him, then he will not feel the responsibility to speak, especially to speak the truth. This has to change. But how? You have to call forth and enliven in the liar (Raskolnikov) experiences and feelings in which he most feels like himself, of which he is proud, which elevate him above the ordinary world. Raskolnikov would like to make humanity happy. Why should he not make the investigating judge happy? Here is an extraordinary trap in which the bait becomes a misfortune for the investigating judge himself, while the force that is supposed to lead to the confession is the same compassion that lay at the root of the crime.

Porfiry says:

"I am, you know, a bachelor, an unworldly and unknowing man, and, moreover, a finished man, a frozen man, sir, gone to seed, and ... and ... and have you noticed, Rodion Romanovich, that among us—that is, in our Russia, sir, and most of all in our Petersburg circles—if two intelligent men get together, not very well acquainted yet, but, so to speak, mutually respecting each other, just like you and me now, sir, it will take them a whole half hour to find a topic of conversation—they freeze before each other, they sit feeling mutually embarrassed ... excuse me, my dear, I'm so afraid of offending you, but it's simply necessary for me to move, sir. I sit all the time, and I'm so glad to be able to walk around for five minutes or so ... hemorrhoids, sir ... I keep thinking of trying gymnastics as a treatment."[35]

From the horizon in which the faceless That One has been raving there emerges someone who is unhappy, worthy of conscientious consolation and that bit of sacrifice that is the proclamation of the truth. The plane of the dialogue changes. The investigating judge changes from being a hunting dog that was directed to hunt an animal into an animal hunted by the dogs. Was Raskolnikov supposed to be one of them?

But Raskolnikov does not cross the threshold of the trap. Why? There is a subtle boundary of mercy, beyond which mercy stands before a growing feeling of disgust. Instead of extending a hand, a man withdraws it. A man turns away his gaze instead of being pained by the pain painted upon another face. Raskolnikov suddenly knows, because of this, that whoever prepares the prison keys for others out of his own pain can expect no sympathy.

But this does not mean that the place of mercy is now occupied by cruelty. Disgust appears here. A man turns his gaze and wants to have nothing in common with it all. The dialogue of man with man breaks off and leaves no hope for reestablishing ties.

In the end Raskolnikov confesses, but not to the judge and not to the one who said to him, "You are a murderer," but to Sonya. She did not prepare any trap for him.

Political Reason

So far we have considered, above all, the external plot of the liar's dialogue, whose goal was hiding the crime. The premise of this dialogue was acknowledging that the truth is a value higher than lying, which is why lying must depend upon pretending to be the truth. Another premise was the understanding of the truth common to the liar and the one being lied to as the conformity of knowledge with so-called objective reality. The consequence of the lie condemned to pretend to be the truth was the game upon a double stage and a double dialogue—different on the exterior and different for the liar left to himself. The double stage and the double dialogue pointed to the presence in the consciousness of the liar of a double *a priori*—an *a priori* of the lie and the *a priori* of truthfulness. Their relationship to each other turned out to be such that the *a priori* of truthfulness was at the same time the *a priori* of the lie, but not the other way around. The lie of common sense assumed truthfulness as its condition of possibility. From this comes the tragic nature of the liar. The very logic of the lie limits the power of common sense over the truth.

Does it have to be so? Let us once again occupy the position of the liar. Are we, liars, irrevocably condemned to pay homage to a value to which we cannot be faithful? Can we not free ourselves from all conditions that limit our power over the truth? However, this is not about what Nietzsche wanted: he recognized that false judgments are necessary to life. Is it not possible to go a step further and accept that the judgments necessary to life are not at all false? Is it not possible to proclaim that what until now was the truth is a lie, and what was a lie is the truth?

What is the truth? Common sense sticks to the view that what is at stake is the conformity of knowledge to reality. But where is this objective reality? Material reality, from which the stage of our drama is built, is a great reservoir of raw material for us, subject to processing by technical reason. Historical reality, the creations of culture, political systems, and religions are the fruit of convictions, which, for unknown reasons dominate in a given time and in given societies. What is called objective reality is only a momentary *state of things* determined by the past history of knowledge and self-knowledge of man. What then is the truth and what is falsehood? Truth and falsehood depend upon the social recognition of the value of the following thesis: a thesis more valuable for a given society becomes recognized as more worthy of being realized, and therefore also as truer; a less valuable thesis, or even one that is harmful, becomes an erroneous thesis. What is the criterion of the truth then? The criterion of truth is the value of a given thesis. A new path opens up for Raskolnikov: what for common sense was a lie proves to be a higher truthfulness, and what for common sense was the truth, proves to be a lie for higher reason.

Such a conception is only seemingly paradoxical. It has indubitable roots in naturalist scientific thinking. Seemingly only the natural sciences are the result of objective thinking, free from all valuations. Science itself organizes its theses not only according to their relationship to reality, but also according to values that belong to them. In the womb of science we find judgments and systems of judgments, which are the judgments of theories, working hypotheses, research postulates, assumptions with only a heuristic value. The history of science teaches us how the valuation of the sciences has changed over time, how one "Queen of the Sciences" had to give way to another and how this influenced their development or decay. Knowledge goes hand in hand with the valuation of knowledge. May the valuation of knowledge now precede knowledge and mark out its truthfulness.

Let us repeat again: the basic criterion of truth is the value that belongs to a given truth. This thesis is a radicalized extension of thinking that has accompanied science since the beginning and that creates it. Besides that, is it not the fulfillment of hidden dreams? Does it not claim that knowledge is a power, and science the basic creative means? Until now truth had power over thinking, but it did not bring happiness to humanity. From now on, thinking will have undivided power over the truth.

We shall call such a stance *axiological radicalism*.

Axiological radicalism has two consequences. Above all, it throws a new light on the idea of power. The problem of power becomes a significant problem of axiology. Every material puts up a lesser or greater resistance to attempts at realizing value. The resistance is the result of either the natural inertia of matter or because the matter has been determined by other values. What is needed is some power to incarnate values into matter, or raise the matter to the level of valued works. Only man has such power at his disposal, especially the man who is given to leading other people. To build a better future, you have to bind many into one giant organism, moved by one thought and one heart. The key for the realization of values, therefore, lies in the hands of those in power. However, this means that those in power also hold the key to their veracity. They know and they can. Their practice eventually turns out to be the concrete and final criterion of the truth: the truth is what those in power succeed doing, while the untruth is what ends in failure for those in power. With the right power, which is able to concentrate in the right direction the will of nations and overcome the obstacles standing in its way, man can feel the lord of what is true and false. Just like God, or, maybe like an anti-God, but in all certainty, just like Raskolnikov.

Another consequence of axiological radicalism must be a certain way of motivating people to recognize certain values especially worthy of realization. How can one convince another that he should realize a certain value? Referring to "objective reality" would be contrary to the idea of axiological radicalism. This is why Nietzsche speaks of *seduction*. To seduce means to give some promise, revive hope, enkindle the desire for promotion. However, seduction does not preclude more negative behaviors: to threaten, awaken fear, frighten, force to action . . . and there is no violation of innate rights of the human person. If everything is material, then also man. Man must also mature to the level of a creator of values. Those in power must therefore form him so that he can reasonably, but obediently, participate in its great undertaking. Therefore, also on the level of the I–Thou relation certain practices become the concrete and final criterion of truth.

What should we call the reason that achieves the radicalization of axiology outlined by us? We shall call it *political reason*. This reason strives to create the world anew. It does not want to, and it cannot, do this in isolation, but instead draws all people into its work through a certain politics. From this comes our name. But this does not mean that this name exhausts all of its contents. If somebody wanted, they also could detect in it something that ought to be called the demonic side of metaphysics.

The figure of Raskolnikov is the concretization of this type of reason. He is accused of murder. But murder exists where there was brotherhood before. The pawnbroker herself broke off the tie of brotherhood. Therefore, if there was anything, then it was homicide. But, do we not kill during war on the battlefield? Is destroying the obstacle on the road to a happy tomorrow not useful for humanity? If yes, then Raskolnikov does not lie, but says the truth in a "higher" sense than the common sense. Why do we condemn him for something we praise Napoleon for?

A different concretization of this reason is the evil genius from Descartes's *Meditation*. Let us look at it a little closer.

Evil Demon

There are at least two possible interpretations of the evil demon symbol: as a demon of the total lie and as a demon of total power. The demon of the total lie lies magnanimously—it plays with lying like a grown-up did when he was a child, and his happiness lived in a land of fairy tales. The demon of total power plays with power like a man grown up—and the lie serves only as a means to this goal. This does not exclude the truth, if only it serves the cause of power.

The dispute with the demon of total lies is simple. Let us recall what we have already said about it: a complete lie is impossible, because it would have to be equally a lie directed at others and a lie directed at oneself. But, after all, there cannot be a lie without consciousness of lying on the side of the liar and nonawareness of the lie on the side of the one being lied to. Therefore, if I were to lie to myself, I would have to be simultaneously aware of the truth that I am hiding from myself, but this excludes complete self-deception. Instead of lying to myself, I prefer running away from myself. So I run away—run away into forgetting myself, into a theater of illusions, into states of nonawareness. It is better to run away from myself than to completely lie to myself.

The dispute with the demon of power is more complicated. Absolute power tempts all of us, even those who are against it. It is not only power over the elements of heaven and earth, but also power over truth and falsehood. The basic desire of total power is not knowledge, but the building of a new "better" world. Political reason is its first servant and is thus raised to the level of metaphysical reason. This reason is capable of using the commonsense understanding of the truth—it does not reject it, why would it? Will it not be useful to it when it needs to accuse and judge opponents? "What were you doing at the appointed hour of the night? Do you recognize this ax? Are these bloodstains?" How is it possible to answer these questions without common sense? But political reason knows that the truth about what is must bow before the truth of what will be and what should be. It is so obvious that common sense frequently bends uncritically toward the propositions of political reason. It is set exclusively to describe the truth and awakens too late to interfere with political practice. It opens its eyes when the work is done and then becomes enslaved by its spell. It is not true that politics affects common sense using violent means and only in that way takes it into its possession. The political deed does not affect it using any other means than the power of established truth. The Owl of Minerva flies at dusk and brings to light as the truth of history what political reason has built. There is no need for fear for a captive mind to arise. Love for what is, because it is, is enough.

The seductive power of political reason can penetrate even deeper. Its fruit will not only be recognition of already formed truth, but an attempt to imitate the very manner of creating the truth. Common sense then begins to be ashamed of itself. Enchanted by the looming theater, it takes as a model political thinking, and by increasingly renouncing its commonality it shapes itself in the image and likeness of political reason. What does it begin with? It begins by posing the key question of politics: Who is with me and who is against me?

We no longer ask, What is? We do not ask, Where did what is come from? What makes up what is? We ask, Who is with me and who is against me? We stand before a completely new mystery of the world!

Our thinking begins with the suspicion: maybe you are against me? And if you are against me, then I have to find a way to incline you to surrender. Demanding recognition, this type of reason suspects that the refusal of recognition is possible, that is, a more or less open rebellion. Political reason uses, on the one hand, a threat, and, on the other, a promise in order to get recognition and silence a possible rebellion. However, it is difficult to promise if one does not have much. Thus, what can be offered? Participation in power. When you will rule with me, you will be able to induce others to obey.

It is easier to threaten: if you do not submit, you will damn your life, the life of those dear to you, and you will perish. The genius of political thinking manifests itself in the wealth of discoveries made along the line of promises and threats. That is why it needs complete knowledge about man. Admittedly, that is a great deal of knowledge in some cases.

The political dialogue with subjects, or candidates for future subjects, turns between a threat and a promise, calls into being a particular type of speech, which is a speech of pressure. It does not refer to common sense, but to political truth, which still does not exist, but which ought to be created. This speech encourages and discourages, strengthens and weakens, arouses enthusiasm and arouses fear, kindles and puts out fires, seduces and deceives—in other words, it agitates. What is said becomes less important; it is more important how it is said. However, it is followed by the shadow of an initial suspicion and all of its consequences: from suspicion come accusations, from accusations come denunciations, and from denunciations it is only a small step to murder. How much charm such thinking and speech have! The basic categories are easily grasped, they stick to the imagination and there continually give birth to new fruits. How much joy is supplied by unexpected discoveries, rightly known as "unmaskings"! Here someone was, as it turns out, only seemingly with us, but in reality was against us. A foreign plug! A spy! Saboteur! Can the discoveries of mathematicians, physicists, and chemists really compete with such discoveries? Political thinking gives the conviction that we are able to judge the existing world. It gives us joy from this judgment. This is accompanied by the great joy of creating, which makes the sadness of destruction that must unfortunately precede creation fade away. Political thinking is contagious; it spreads not thanks to unveiled truths, but like a plague—through contact itself. No wonder that even the most sophisticated intellectuals succumb to it—even intellectuals such as Raskolnikov.

Victory

Who won in the dialogue of interrogation? Raskolnikov won. His victory consists not only in the fact that he did not let himself be pulled into the trap, but, above all, that he was capable of convincing himself that he did not commit a crime in killing, but instead contributed to the progress and happiness of humanity. A change in the concept of truth was the means to his victory. Truth no longer is the agreement between knowledge and the reality knowledge is concerned with, but the agreement between the reality created by man with the previously undertaken ideal project of rebuilding it. Raskolnikov cannot explain all of this to the investigating judge, because the investigating judge is incapable of understanding anything. He has predetermined thought-patterns in which he wants to confine Raskolnikov's views. The investigating judge is part of the world that should disappear.

Raskolnikov's victory does not depend only upon saving his life. The dispute we are witness to is a dispute over holding power. To gain power one must present oneself as being just among the unjust. Victory depends upon self-justification. To justify oneself means to show that you are not a liar. Raskolnikov, thanks to including political reason into his discourse, shows that he is not a murderer. Therefore, he is not a liar. His act was actually a heroic act. Even though the investigating judge has a different opinion about this, that fact has no greater significance. Raskolnikov is therefore worthy of holding power. Thanks to his ability to foresee and his heroism, he can be the leader who leads society toward a better future.

Raskolnikov did not renounce the truth. He only changed its meaning. He is fully aware how great a role is played by truth in the life of men and nations. He does not intend to rule other than only through truth. Raskolnikov precisely distinguishes what will take place tomorrow thanks to his politics and what has already happened thanks to him. What will be, what will be called into being, depends upon the truth of political reason; here the absolute precedence of axiology applies: the more valuable the project of tomorrow, the more real it is. What has already been created is subject to evaluation and description according to the categories of common sense. No reasonable person should contradict the achievements of political reason. If someone were to dare raise doubts, he might encounter an even better investigating judge who will point out the lie to him. Thus, the truth is the foundation of Raskolnikov's power.

Raskolnikov won.

However, we know from Dostoevsky's book that things happened differently. Why? Was it because he was too weak to carry the weight of his deeds? Or, because his argumentation failed somewhere? Or, maybe he lost by accident, because of the homicide of unfortunate Lizaveta? Finally, perhaps Sonya, whose opinion he valued too much, is at fault for everything?

Dostoevsky shows a losing figure. But we do not believe him: Raskolnikov won and has power. What now? Did his fears cease? How did his cares end?

Victor's Demon

Let us once again take a look at the course of the interrogation dialogue: this dialogue began from a defense and ended with the seizure of power over man and the truth. It brought with it, through the power of its logic, a specific relation to another man—a relation of opposition. The interrogator is the opponent of the interrogated and the interrogated is the opponent of the interrogator. Where there is an interrogation, there is a dialectic of oppositions. That is why there is no other way: somebody must fail and surrender, and somebody must become a master. The stakes of the dialogue are dominion or slavery. This matter is also served by changes in the concept of truth. Truth . . . ? Yes, but such a truth, and as much truth as is needed to rule.

Let us ask now, Where lie the main dangers for power gained in such a way? Where do the dangers for Raskolnikov-leader hide? Where may a flame of rebellion still burn when everything has been subjected to him?

The answer is in the dialogue of interrogation itself.

The dialogue of interrogation does not end at the moment when power is seized, because power is always inherently threatened. You can never be sure enough of yourself. The subjects must be continually interrogated. Raskolnikov interrogates well because he himself was interrogated. But by interrogating he imposes upon himself and upon those subject to him a relation, which, necessarily entails this dialogue—a relation of opposition. He is against them, and They are against him. What does it mean to be an opponent? What body does this abstraction take on? To be against means to set yourself on revenge. Eye for an eye and tooth for a tooth. Whoever interrogates is interrogated. The truth he fights with will be the truth with which he is fought off.

It is not true that there is no dialogue between absolute power and its subjects. There is a dialogue. But it is the dialogue of interrogation. At one time, those who hold total power interrogate a society of subjects, and at other times, the society of subjects interrogates those in power.

In this way, Raskolnikov feels that everything he invented turns against him. If he invented a double stage, then he has a double stage. If he invented a double dialogue, then he has a double dialogue. If he demonstrated how it is possible to jump on breaking axiological axes, then he has before his eyes a wondrous circus. If he demonstrated how to circle around a crime, then he now sees how his subordinates circle.

When he sets traps for others, then he sees how others set them for him. But the greatest shock is caused by the change in the concept of truth and the change in the nature of thinking that goes along with it. If all of reality is only material with which one must do something sensible, then he himself, Raskolnikov, and his power are also materials. Cannot this power be changed? One must try, maybe destruction will succeed. When the practice of power in relation to society is the final criterion of the truth, then the criterion of truth is also the practice of society in relation to those in power. Political thinking is the pinnacle of thinking ... Therefore, Are the authorities with me, or against me? The one who interrogates me is always against me. Therefore, I also cannot do otherwise. If those in power with their reason continually suspect that I am seemingly a subject, then I also have the right to suspect that they are seemingly in power. If political reason threatens me, then I also threaten it. If it promises, then I also promise, and my promises have the same value at the promises of those in power. When they do not keep them, then I also have the right not to keep my promises. Those in power accuse me. I accuse those in power. Those in power condemn me. I condemn the ones who condemn me. Those in power can destroy me. But I also can do the same, even here and now, by erasing awareness of them. Retaliatory thinking has its charms. Perhaps they are bigger than that of the constructive, or seemingly constructive, thinking of those in power. This thinking further develops foresight, cunning, caution and courage, penetration and deceit, as well as all other underground abilities of the human body and spirit. It also brings many joys, the joys of victory. For in a fight with a great opponent, even the smallest victory counts as a great success. The principle of retaliation is key. The game takes place upon a double stage, a double dialogue pairs with it—different for those in power and their subjects among themselves, and different for those in power with their subjects and the subjects with those in power. Those in power are Them. The subjects are the Us. But the converse can also be true—Us, we are those in power, and the subjects are Them. Who among us is higher and who is lower? We are still moving along a broken axiological axis, once higher, once lower—despising and despised. Between Us and Them there is a whole system of traps—accidental traps and traps with a variety of baits. Who will outwit whom? Who will get caught in the act? Speech grows around all this. It is the speech of pressure: promises pass into accusations, incentives become entangled with threats, unmaskings with denunciations. This kind of speech shows us the structure of political thinking: Who is with me, who is against me? Who am I with and who are you with? And this is how the elaborate structure of lies grows—lies that come from pure revenge. Here are the lies that only those in power believe. Here are lies that only the subjects believe, and also the lies that nobody believes. Special knowledge and unique skills are needed to not lose oneself in this edifice.

Does what really is no longer exist? Reality *really* is the circle of existence drawn out by consciousness of the crime. In the beginning there was some crime. Who committed it? When? This is not known, the interrogation continues. We are still following the tracks. We do not even precisely know what kind of crime it was. But paradox depends upon this, that what we do not know exists for us more than what we know about—it is more real from what is here and now, and can be stronger in action than the ideals of political reason, which require such great sacrifices.

The significant achievement of the dialogue of interrogation is only this: it reveals to us a circle of criminal existence from which we cannot escape. Is there anything more real?

This is how the kingdom of Raskolnikov perishes—by slow degradation. His political reason striving to change everything into material is suddenly in a situation where that *something* from which *everything* was supposed to arise is still *nothing*. But in that case he himself is *nothing* with his whole desire to become someone through controlling everything. It is not the truthful God who turns out to be the destroyer of this kingdom. The demon of lying bends under the weight of the demon he provoked.

C. Going Astray in the Element of the Good

Our attention is still focused around the mystery of encounter. To encounter, above all, is to encounter the other person. We also speak of the encounter with God or a work of art, but more in a metaphorical, nonliteral, sense. The experience of the encounter or, more precisely, the lived-experience of an encounter, puts the one who encounters someone within the personal truth of the encountered person. The power of persuasion this kind of lived-experience carries within itself cannot be compared with the power of persuasion of any other experience. When I encounter, I know that the other person exists, and that he faces me just as he really is, without masks or veils. Usually, I cannot describe what I see and feel; even so, I know that from the moment of encounter, my life has taken on a new meaning, while the surrounding world has gained a new principle of organization. The lived-experience of an encounter is not only the summit experience of another person but also the summit of all experience.

The encounter requires descriptions from various angles. I have already turned our attention toward the ambivalent role of beauty, which sometimes seems to open up an encounter, but later often leads the one encountering and the encountered toward wastelands. I would like now to take up the question of the role of evil—the evil incarnated in the one whom I encounter—which is sometimes the cause of reversal and retreat, of breaking all contact with an *evil person*. Does such a retreat make encounter impossible? Does it not indicate, at least indirectly, some truth about the encountered person? When we take up a topic formulated thus, we cannot avoid the question about the essence of the phenomenon of evil. What is the evil incarnated in the other? What exactly does the evil person threaten me with? Questions such as these impose themselves all the more, because the experience of the evil person is not only a certain way of experiencing a man as a man, but simultaneously it is a primordial way of experiencing evil as evil. The experience of objective evil—evil things, evil events—seems derivative, nonoriginary. Phenomenology was supposed to be, according to Husserl's aims, a science of the essence of phenomena, based upon originary experiences of the object. If so, then it has to include the experience of encounter in a special way if it wants to study the essence of the phenomenon of evil.

Considering the phenomenon of evil through the prism of the I–Thou relation has important consequences. This is because it signifies a stepping beyond the ontological plane of investigating evil. What characterizes the ontological manner of thinking about the question of evil? In general, it depends upon an attempt to reduce the concept of evil to concepts derived directly or indirectly from the concept of being. In these investigations, it is presupposed, more or less clearly, that the concept of being is a more luminous concept, more general, whereas the concept of evil is a murky and more concrete concept. This assumes that the fundamental distinctions pertaining to being should in some measure be applicable for conceptions of evil. It is said that what is, is good, however much it is; being is a good and evil is nonbeing. The key question of ontology is always, though formulated in a myriad of ways, the question of evil's manner of being. Ontology, in order to know what evil is, asks, above all, about in what manner evil exists. Within ontology, the question of the manner of being takes on the character of an essential question. This kind of question already contains its answer. Because, in principle, there are only three possibilities: evil is being, evil is nonbeing, or evil is the lack of harmony between some beings. Does this exhaust all the possibilities of answering the question as stated? Is there no other choice? Such presuppositions do not seem adequate. Perhaps the application of the phenomenological method to the study of evil will reveal other perspectives?

The phenomenological way of asking about the essence of evil seeks to clarify the phenomenon of evil, and distinguish it from phenomena that are most intimately bound to evil. It is more essential to capture the differences than to show the similarities. Evil threatens, but it simultaneously lures. We cannot say that evil is something real, because if it were, then it could not tempt in order to materialize. Nor can we say that evil does not exist, because that which is not cannot threaten, fill with anxiety, and horrify. What can we say in this situation? We must strive to show evil as a phenomenon, abstracting—if only momentarily—from evil's relation to being and nonbeing. Evil is like something that is given, and not like something that is defined. In a concrete interpersonal experience, evil is less an axiom of our thinking than it is an axiom of our experience. Upon this axiom there rest other, more derivative, experiences of other people. The experience of the evil incarnated in the other belongs to *axiomatic experiences*—it can be found alongside such experiences as the experience of beauty, goodness, and holiness—that mark out the meaning and the course of other associations with men. Of course, I am only considering those instances in which the evil of the other is given in an indubitable way. I know that the other is an *evil person*, the only thing I do not know is what this means, what his *evil* depends upon.

Evil is a given. I no longer ask whether this is a semblance or not. I know that I have experienced this in a sufficiently clear way—some evil is incarnate in the other person. I experienced his evil in such a way that all doubts disappear as to whether the other is, or is not, evil. I repeat: evil is a given in an axiomatic experience whose power of persuasion is beyond rebuttal. This evil threatens me, but it simultaneously entices me. It pushes away, but it also pulls me in. It threatens, but some temptation is present in this threat. It wants to deprive me of hope, but it also promises some hope. The serpent of biblical paradise says, "You shall be like gods." Evil appears within the horizon of some ambiguity. It is the forbidden fruit around which everything circles. When God speaks, the picking of the forbidden fruit is a sin. When the mysterious tempter speaks, the picking of the fruit appears as a good. How is it really? Whom should we believe?

Whatever one might say, evil appears here within the horizon of a discourse between beings that are capable of dialogue. The fruit "in itself" is neither good nor evil; it is beautiful at best. It is only the act of picking, itself an element of a dialogue, that shows the invisible meaning of the fruit. For the tempted person, evil appears as an integral part of a conditional whose general meaning can be expressed thus, "If you commit act X, the good Y awaits you; if you do not commit act X, good Y will elude you, but you will encounter evil Z." As we can see, act X is what everything is about. This act is at one point recommended, at another point it is forbidden. How do things stand? Both the temptation and the threat direct themselves toward being, which is in turn directed toward the future, touching within it the experience of hope. Temptation enlivens hope, while the threat undercuts hope. Obviously, the same hope is not at stake, but rather that man abandon one hope and reach for another. Only the following hope matters for the tempter in the garden: to be like God. Evil persuades in different ways, according to its knowledge of the pains and joys of man. Pain and suffering incapacitate man, undercutting all rebellion within him. It is as if evil knows about this and from it comes its striving to take control over the pains of a man, and through controlling pain it aims to take control of the whole of a man. It also knows that pain drains man's powers, that a man troubled by pain falls into inertia. To get around this inertia, and to push man into action, evil must give him some hope. From this comes the promise that man will be "like God and know good and evil." Evil in itself, by threatening and tempting, presupposes that in man there is some space of freedom. The more evil threatens and tempts, the more it reminds us that man has some space for choice, some freedom. Therefore, the involuntary gift of evil is the experience of freedom—freedom exposed to a trial.

Besides future evil, which is the content of the temptation and threat, we are also given past evil, already effected. Past evil also appears within the context of some wider whole. We say, "If I did not commit X, I would not have met evil Z." Act X turned out to be something like an opening for an evil that was waiting at the gates. The characteristic feature of evil is that, once it is realized, it does not pass, but in some way continues to exist. The endurance of past evil is closely tied with the endurance of suffering, a suffering that questions not only the fact of my life and my existence, but also the "moral right" to exist, the very right to exist. Suffering is a matter that makes my otherwise healthy existence unbearable to me. I know that what I have become is not what I should be. I would like to hide, go away, cleanse myself, and atone. Consciousness of evil that has come into being within me, and was brought by me into this world, reduces itself to the agathological knowledge of my existing in an unjustified existence, and so my nonexistence would be justified. I know that I should not be, but despite that, I am. There is some kind of contradiction in this. Consciousness of this contradiction is pain, the pain of the evil existing within me.

It turns out that the phenomenon of evil is determined by several elements that define its conditions of possibility. Above all, it cannot be thought without some kind of suffering. Suffering is not only a symptom of evil already committed, but also of the evil that threatens. The experience of evil likewise cannot be thought without some pleasure, bliss, or joy. Evil lures, evil tempts, and evil deceives. Evil as both the source of suffering and bliss is ambiguous, simultaneously truthful and lying. This is why evil cannot be understood without illusion. Irrespective of the kinds of evil, the motive of illusion is, as it seems, present in every evil. This motive makes us think about the shrewdness of evil and at the same time its *dumbness*. Evil is shrewd because it tempts and entices. Evil is dumb, because it has to utilize illusions. And now, at last, we come to the other person. If there were no other people, would evil be evil? It seems that evil—regardless of where it comes from—always appears in the space between people as a specific reality, dialogically conditioned. As an "interpersonal reality," evil separates and brings people together, joins and divides, it destroys some completely but allows others to endure.

Evil first appears—even before it is realized—in two experiences that are contrary to each other: in the experience of threat and the experience of temptation. Threats cause an escape response, temptations spur attraction; however, one cannot be separated from the other. For the sake of our analysis, however, we shall consider these two aspects of evil separately, starting with the threat and the flight elicited by it.

We will concentrate our attention on three questions: What is the escape from evil? How does it differ from misfortune? What does it mean to say that evil is an interpersonal reality conditioned dialogically? These three questions will help us frame our inquiry about the boundaries of evil, and thus the relationship between good and evil, which, in turn, will open up the path to analyze the experience of evil through the prism of temptation. We will, of course, have the evil with which the other constantly threatens or tempts us in mind. Since we continue to consider the encounter, we will leave behind the matter of evil past, evil that constitutes the motif of separation, beyond the scope of our reflections. We will address this matter in the chapter on separation.

1. Evil in the Domain of Dialogue

One scene from Shakespeare's drama *Richard III* is the literary illustration of the situation I will attempt to shed light upon here with the help of the phenomenological method. Lady Anne meets Gloucester, whom she sees as the personification of evil (and ugliness). He is, in addition, the murderer of her husband and of her father-in-law, Henry VI. It would be difficult to imagine a greater opposition. There is no doubt that Gloucester is *the incarnation of evil*. At the sight of him, Anne blurts out, "Foul devil, for God's sake, hence, and trouble us not," and then adds, "Either heaven with lightning strike the murderer dead, / Or earth, gape open wide and eat him quick, / As thou dost swallow up this good king's blood / Which his hell-govern'd arm hath butchered!"[36]

To flee is to distance oneself, or to put someone else at a distance. Anne flees. She did not seek out this encounter while following the coffin of the murdered king; Gloucester himself cut her off. Now she wants to distance the murderer from herself. Here we distinguish two different forms of flight of man from man—flight from the *sight* of the other and flight as the severing of *dialogical ties* with the other. Which of the two is a flight from evil in the strictest sense?

The Flight of Man from Man

We will first consider the case of flight from the sight of another, then flight as the severing of dialogical ties.

Flight from the sight of another seems to express itself in the phrase, "I don't want to know you, I don't want to hear about you, and I don't want to see you." Flight from the sight of another presupposes the existence of an intentional relation between man and man. The other person is there while I am here; there is a distance between us, which, however, does not rule out some form, or some degree, of visibility to each other. I see a person, hear him, recall and imagine him to myself, in other words—I *have* someone within the scope of object-oriented acts of consciousness. Escape from the sight of another begins with a *get out*: get out of my sight, my memory, or imagination. Here, to flee means the following: to distance oneself or to distance another beyond the reach of intentional experience, to cast someone beyond the reach of the surrounding world. Can such a flight succeed? I will not resolve this question here, but the attempt to flee in this way is enough for our present considerations.

Flight, as the breaking of the bonds of dialogue, is more radical and touches upon deeper levels of the soul than flight from sight. When we say, "I don't want to have anything to do with you," then we want the other person to stop posing questions to us and to not expect any answers from us. "Don't talk to me, I'm not saying anything to you, nor will I." Why? Because there is either no relation of understanding between us, or it has ceased, which is the very condition of possibility for the exchange of words. It is not easy to describe more closely the dynamics that underlie such a relationship. Its character and quality show themselves only in the breakdown of dialogue. One thing is certain: this is not an intentional relation, but a dialogical relation, where a human being is not an object of experience, but a participant in a dialogue. The existence of a dialogical relation is revealed by the first act of a conversation between two people. This act is usually a question and a response. The question points in two main directions: What do you judge about this? The words "about this" (sometimes "about him," that is, a third party) express an intentional relation, whereas the words "what do you" indicate a dialogical relation. The latter does not have an objectifying character. The other person given in its horizon is a subject, not an object; he is a subject for whom there are, or there can be, objects. The dialogical relation precedes words and conventions of dialogue. It is an openness toward the other—a readiness to listen and speak. Such a readiness conditions the dialogue. Whoever flees from another person, breaking the bonds of dialogue, strives to radically close himself to the other.

These two varieties of flight are usually interconnected. One cannot flee without breaking the bonds of dialogue and one cannot break the bonds of dialogue without distancing the image of the other beyond the boundaries of visibility. Flight also does not preclude a form of longing for whomever we are trying to escape. The painful remembrance of another person awakens in us not only the desire for severance but also the desire for another, better, encounter with him. Those in flight erase the image of the other, but they long for dialogue; they break the bonds of dialogue, but they long for the image. A paradox is hidden in the very concept of flight: as long as I flee, I see the shadow of the other next to me. In this way, in fleeing I involuntarily return.

The two varieties of flight of man from man reveal to us the two basic forms of human relations: it is different toward the environment than it is toward people understood as dialogue partners. The difference between an intentional relation and a dialogical relation is thrown into sharper relief through the experience of flight. Both these relations cannot be reduced to each other. However, they do not mutually exclude each other in such a way that one would not be possible where the other one is already taking place. To be more precise: the dialogical relation can overlap with the intentional relation, and vice versa (one can look and talk), none of which means that one type of relation must absorb the other. To better foreground the differences between them, we will once again use the dramatic metaphors we already used in earlier chapters.

The general world of the human drama is first the reality of the stage. The stage is the stage of dramatic action. The stage is composed of things, objects, landscapes, and other human beings who are made present through intentional experiences. The stage is a place of possible movement. When I move across the stage, I must consider the obstacles that lie upon it: I must avoid a puddle, a fallen tree upon a road, and also another person coming at me. The stage is the place of possible movement. I am tied to the stage upon which my drama unfolds exclusively through an intentional relation, or a relation that can become exclusively intentional. I know that I can aim various intentional acts toward the stage, even though I am not currently doing so. This relation is ruled *a priori* by the category of space. The objects, things, and people are always *somewhere*, somehow tied to places where they remain motionless or, to some degree, moving through them. The objects and people located in space are ruled by the principle of one-next-to-the-other. According to it, it is impossible for two bodies to simultaneously occupy exactly the same place. In the intentional consciousness directed at another person, a consciousness that objectifies man, the experience of his body is of particular significance. Upon the spatial stage, spatial humans live, move, and die. These people are first only given as objects—much like things—to external perceptions, thanks to the mediation of the harmonious interplay of consistent appearances. Husserl has pointed this out. The fundamental rule of this experience is the rule of distance: me here, you there. The effect of the intentional experience of man is the perpetuation of his sight as the sight of a component of the general landscape of the world. Man is part of this landscape. When this human disappears from it, then the memory of the landscape where we saw him will bring forth his presence. The lack of a person among things where he used to spend time creates the impression of an empty stage.

But the world of the human drama is also something more: it is constantly developing, multidimensional, variegated, and conflict-filled dramatic elements and plots, tied up with others and constituting, in the broadest sense, a lifelong dialogue of a man with others. The man-to-man relation here does not have an intentional character, it is dialogical. The other person within it is not the object of acts of perception, but is the Thou of an actual or potential conversation. The category of space no longer plays the leading role here. Its place is taken over by the category of time. It governs the exchange of words, the exchange of thoughts. Words and utterances must occur one after another if there is to be an exchange of words, if human speech is to become a conversation. Here the other person is no longer part of the spatial landscape, but an integral part of historical time—he is an *existence*, who leaves behind some past and has a future ahead of him. Man is a character of a drama. Man is joined to man through the mediation of dialogue, in which the key role falls to questions and answers. I ask and I expect an answer. I listen to the questions directed at me and I provide answers. Between the moment of the answer and the moment of the question, a moment of tension elapses in which the experience of a particular responsibility is constituted: the consciousness that I—the questioned—should give the other some answer. This experience demands a deeper explanation. For now let us only say that nothing like it is constituted in being between things (rocks, trees, everyday objects), but with beings who are capable of conversation, therefore above all with people. The experience of responsibility also does not have a strictly intentional character. Intentional acts are object-directed; for example, the act of questioning is directed toward what we are asking about. What we ask about is given to us as an object. On the other hand, the person we ask is not an object, he is a participant in a dialogue. I am tied to the participant of a dialogue in a nonobjectifying relation of responsibility. He is the basis and beginning of mutual participation in a dramatic engagement, which, with the passage of time, reveals itself as ever-more, or ever-less, mutual.

The difference between the intentional relation to the world-stage and the dialogical relation toward a human Thou was already pointed out by Martin Buber, when he was either directly or indirectly polemicizing with Husserl's theory of intentionality. Michael Theunissen in *Der Andere* demonstrated the opposition of both these two manners of thinking and the attendant difficulties. Without going into the particulars of this debate, we can make some kind of assessment. The analyses of the apprehension of the other person that Husserl left behind were, in the main, devoted to the intentional experience of the other, treated as if he were part of the stage. The analyses inspired by Buber, and the rest of the Philosophy of Dialogue, were, above all, analyses of the I–Thou relation. In both approaches we are dealing with studies of experiencing the other person, but the manner of conducting these studies is completely different, and the different results of the studies come from there. We shall return to this later. Here we begin to see the outlines of a very important problem: What is the relationship of dialogical openness to intentional experiences directed toward the other person? Which is more originary? Which is the condition for the other?

Let us return to the problem of flight. We can now somewhat better understand the difference between flight from the sight of someone and flight that leads to breaking the bonds of dialogue. We desire to change the stage in fleeing the sight of the other. We do not want the *evil person* to appear upon our stage. The sight of him pains our eyes, deforms the landscapes around us, and is an obstacle to our movements upon the stage. We want to deny all traces of experiencing a link, all traces of responsibility, by breaking the bonds of dialogue. We do not want to ask. We do not want to give answers. We want to take part in neither a factual nor a possible conversation. Yet, both flights have one and the same source: the conviction that the other person is evil in some sense. This conviction—the conviction about the *malice* of the other person—prompts the flight reflex and the attempt to erase all traces of presence.

But flight, as I already said, conceals a kind of paradox: in fleeing I simultaneously confirm a presence. The louder I speak of the need to take leave, the more I confirm that the other is there. The exiles return—they return in dreams, in fantasies, in a remembrance. This is why we can say that flights are simultaneously an opening of horizons for successive encounters. The evil that threatens also presents itself as a temptation.

A question arises: Which dimension, the intentional or the dialogical, is the proper dimension where evil appears? The answer does not seem difficult: evil in its broadest definition can come toward us both from the stage and from another person. Let us repeat: broadly understood evil. Here it is necessary to refine the concept of evil. The evil that comes to us from the stage is different from the one that comes from people. The evil that threatens us from the stage has an ontological character, while the one that comes from the other man is ethical, or, perhaps, even metaphysical. We will attempt to explain these distinctions.

Evil and Misfortune

The ontological interpretation of evil understands evil as a lack that appears in some being. Let us pause with the phenomenon of threat. What does ontological evil threaten man with? It threatens to deprive him of an already possessed quality, or one that is within reach. In other words, it threatens him with the lack of something. To be exposed to ontological evil is to be exposed to some deprivation. The home that I own can go up in flames; I can lose my health, or even my life. What does this mean? It means that the ontological interpretation of evil essentially depends upon a substitution of the concept of evil with the concept of imperfection. For ontology, evil is equivalent to the imperfection of created beings. Imperfection does not exist independently, but only insofar as there is a being in which a perfection should come to exist. This leads to a phenomenologically paradoxical thesis: evil as evil does not exist, and the very nonexistence of what should come into being is evil.

Two problems are especially important here: What is the range of the ontological interpretation of evil, and does this interpretation take into account the whole content of the experience of evil?

It seems, above all, that the ontological interpretation of evil neither does nor can go beyond an intentional-objectifying consciousness of the world. It is derived essentially from the experiences of the stage and is adapted to those experiences. It assumes that we have an object-directed consciousness of things and people (including ourselves) as beings composed of many qualities. These beings truly exist. Here evil is what should come into being in what already exists.

Existence is acknowledged implicitly as the fundamental good, which cannot be questioned as such. On the other hand, evil is on the side of the nonexistent. The intentional consciousness of the world presents people and things to us within the horizon of existence. The horizon of existence is likewise the horizon of the good. To desire the good is always, in the final analysis, to want the existence of something. To be exposed to evil is to be exposed to a potential loss. Upon the world-stage there are powers capable of depriving me of what I have and what I ought to have. What exactly is that most fundamental quality of which I could be deprived? It is my existence, my life. Death is the evil above all evils for the ontological interpretation. Death is the archetype of the ontological philosophy of evil. It is the end of life as given in the mode of an intentional representation. I see the world and I strive to represent myself as absent from it. The ontology of lack derives its main principle from attempts at such representations.

The temporal beginning of imperfection, that is, the moment when some more or less fulfilled being, some more or less finished whole, is deprived of his proper perfection, is a moment of misfortune. Misfortune is the moment when imperfection enters the world and remains within it as a lack. There are many causes of misfortunes; another person, even I myself, can be its cause. The misfortunes caused by an uncontrollable world are usually acknowledged as chance accidents. Chance accidents are events that occur outside the ordered course of events. Lightning striking a house, a flood, an earthquake, and so on are all misfortunes. Actually, from the scientific point of view, none of these events are accidents, but science's point of view is not the point of view of the person struck down by misfortune, a person who continues to consider it as a disastrous accident. Misfortunes are the questioning of man's basic project of living in this world by the inscrutable powers of the world-stage. Man runs the course of a peaceful life upon the stage of the world, when, at a given moment, the stage revolts against his presence; the joyful certainty of possessing the world instantaneously disappears from the soul of man. In this way misfortune speaks to man with a twofold negation: you did not anticipate and you did not control. In this way misfortune makes man aware that he is a finite being.

How does evil in the strictest sense differ from misfortune? Evil appears upon a level different than the level of misfortune. The proper place of evil is in the dialogical I–Thou relation, not the world's intentional relation of man–stage. This statement is crucial for our problematics of evil.

Before we attempt to more precisely explain the difference that is sketching itself out, let us once more turn our attention to the scene from Shakespeare's drama. Gloucester attempts to convince Anne of the real source of his crime and thus attempts to prove his innocence. What he says is meant to prove that his crimes are not an evil deed, but a misfortune. Gloucester explains that he loves Anne. His love is like a storm, like a flood, like an earthquake. Anne's husband stood in the way of this love as a *chance obstacle*. This is one of the first misfortunes. Gloucester did indeed kill, but Anne cannot blame him for it. Was it not her beauty that drove him to madness? By suggesting misfortune, Gloucester attempts to cover up the essence of evil.

Let us return to the distinctions we introduced.

Dialogical Evil

We are still on the general topic of the threat. I have already mentioned the ambiguous situation a threatened man is put into by a threat. Threat is expressed in the conditional form, "If you do deed X, you can expect good Y, but if you do not fulfill this deed, then you will not attain good Y, and you will encounter evil Z." The words "deed X" should be understood as broadly as possible, that is, they should include the renunciation of something: "If you do not pick the forbidden fruit, then you can expect good X, but if you pick it, then evil Z awaits you." The deed-renunciation X is ambiguous, it is disputable. Eve looks at the fruit and sees it to be beautiful and delicious. The evil of the deed is not as evident as the beauty and the taste of the fruit. The tempter takes advantage of this and says, "You truly shall be like God." Evil not only threatens, it also promises. Evil enters between people and exploits the ambiguity of objects and events—an ambiguity that emerges from the very existence of different points of view on the same thing.

Once again we will attempt to exclude ontology. Looking at the fruit as such, Eve sees no evil in it. In other words, an ontological consideration of the structure of the world as a stage detects no evil in it. St. Augustine exploits this fact in his polemics against the

Manicheans: "For all things in proportion as they are better measured, formed, and ordered, are assuredly good in a higher degree; but in proportion as they are measured, formed, and ordered in an inferior degree, are they the less good. These three things, therefore, measure, form, and order—not to speak of innumerable other things that are shown to pertain to these three—these three things, therefore, measure, form, order, are as it were generic goods in things made by God whether in spirit or in body."[37]

When does the fruit of "good and evil" reveal its evilness? Only when it becomes the topic of a dialogue between man and man, with God, and with the tempter.

Therefore, speaking generally and in a nonbiblical language, evil is not a thing-in-itself, instead it should be categorized as a phenomenon. Evil is something that *appears*, rather than something that *exists*. However, it is a very specific phenomenon. It cannot be thought without a moment of some falsehood. Evil is not a phenomenon conceived as an adequate manifestation of the thing hidden behind it; evil does in fact reveal something, but it does not reveal the truth of things. Yet, it is not a total illusion behind which lies an utter void and nothing more. Through the ambiguity of the fruit of paradise is revealed both a truth and a falsehood about man, God, the tempter, and the thing-in-itself. The phenomenon of evil is situated somewhere at the intersection between illusion and manifestation. As an illusion, evil has something of *foolishness* within it, but as a manifestation it has something of the *threat* within it. What, then, is this specific phenomenon of evil? It seems that the specifics of the phenomenon of evil are well rendered by the Polish word "zjawa" [specter]. Evil is a *specter*, an *evil specter*, but the adjective only analytically expresses what is already hidden within the concept of *specter* itself. The specter simultaneously lies and tells the truth, it threatens and seduces, takes away one hope only to resurrect another. The reality of the *specter* is not a reality of being, nor a reality of the lack of being. The specter is an inter-reality, which is born *between* man and man as the fruit of mutual dialogical structures.

Let us look a little deeper into the structure of the specter by considering only the aspect of the threat.

The threat puts man face-to-face with a future evil. Time, more precisely, the temporal future, is the fundamental condition for the possibility of a threat. A threat is threatening for a person who experiences the flow of time. The threat shuts off, to a certain degree, a person's future. Space also plays a substantial role here. The evil contained within a threat comes to man from the outside, from the space surrounding man, which is already peopled. The threat introduces a kind of division in a man—it divides his personality into a more external part, which concentrates upon its very own self in fear and trembling, and a more internal part, which is most exposed to the touch of evil. The imagination is yet another highly important aspect of the specter. Threat awakens fear and dread—primarily through awakening the imagination. Without the imagination, the threat would not be so frightening. Imagined evil has "something uncanny" about it. It frightens with a mysterious power, it frightens with cunning and deception. It forces a man to acknowledge his weakness before a direct fight even takes place.

The specter is undoubtedly conditioned by the ontology of the stage. It emerges as the boundary of future time, a time that results in various projects upon the depths and the heights of the stage. The time of the stage is conditioned by space. This is why the threat can manifest itself as a roadblock. We sometimes say, "I was dumbstruck by this threat." The knees of a person who has been "dumbstruck" go "weak." He is "stuck in place." The specter questions the project of man's being in the world in this manner. Ultimately, it strives to deprive man of his place upon the world's stage. The man touched by a threat becomes an "exile." The "Holy Land" does not want to carry him along anymore. The stage, so far obedient and calm, rebels now.

Despite all of these conditions, the interpersonal space of dialogue is the significant source of the specter. The stage of the world is where various projects of many different people and communities intersect. Specters are born somewhere at the intersection of these projects. Adam and Eve's project of being, the project of likening God to man, and the project of the mysterious tempter are projected onto the fruit of paradise. The fruit truly is beautiful and good, but because of the intersection of many projects it starts to be something more than it is; it comes to mean something more and say something more. In this way it becomes the start a chain of evil, a chain of evil events. The fruit is the possession of God. Eve's project turns it into a possession of humanity. The change in its meaning becomes possible because of the deception introduced by the tempter.

The fruit is the real foundation of the specter—the forbidden fruit. When we look at the situation externally, we see that the sources of the specter are competing projects of ownership. Who owns the fruit? The fruit is part of the stage. Man is convinced that he possesses the whole stage. Meanwhile, God has reserved some fragment of it for himself. Hence the double meaning of the fruit. The fruit simultaneously portends happiness and misfortune. But is it really only a matter of two different ownership projects? Does the conflict revolve exclusively around possession? Is everything to be resolved in terms of the commandment "Thou shalt not steal"? Certainly not. Something more is hidden at the foundation of the ownership project.

The conflicting ownership projects presuppose not only the negation of the right to own but also the negation of the right to exist. The position of "you have no right to own" leads to the position of "you have no right to be." From the principle of "Thou shalt not steal" we move on to the principle of "Thou shalt not kill." From the perspective of this shift, theft turns out to be a form of killing. Both formulas point us toward the real heart of the matter, but they do not reveal it. To kill means to deprive someone, first and foremost, of the right to exist. God says, "If you eat the fruit, you will deprive yourselves of the right to be." The snake says, "If you eat the fruit, you will be like God." The man who reaches for the divine denies God the right to be within what is divine. The controversy is about axiology, conceived as deeply as possible, that is, about the principles of agathology. The ownership project presupposes, as its condition of possibility, the project of being. The project of being is not only the project of how to be, but above all the attempt to be, that is, to exist in a justified existence. All evil, in the final analysis, is an indicator that the man touched by it exists in an unjustified existence. He is, but without the right to be. All the good that is the portion of man is a symbol of the fact that a man exists in a just existence. Existence itself is a problem for man. It is a problem because it can be both the existence of good and the existence of evil. Scheler said that "the existence of negative values is itself a negative value." He also said that "the existence of positive values is itself a positive value." The existence of evil is evil. Only the existence of the good is good. Man has a problem with his own existence because he desires it to be the existence of good.

However, none of this settles the matter. The crucial task of the threat (much like temptation) is to incline a person to acknowledge and to accept evil as his own. The threat is a form of persuasion in which the main argument is fear. The specter, above all, frightens. It frightens using something that is somewhere beyond the fruit, what is to happen, what will occur. The specter speaks in man's own voice. This is the meaning of what it says: "The fruit is beautiful and delicious, while evil is apparent, it is so insignificant that it does not count in comparison with a future good." The specter destroys one hope, but it enlivens another. It operates within the realm of hope. It diminishes the meaning of what is to appear in the future. Why? So that man will pick the fruit himself. If man did not do it himself, if the wind were, for example, to knock the fruit off the tree, then it would be a misfortune at worst, but there would be no evil. Evil needs man in order to occur. It occurs thanks to the hands of man. Let us note: misfortune destroys as violence, whereas evil destroys through persuasion. It is incapable of destroying a man if man does not destroy himself. Hence evil is not only a trial for reason, but also a trial of the will. At this point the specter reveals its powerfulness and powerlessness simultaneously. Powerlessness, because in itself the specter cannot do anything. But also powerfulness, because it can make use of dormant powers within a man and incline him to, against himself, destroy himself.

Summary

The important achievement of these analyses is the insight they afford into evil as a specter. Evil is neither a being nor a nonbeing, instead it belongs to the category of phenomena—it is a specter. Phenomenology as a science of phenomena is specifically called to study the nature of evil as a specter. The specter of evil reveals itself in the form of the threat and temptation. So far we have confined ourselves to only analyzing the threat.

The specter appears in the space of the dialogical I–Thou and not in the bosom of the intentional dimension between man and the stage. Various projects of ownership condition the possibility of the specter. In turn, the condition of the possibility for the various projects of ownership are projects either to acknowledge or to deny another person's right to exist. The threat is always a denial of the right to exist. One who threatens says, "You are evil and you have no right to exist." The one who is threatened defends not so much, and not only, the brute fact of existence, but also its goodness. We do not know precisely what evil is, nor what good is, but we do know one thing: evil causes a man to become an unjustified existence, while good causes him to exist in a justified existence. Good and evil constitute the true metaphysics of human existence, they are what *meta-physica* is.

An introduction to the phenomenology of evil shows itself to be indispensable for man's understanding of the specific experience of man by a man—an experience where another human being turns out to be a carrier of evil, whereas I who encounter him can neither flee from him nor come near him. Living on the edge of encounter and departure, I see more clearly what both one and the other are, namely, what reveals itself as impossible: encounter itself and departure itself.

2. Enslavement to Fear

The encounter with an evil person can develop in various directions. Above all, the possibility of fleeing opens up. However, let us assume that this possibility does not materialize. Can one really flee from a person?

Another possibility is fighting against the evil man. However, let us suppose that it also cannot be taken up. I am constrained, weak, and I cannot fight. One thing remains: I can face the danger in a spiritual manner, look straight into the eyes of the threat, pose the question about what exactly is its meaning. Thus, In what does the other man threaten me and with what at all can he threaten me?

At bottom, the range of basic threats is not too great. Everything comes down to three of them. The one who threatens can kill me—that is the first possibility. The one who threatens can cause me longer- or shorter-lasting suffering—this is the second possibility. Finally, he can destroy me morally, can condemn me, deprive me of dignity and all respect that I enjoy from people. But the threat is almost never a goal in itself—the one who threatens, threatens in order to achieve some other goal. What is the goal of the threat? It is some more or less permanent, more or less profound, enslavement of a man. The one who threatens me strives to make me, for some time and in some domain, subject to his will. The threat remains in a close relation to enslavement, and resisting threat is a form of struggle for liberation.

In this way we find ourselves in the sphere of the problem of encountering an evil person. This person threatens me, wants to put me into a state of some enslavement. Let us consider the deepest existential sense of this type of threat. We will call upon for aid passages in texts devoted to enslavement that come from Hegel and Dostoevsky. Just as all threats are not the same, so not all enslavements are the same. We will also look at the conditions of possibility for liberation from threats and violence. For this purpose we will once again read, from a different perspective, Descartes's famous metaphor of the evil demon, which, considered through the experiences of the enslaved, reveals unexpected contents.

The Basic Meaning of Threatening with Death

We are now interested in the matter of death. However, we are not concerned with developing a full, that is, as comprehensive as possible, phenomenology of death. The problem of death finds itself in our field of interest only inasmuch as the representation of death is the subject of the threat that man puts in front of another man. What does death become when it is made into a threat directed against a man?

Death as the content of a threat stops being the end of man's life so common in nature, instead it is a homicide, a death willed and at the hands of another man. Each of us knows that death must come after him, but nobody has certainty when it will happen. It is different with a threat. Here another man chooses for me the time of my death; he wants to inflict death upon me somehow. Death takes on a dialogical character. It can be compared to a word directed at me by another—it is to be an event laden with a certain meaning, just like a word. This word has an exceptional character—it is the last word going out from him toward me. After him there will only be silence and darkness.

The threat of death, just as every word, is located in a wider semantic context thanks to which death—death at first conceived as a phenomenon of nature—reveals in a clearer manner certain contents, and leaves others as if in hiding. The act of threatening with death is an act in which a certain hermeneutics of death fulfills itself.

The semantic context of the threat can be expressed in the following conditional mode: "I will kill you, unless you act as I command you." What does such speech mean? Above all, it presupposes that the one who threatens me in this way thinks that death is something evil for me. Conversely, if a threatened person would see some good of his in death, then there would be no threat. The assumption of the threat of homicide is the unity of convictions, shared by the threatened and the one making the threat, about the evil character of death. The axiology of death must be held in common, otherwise everything could be different. Second, death is not a goal in itself, the final goal of the threat is some enslavement. The threatening person is not concerned with killing, he is concerned with subjugating. This obviously does not exclude the possibility of killing for the sake of killing, or killing to satisfy hunger, but, in general, in such situations there are no threats then, there is no dialogue, there is no common axiological plane. There, where there is a threat of homicide, there is also enslavement.

Enslavement presupposes the persistence of two elements: the enslaver and the enslaved, the master and slave. Both elements oppose each other, but they are also connected. What connects the one making the threat with the threatened, the master with the slave? They are joined by a consciousness of some possession. If man did not have consciousness of possession, there would be no conditions for the possibility of a situation of enslavement. And so, what does it mean to be an enslaver? Being an enslaver, that is, a master, means being the owner of that which is the property of another man, an enslaved man. And what does it mean to be the enslaved, to be a slave? To be an enslaved man means to give to another man something that is in my possession. In other words, the possibility of enslaving emerges where the mysterious experience of *to have* lives and reigns. It ends where the domain of *to be* begins. To be a master means to own someone. To be a slave means to not have, but to remain in someone's possession. We know that life is one of the most fundamental possessions of a man. Thus, whoever takes possession of human life, whether directly through the threat of murder or indirectly through possessing the means for life, also takes into possession a man, makes him a slave, and becomes his master. The experience of life and death plays a key role in enslavement.

As we know, pictures of death vary from culture to culture, or even among various people who live in the same cultural circle. Don Juan has a different picture of death than a Christian saint. It seems that there is a certain close-knit tie between the character (content) of a representation of death contained in a threat and the eventual character of enslavement resulting from this threat. Generally, the greater an evil death is for the enslaved, the deeper the enslavement resulting from the threat. It is possible to imagine a radical enslavement, which appears when death is considered an absolute evil. Where death appears as a relative evil, or limited in some other way, then the threat of homicide is also relative and enslavement is not as radical.

One of the classic philosophical texts describing the phenomenon of enslavement, as both a historical and existential phenomenon, is a fragment from Hegel's *Phenomenology of Spirit*. Hegel explicitly and emphatically reveals the relationship between enslavement and the experience of death, more precisely, the fear of the threat of death. Hegel writes, "For this consciousness has been fearful, not of this or that particular thing or just at odd moments, but its whole being has been seized with dread. In that experience it has been quite unmanned, has trembled in every fiber of its being, and everything solid and stable has been shaken to its foundations."[38] The fear before death becomes for the enslaved consciousness the most essential, as if absolute, form of fear. At the thought of death, it "has trembled in every fiber of its being." The evil of death presents itself as an evil against which there is no appeal. The enslaved person, according to Hegel, seems to believe that death tears him away from all values, negates all hope for tomorrow.

Life is an absolute value for him. The sources of life are thus, in his conviction, the independent existing things of this world, the real fruits of a no less real earth. The enslaved is tied to the earth like a tree—if one of them were to suddenly gain consciousness. He is convinced that thanks to the independence of the things he feeds on, he himself is an independent being. His enslavement turns out to be a result of his realism. He believes in the reality of his own being, because he believed earlier in the reality of the objects with which he satisfies his most urgent needs. This is why he is unable to expose his life to danger in his fight against the master. He is also incapable of tearing himself away from the earth. He devotes his freedom to rescuing his own absolute value: life. He becomes the property of someone who succeeds in convincing him that he is the owner of the earth and its fruits.

The consciousness of life and death about which Hegel speaks is a natural consciousness. I want to say by this that the master does not create for the slave some sort of especially frightening representation of death to frighten him more and thereby to more deeply enslave him. The master knows the same about death as his slave. On this level there are no illusions that lessen or increase the threat of death. The difference depends upon the degree of courage. The slave is the one who at some moment acts cowardly. Cowardice knocks him down a step below the master. The master is not a coward, he is able to put his life in danger in combat. This is why he has the moral right to a higher place.

Hence the special character of enslavement: the slave must labor for the master, but has no obligation to sacrifice his life for the master. One cannot demand from the slave to do for the master what he most fears, to sacrifice for him his own absolute value: life. It was fear of death that made him a slave. He must not be given an opportunity in which he could overcome this fear in himself. However, one can demand that he give the fruits of his labor to the master. The one who is capable of exposing his life to danger becomes a master in spirit. Therefore, labor must be the fate of the slave. According to Hegel, this fate is not hopeless. A path of liberation draws itself through labor. Labor gives the slave a deeper knowledge of the earth—the stage of his drama—it familiarizes him with the earth, it undercuts in him a primary faith in the independence of things. Things reveal themselves as merely material, and he, the slave, reveals himself as a creator. Labor cures the slave from the sickness of naïve realism. This is why the future belongs to slaves.

However, let us leave to the side the whole matter of liberation. Let us penetrate a little deeper into the tangle of relations between man and man, which makes a master out of one and a slave out of another. This tangle has a dialectical character, it is an example of the *unity of opposites*. The master is the opposite of a slave and a slave is the opposite of a master. However, opposition is only possible where there is some community underneath it. Essentially, the master would not be a master without a slave, and a slave would not be a slave without a master. The one concept finds its confirmation in the other.

The slave becomes the victim of his own realism. Let us give Hegel a voice, "The lord relates himself mediately to the bondsman through a being [a thing] that is independent, for it is just this which holds the bondsman in bondage; it is his chain from which he could not break free in the struggle, thus proving himself to be dependent, to possess his independence in thinghood."[39] The slave is first a slave to his owning of things and, so long as a thing is only a possession, he does not yet feel any master over himself. However, when someone else becomes the owner of things, then by reason of his ties with things the slave becomes the property of the owner of things. According to Hegel, the rationale for this situation is *desire (Begierde)*, a word that signifies all the most basic vital needs. A man must have food, drink, and shelter. Desire is for him the ownmost internal reality, he feels himself in desire and understands himself through it. For him the projection of desire picks out from the surrounding world, above all, that which satisfies or can satisfy desire, that is, bread, water, meat, shelter, and so on. The objects of desire are for him the model of a reliable existence. To lose that world of desires is to perish. To live means to have things conceived as the objects of desires.

On the other hand, the master, through the act of putting his life at stake, has torn himself away from a direct relationship with things. The master values chivalry more than the world of the slave's needs. Chivalry is for him something more true and real than bread, water, and shelter. The object of the master's desires is no longer anything that can be found upon the stage of the world as a part of that world. But even the master has his obsessions. The obsession of the master is *recognition* from others—the recognition of the master as master. In order to achieve this recognition the master must take possession of the desires of the slave, he has to own his desires. The master must squeeze between the slave and the things the slave desires and make him, when desiring things, in the act of desire itself, recognize him as master. The master achieves this by becoming the owner of things. The slave cannot drink water directly from the source, but should drink it from the hands of the master, simultaneously expressing gratitude toward the master for that gift.

The great Hegel expert Alexandre Kojève writes the following on this topic, "Man's humanity 'comes to light' only in risking his life to satisfy human Desire—that is, his Desire directed toward another Desire. Now, to desire a Desire is to want to substitute oneself for the value desired by this Desire. For without this substitution, one would desire the value, the desired object, and not the Desire itself."[40] The master, who has risked his life, has thereby changed his relation to the stage, to the totality of independent things. He only takes those things that bring him joy. The master, it is true, has things, but he does not desire them. The object of his desires is another human being. The master is solely the possessor of this inasmuch as such possessing opens up a path for him to the souls of the slaves. He attaches slaves to himself through fear and gratitude. Forced gratitude—this is the psychological plane of their coexistence.

The dialectic of mediated recognition is for Hegel the core of an enslaving relation. It contains something paradoxical. Following a deeper analysis, proposed by Hegel, it becomes apparent that the slave is only seemingly a slave to the master, in reality he is enslaved by his own *realism*, through the fear of death resulting from his faith in the reality of the world. One ought to distinguish the relative master from the absolute master. Death is the absolute master, all other masters are relative masters. The situation of the master is not much better than the slave's. The master is also, in his own way, enslaved, but by his own *idealism*. The slave, who has feared death, created the reality of the master's with his fear. In turn the master searches for the foundation of his faith in himself in the faith of the slaves. What is the faith of the slave worth for the master and what does it mean? What meaning can the recognition flowing from a frightened heart have? The master lives overwhelmed by an obsession with a fight in which he has the hope of finding the confirmation of his own mastery. In the fight he finds an opponent who is equal to him. He wants the opponent to confirm his mastery. But is this possible? Let us assume that the master wins. The victory can signify either the death of the opponent or his enslavement. In both instances, acknowledgment is a semblance of recognition. The silence of the slain is a refusal of recognition, the recognition of the enslaved is an illusion. Let us assume the master loses. He will then become, possibly, a myth, legend, poem, but will lose all possibility of drawing joy and pleasure from things. The paradox of both types of consciousness is that they desire to have something that they cannot have: one desires things, the other people. The masters stand in the way of slaves possessing things, and the slaves, who are treated like things, stand in the way of the masters realizing their obsession of possessing people.

Therefore, partial illusion is the condition for the possibility of enslavement. It seems to the slave that he has become a slave because of the fault of the master who wanted to kill him. It seems to the master that he has become master thanks to his own bravery. The truth is different: the slave himself created a master for himself in his soul. Without mediated recognition, which is made by the slave, his enslavement would not exist. However, the illusion does have its limits, it is an illusion about the source of enslavement, but it is not an illusion about the fact of enslavement. Neither the master lies to the slave about his enslavement, nor does the slave lie to the master about the fact of his mastery. The slave does not pretend he is a master, and the master does not pretend he is a slave—both recognize themselves in the concepts of mastery and slavery, which are intelligible to them both as such, and, thanks to this intelligibility, they access the intelligibility of the world. One and the other finds his place in the world, meaning the space of some freedom proper to him. This freedom is for the masters an arbitrary freedom, for the slaves it is a freedom in the frame of the obligation to labor. Each has gained the sort of freedom they can afford.

Hegel's thinking breaks off at this point, leaving plenty of space for commentators.[41] We will not enter into the many interpretive possibilities, nonetheless we will pose several questions. Why is a radical, truly liberating—meaning, liberating from within—rebellion of the slaves not possible? Where does the internal power of the structure of enslavement come from? Is enslavement exclusively a logical paradox, or something more? Enslavement lasts, moves from one generation to the next, sometimes becomes a need of the human soul. Is the very intelligibility of the world, and the ability to understand social life given through this intelligibility, the source the durability of such structures? Today we are aware that the structure of enslavement has a wider reach than just the structure of the system of slavery. It is not only the analyses of Marx and Sartre that tell us about this, but, above all, the scholars from the psychoanalytic school. The picture of enslavement they paint also seems less paradoxical (less dialectical) and more tragic (antiethical). Erich Fromm wrote the book *Escape from Freedom* where he opposes the Hegelian concept of historical progress. Man does not strive toward freedom at all, freedom is an unbearable burden, instead he strives to get rid of freedom, to throw off the weight of responsibility. The problem of enslavement still needs to be deepened. Let us take a small step in this direction, however, without going beyond the basic horizon of Hegel's thinking.

It is necessary, above all, to deepen the tragedy of enslavement in order to better understand the paradox of this situation. Tragedy does not consist on both sides of falling victim to illusions about the sources of their state, because such an illusion does not get in the way of them living and understanding their world. On the contrary, in some way it makes possible both one and the other. Tragedy also does not consist in the slave having to work for the master, because in the same work he also works for himself, and besides, the master, in putting his life in danger, gives to the slave something that is owed to him from the master. The burdens are therefore double-sided. Actually, we do not know why we speak here of enslavement. Are the masters not also slaves? The sources of the tragedy lie deeper, on the level of elementary experiences of good and evil, experiences that have a thoroughly ethical character. To capture the sense of these experiences we have to understand a new representation of death, and this representation makes it so the slave is unable to raise his hand against the master, and the master refrains from killing slaves. Who exactly has the slave become for the master? Who has the master become for the slave?

After the slave loses his freedom, the master becomes an ethical principle for his life. Before the slave fell into enslavement, the earth was the principle of his life, along with those self-sufficient things that he found on the earth—the stage of his drama. But this principle did not have an ethical character, it was the ordinary principle of the existence of all living beings, plants and animals. Now, when the master has appropriated the land, he himself has become the life-principle of the slave. The new principle of life has an ethical, dialogical character. The fear of flood and crop failure has turned in the slave into fear of the master's anger, of the master inflicting hurt, of the breaking of the bonds of dialogue with the master. Man can rebel—in any case, it is possible to understand his rebellion—against this or that life situation, but the reason for such a rebellion is the assumption that the very principle of life, the very conviction that one can and must live, remains important. The struggle to improve life is a struggle in the name of life and not against life. To be a principle of human life means taking part in parenthood. Parenthood is a category emerging from the ethical, not logical, sphere. Whoever has participated in it, has participated in an ethos. The power of the enslaving structure precisely comes from the fact that the one enslaving (master) gains participation in parenthood—becomes a parent for the enslaved. When the one who is a parent becomes angry and threatens with death, then this threat has a particular meaning: it touches the filial Thou of man and is a form of a curse cast by a father upon a son. The progenitor who curses seems to have the right to kill. His curse is based upon values that are higher than life—it is the group of values that give meaning to life, which are its reason. Hence the specific fear of the enslaved, which makes him incapable of rebelling. His inability is something more than cowardice. The cursed son has only one way: to return to the father like the Prodigal Son did. And so, through participation in the symbol of the father, the master not only enslaves but also disarms. This is the essence of the tragedy. It is tragic that the father-master, by making himself into a principle for the enslaved, makes of him his child and threatens the child with death because he wants to be a full human being. The principle of his life becomes a principle of death. The path of the son's to freedom must henceforth lead through the fault of parricide.

There seems to be no way out of this situation. The structure of enslavement has deeper roots than the roots of dialectical logic. It is both a continuation and distortion of the family ethos. The ethos of the family must be renewed in order to endure enslavement. Historically, it was necessary that a new vision of God and man be born, so that between man and God a relation of sonship should emerge—only when the old Law could give way to the new Covenant. But these are matters of a different order into which we cannot enter.

At the very beginning we asked the question: What can the other man threaten me with? We considered the first answer: death and enslavement flowing from the fear of death. The shape of the enslavement is decided by the representation of death. The representation of death, which we had in mind with Hegel, was understood simply as a moment in which life ends and all bonds with the earth break. When it came to death, the master and the slave agreed with each other. However, another situation is possible: a man threatens me with an elaborate death, threatens me with a drawn-out suffering. Suffering is slow dying. Let us now consider the situation of enslavement resulting from a threat of slow dying. A speech of the Grand Inquisitor from Dostoevsky's *Brothers Karamazov* will help us in this.

Enslavement through Suffering

In Dostoevsky, the key formula of the threat—not formulated clearly—seems to be different: "If you will not act as I command you, then you will die slowly, you will suffer." In fact, the speech of the Grand Inquisitor does not contain many threats, only promises come to the fore. But this is only on the surface of the text. The main threat is present, it hangs like a heavy cloud over the whole spiritual landscape of the enslaved.

There is a significant difference between enslavement in Hegel's text and enslavement in Dostoevsky's text. In Hegel the enslaved man is a slave of violence, in Dostoevsky he is a slave of illusion—illusion not only about the sources of enslavement, but also about its fact. The condition of the possibility for enslavement is, as I have said, a particular approach to the ownership relation—somebody else becomes the owner of what is still my property; somebody else rules over my life. In Hegel, life is at stake in the game. Life is the property of a man, but in a situation of enslavement it becomes the property of another, the enslaver. To cause this change in ownership the master had to put his life in danger in a battle and the slave had to withdraw from the battle, turn coward. In Dostoevsky, the matter presents itself differently. Slavery is the work of masters who never had to put their life in danger. The master in Dostoevsky is not the hero of a war, but a genius of illusion. The character of the Grand Inquisitor is the symbol of a master of illusion. The mastery of the Inquisitor, who is not able to put his life in danger, must reach deeper than the mastery of the parental-knightly type, because what is at stake is not only that the slave works in place of the master and for the master, but also that in a time of need he would die voluntarily in place of the master. The art of enslavement must take a step further here.

What must be done to achieve such a degree of enslavement? You must base enslavement upon layers of the soul deeper than the consciousness of life, you must promise a man something more than food, drink, and lodging, but above all, you must threaten man with a greater evil than death itself. The man should understand that the choice of death in the defense of the Grand Inquisitor's life is for him an escape from an even greater evil than death. The Grand Inquisitor promises people real happiness — and what does he frighten them with? What internal powers does he reference?

In Hegel, the game over enslavement is carried out upon the plane of experiencing the value of life. In Dostoevsky's text, it is carried out on the plane of the conscience — it is a dispute about the independence or dependence of the human conscience. Enslavement clearly moves from the vital level onto the ethical and religious level. The enslaver turns out to be not the one who gives bread, drink, and lodging, but the one who *besides* this and above *all* releases from the feeling of guilt. We read: "But he alone can take over the freedom of men who appeases their conscience. With bread you were given an indisputable banner: give man bread and he will bow down to you, for there is nothing more indisputable than bread. But if at the same time someone else takes over his conscience — oh, then he will even throw down your bread and follow him who has seduced his conscience."[42]

Something more than external violence is needed to enslave the conscience, something more than illusion about the sources of enslavement — what is needed is radical illusion, illusion about the meaning of the existing situation. The speech of the Grand Inquisitor contains the basic element of the schema for such an illusion. The first is illusion about the value of human nature as such, the others are the illusion about the happiness of man and — the one that weighs us down the most — illusion about death, which is transformed into a process of long-term dying. Let us consider them one by one.

Lowering one's self-worth is the condition for making the decisive step — of entrusting the value lowered in this way to someone who seems to be more valuable and more worthy. His value becomes the basis of my value. Recognizing the value of the other, whether overt or hiding, makes me simultaneously worthy and unworthy of myself. The value of me as myself is a value based upon his value — I feel worthy of myself, because I participate in his worthiness, but for the same reason I am not worthy of myself, because I will never equal the worthiness of my master. Out of the depths of my ambiguity and uncertainty, I am ready to entrust my conscience to the other.

The promise of happiness is the second moment of the new illusion. Since man is not able to achieve a great happiness, let us permit him to stop at a small happiness. Man should desire his small happiness as if it were his great happiness. Therefore, he must be convinced that his happiness, although limited, is the only one possible human happiness to gain. We read:

> Then we shall give them quiet humble happiness, the happiness of feeble creatures, such as they were created.... Yes, we will make them work, but in the hours free from labor we will arrange their lives like a children's game, with children's songs, choruses, and innocent dancing. Oh, we will allow them to sin, too; they are weak and powerless, and they will love us like children for allowing them to sin. We will tell them that every sin will be redeemed if it is committed with our permission.... We will allow or forbid them to live with their wives and mistresses, to have or not to have children—all depending on their obedience—and they will submit to us gladly and joyfully. The most tormenting secrets of their conscience—all, all they will bring to us, and we will decide all things, and they will joyfully believe our decision, because it will deliver them from their great care and their present terrible torments of personal and free decision. And everyone will be happy.[43]

Finally, the third moment—the threat. What happens if man does not bend, what punishment awaits him, what evil? It cannot be death, because one cannot threaten with death those who are supposed to be ready to sacrifice life in the defense of the new masters. They must invent a more terrifying evil. The suffering of a slow death is such an evil. It hurts not only as an external pain, but also as a spiritual suffering, as an unwavering remorse.

The suffering of slow dying is a type of slow process that lasts in time, it is a withering away. In this withering away, what dominates is not so much death itself as the consciousness of death. Man is imbued with the painful consciousness that his life ebbs away among such circumstance in which no property of his soul and body, no talent, no ability, and no hope can achieve, so to say, the natural fullness proper to them. Man is condemned to half-heartedness, to insignificance. This is combined with consciousness of debasement in ethical character. Man lives in a state of uncertainty and fear, because none of his moral virtues is able to be fully a virtue, each one can be exploited against man himself or those close to him. Truthfulness can be exploited as informing, diligence can multiply unjust profits, friendship with one man can become the betrayal of another. Something that undercuts all hope hides in all this besides. Man says, "It could be worse." Man was given enough hope to not commit suicide, and enough hopelessness to not start a rebellion. Indeed, it could be worse.

All that remains is surrendering the conscience. The conviction is born that man can do as much good as the good he does in service. The threat is joined by the promise of some creativity—creativity within the limits of surrender. The man who commits an act of surrendering the conscience thus makes the choice of his future enemies: from now on he will have the Inquisitor as a defender and friend, the enemy will be every man, especially a slave, who dreams about some freedom. The pain of one's own strangled freedom turns slowly into joy that comes flowing from choking out the freedom of others. Man believes that he is not a slave [*niewolnik*], but a *follower* [*zwolennik*].

The change in the way a slave values a master is an important culmination of the situation. Who does the Grand Inquisitor become? Certainly, something more than a father. A father is only a principle of human life, whereas the Grand Inquisitor is the owner of human consciences—the one who decides between good and evil. The Grand Inquisitor appropriates attributes of the ultimate ethical principle: he becomes God or, rather, anti-God. That is the meaning of his speech. He declares it against the Son of God as an accusation against the work of creation and the work of redemption. The logic of the speech is built upon the logic of demonism.

We read: "For the care of these pitiful creatures is not just to find something before which I or some other man can bow down, but to find something that everyone else will also believe in and bow down to, for it must needs be all *together*. And this need for *communality* of worship is the chief torment of each man individually, and of mankind as a whole, from the beginning of the ages. In the cause of universal worship, they have destroyed each other with the sword."[44] Further on we read: "Have we not, indeed, loved mankind, in so humbly recognizing their impotence, in so lovingly alleviating their burden and allowing their feeble nature even to sin, with our permission?"[45] And yet one more motif: "For only we, we who keep the mystery, only we shall be unhappy. There will be thousands of millions of happy babes, and a hundred thousand sufferers who have taken upon themselves the curse of the knowledge of good and evil. Peacefully they will die, peacefully they will expire in your name, and beyond the grave they will find only death. But we will keep the secret, and for their own happiness we will entice them with a heavenly and eternal reward. For even if there were anything in the next world, it would not, of course, be for such as they."[46] This has a profound meaning: the Grand Inquisitor is to remain innocent in the eyes of his slaves. After all, he suffers for them. Power does not give him pleasure, like it does to the masters from Hegel's text, but a cross difficult to carry. The rebellion of the people becomes in this situation an act of ingratitude bordering on sacrilege.

What is the essence of the new relation of enslavement? Here we could also use Hegel's language and speak of a mediated recognition, but the level of this recognition is deeper than before. Comparing Dostoevsky's text with Hegel's text, we can say that Hegel had no idea what a real slave looks or can look like, and his vision of enslavement is an idyll compared with Dostoevsky's vision.

The enslaved from Hegel's texts recognized in the master the *raison d'être* for his life, he saw in him his father. The enslaved from Dostoevsky's text sees in the Inquisitor not only his parent but also, and even above all, the *raison d'être* of his ethical dignity — his holiness. Only the Inquisitor knows what is good and what is evil, he decides about heroism and betrayal. All ethical concepts focus around the axis the great master of illusion has established for the enslaved. The slave from Hegel's pages could not rebel because it signified for him falling into fault of fratricide. Here a deeper fault threatens — blasphemy and sacrilege, that is, the fault of a coup against holiness. Blasphemy is mockery directed against the holy. Sacrilege is an attempt to control holiness with violence — to conquer and overcome it. Holiness is what radically transcends the possibilities of man. Despite this, the blasphemer and the sacrilegious make an attack against holiness.

It is not harmful to the highest holiness, but it harms the blasphemer and the sacrilegious, because it reveals their stupidity. Who then is the one who attacks the Inquisitor? It is someone who is morally insignificant, a *nobody*, a creature unworthy of his own existence.

Therefore, the meaning of the outlined transformation of values is simple: from now on, meaning from the moment of rebellion, the rebellious slave will exist in an unjustified existence, his dignity will be below his existence. His nonexistence will be justified. The highest art of the master's illusion was that he stood in the place of what is highest, and in the same way he appealed to what is best and most profound in man. In this way he placed himself beyond the reach of rebellion. From now on he is no longer even interested directly in the eventual suppression of the rebellion. The Inquisitor will never expose his life, because there are no opponents worthy of him anywhere. It will be done for him by other slaves. The Inquisitor does not light the pyres. His significant task is creating illusions—writing the script for a play that others will perform.

I spoke about the conscience earlier. What is the nature of the bond between the master and the slave on the level of the conscience?

The Grand Inquisitor, like the Hegelian master, has an obsession with being recognized by other people. The Hegelian master directed his desire toward human desire. The Inquisitor desires the loves of humans from which human consciences originate. To have love means that to be a possessor of love, one must take man's freedom from him. The Inquisitor does not love people, but he wants to possess their love, because only through possessing their love can he perpetuate his rule. However, at this point a paradox comes into being that is similar to the paradox present in Hegel. What is the love of the enslaved worth, the love of people who are deprived of a conscience? Such a love is essentially worthy of contempt. The Inquisitor lives in the shadow of a constant need to despise his own slaves—a contempt that destroys his own soul. In turn, who is the Inquisitor—the one who is ready to give people everything except freedom—for his subjects? He is an apparent master, a master worthy to be scoffed at. Scoffing is the chief sin of the Grand Inquisitor's subjects—a sin the Inquisitor encourages. The new relation between the master and the slave is therefore a relation of recognition in contempt and scoffing in recognition. Contempt and scoffing have two ends. Despising others: I at the same time have contempt for myself for my relationship with the other. Scoffing at the other: I at the same time scoff at myself for my relations with him. Here nobody can be themselves fully. The community of the Inquisitor with the subject and the subject with the Inquisitor is a hell whose flame does not burn the soul of man from the outside, but right in the middle of it. The Grand Inquisitor proves to his subjects that they—if they rebel—will exist in an unjustified existence, but in proving this and creating the system of illusions serving it, he himself feels and discovers that from the same he himself begins to exist in such an existence—he exists without an ethical reason. He wants to be loved, but he cannot love. Therefore, he can do one thing: possess.

Threat of Condemnation

We must now take a better look at the moment of condemnation, which, as it turns out, lay at the foundations of the two threats mentioned above. What were the threats described above? They were the expression of conviction that the one threatened has no right to exist. First, the right to exist was denied, then there was a threat of death or dying. Death turned out to be the punishment for parricide, sacrilege, and blasphemy. To deny a man the right to exist is to condemn him. It must be added that condemnation can appear without threat of death and dying, that death and dying are not necessarily consequences of the act of condemnation.

The situation of condemnation is drawn by Kierkegaard in his conception of the "sickness unto death." He writes about despair:

> But in another sense despair is even more definitely the sickness unto death. Literally speaking, there is not the slightest possibility that anyone will die from this sickness or that it will end in physical death. On the contrary, the torment of despair is precisely this inability to die. Thus it has more in common with the situation of a mortally ill person when he lies struggling with death and yet cannot die. Thus to be sick unto death is to be unable to die, yet not as if there were hope of life; no, the hopelessness is that there is not even the ultimate hope, death. When death is the greatest danger, we hope for life; but when we learn

to know the even greater danger, we hope for death. When the danger is so great that death becomes the hope, then despair is the hopelessness of not even being able to die.[47]

Why am I condemned? I am condemned and worthy of being condemned because I became a parricide (Hegel), a blasphemer and sacrilege (Dostoevsky). What does it mean to be condemned? It means that I still exist, I am, feel myself, other people, and the stage of the world. It also means that I no longer have a right to exist. I am, I live, I feel myself, and others, and the stage of the world—without right. I am someone who is evil. Therefore, my nonexistence would be justified. Being aware of condemnation, I essentially have consciousness that I should not exist. The formula for condemnation contains the word "You": "It is you who are condemned." The formula touches me in my axiological I.[48] At the point where I most feel like myself, I at the same time feel that I am someone worthy of contempt. I am not worthy of my name, existence, the earth beneath my feet, and answers to questions addressed to others. I am dust, I am nothing, I am the miscarried fetus of chance.

Condemnation is radical when, as if beyond the constructed system of external values, it affects the direct sense of self-worth. This feeling has the character of an axiomatic experience. Upon it, as upon a mathematical axiom, rest all the other axiological terms. First, I am a value for myself, in myself, at my place. Condemnation aims to question that axiomatic experience of oneself as value. It says: since you are not a value for the other (i.e., for the master), you are not any value, you are a collection of monstrosities. Condemnation takes away value and creates a feeling of antivalues. Nothing will be able to rescue the condemned anymore. Even if the condemned will perform something externally good, it only leads to a greater lostness, because to the existing faults it adds the fault of hypocrisy.

Therefore, everything is an expression of condemnation—death and dying. It is not important what you threaten with, what matters is that the one who threatens condemns. Condemnation is the fundamental condition of possibility. This condition is visible in every threat. Everything in a threat is reducible to one thing: if you will not submit to me, then I will condemn you and force you to condemn yourself. When man condemns himself, the path toward enslavement stands open before him. Enslavement begins with debasement. Everything else is secondary.

Limits of the Threat and Possibilities of Liberation

Evil usually appears as the content of a threat—a threat directed at us by another man (evil originating in the external world, i.e., an earthquake, I have called a misfortune). Evil appearing as the content of a treat is a specter. Evil existing in the manner of a phenomenon is a particular reality, it emerges from interpersonal space—space ordered by the rules of dialogue. Therefore, evil is not originally in me or in you, but is *between* (Buber's *Zwischen*) you and I. If there were no other people, then misfortune would be possible, but there would be no evil. If I did not exist, then the specter would have nobody to frighten, therefore there would be no threat, which is an integral ingredient of the phenomenological essence of evil. Evil, as I attempted to show, emerges at the *crossings* of projects of being in the world—mine with yours, many others with ours. Evil has a tendency to personification, which is why when encountering evil, we usually search for a person in whom it would be possible to anchor it. Sometimes for us, such a person is a concrete person, sometimes a collectivity, and, at times, as in religious thinking, some mysterious demon. The subject of our considerations is, however, the instance when the carrier of evil for us (it seems to be) is a concrete human being, because we are still interested in the experience of the encounter. Such a man approaches me and threatens me. With what, in the final analysis, is this man threatening me and what can he threaten me with in the future? He can threaten me with an act of *condemnation*. If I am to face his attack against me, then I must, above all, free myself from the specter of condemnation. Everything else will come later. In other words, I have to find in myself the foundation for the autonomous value of myself.

Let us once again look at the phenomenon of the threat. It has double boundaries—external and internal. The external boundary of the threat circumscribes the horizon of possible threats. I can respond with a similar threat of death to a threat of death, and to a threat of dying I can respond with a similar thrusting into dying; I can also condemn the one who wants to condemn me. In following the same path as my opponent, I enter into a dispute with him. I can conduct this dispute on many levels and with many methods. There can also be many different results to the dispute. In effect, life itself shows whether the threat was justified or not. However, internal boundaries are more important than external boundaries of the threat. What do they consist in?

Enslavement is the goal of the threat; in order that this goal might be fulfilled, the threatened man must make an internal act of choosing, he must give up freedom. The one enslaving does not move a man like a tree log from one place to another, but wants to force him to change his place by himself. In this way the striving to enslave is connected with the remembrance of freedom. The more vivid the intention to enslave, the more open is the presupposition of freedom. Enslavement from Hegel's text assumes the possibility of freedom at the level of life—giving one's life or preserving it for oneself. Enslavement from Dostoevsky's text assumes freedom on the level of the conscience— preserving one's conscience or giving one's conscience away. The threat of condemnation reminds us of the choice between the highest Good and the highest Evil. Great threats are an attempt to muffle the great sense of freedom. But, precisely where great threats are needed to muffle freedom, the great feeling of freedom makes itself known.

All three types of threat required man to acknowledge their rightness. This is a very important moment. Evil differs from misfortune in that it cannot harm a man if man does not harm himself. No one can become an enslaved man unless he acknowledges to himself that he is enslaved. It is similar with condemnation. No one can put a man into a state of condemnation if a man himself does not admit to himself that he deserves to be condemned. Dialogical evil propagates itself through the word. Like every word, it requires recognition, understanding, and confirmation. The word gives, and takes away, meaning to deeds. Man can recognize, or not recognize, what another man is communicating to him with the help of words. In the depths of his spirit he is the master of his axiological recognitions. Freedom determines the interiority of man.

The independence of man toward what words contain can be expressed with Descartes's famous principle—*cogito ergo sum*. This principle is interpreted in a myriad of ways, usually it is considered as a shortcut expression for the philosophy of the subject, and from this as the beginning of modern idealism. This is only one of the possible interpretations, a rather superficial one. This principle reveals before us new layers of meaning when we place it in the general horizon of the drama of man suspended between good and evil. Then we will be able to accept that the evil genius of the philosophy of Descartes is a sign and harbinger for Dostoevsky's Grand Inquisitor. Just like the Grand Inquisitor, he rules using illusions, this is how the evil genius deceives and confounds; he is proficient in the same craft. Therefore, Descartes's philosophy ought to be rather interpreted in the categories of dialogue rather than the philosophy of being. The thought of Descartes captured in these categories will turn out to be the first radical philosophy of liberation from the rule of the inquisitors.

Let us look closer at man. The Cartesian man is someone who was thrown into the middle of a world of ambiguity. The boundaries between truth and falsehood have faded, between good and evil, between the reliable manifestation of things and illusion, between the face and the mask of a man. The original certainty of the stage has been shaken. What should a man do in this situation? He is to go as far as possible along the line of the logic of illusions. By following this path, he discovers that in a situation of radical uncertainty, his first good will be some truth, some certainty of a basic truth. You should not be afraid of your own doubts. Let what is doubtful be treated as if it were false. Let uncertainty and its pain be taken to their ultimate end until they become a certainty that everything is false. Such a radicalization of evil genius's intentions turns out to be salvific because it is a liberation of its influence. Since everything is uncertain, then the existence of the Inquisitor (evil genius) is also uncertain. Since what appears as uncertain can be recognized as false, the existence of inquisitors and other masters of illusion also becomes false. Only after this can the second act follow—the discovery of self-certainty, the certainty of one's own existence. Since I am deceived, I am. My existence is certain; the existence of the master of illusion is doubtful.

But what is such a discovery for a man threatened with condemnation? *Cogito ergo sum* is a discovery of the truth. "I think, therefore I am" means that I am a subject of truth. The truth is a good. If so, I am a subject of the good. Since I am a subject of the truth-good, then I cannot be condemned. My good, that is, my truth about myself, is a value that justifies my being. The truth is the beginning of my liberation. The truth liberates. The truth liberates as much as it becomes a value serving those who search for the truth and have the beginnings of it in them. I am in the realm of truth. I am under the protection of the good, which has taken on the shape of the truth. From this good, from this truth, my new dignity begins. Along with it I am beyond the reach of the threats of men and masters of illusion.

Therefore, all liberation begins from the experience of dignity. Yet, this dignity does not flow either from work, as Hegel imagined (even though the matter requires many interpretations), or from the eventual rebellion, from any form of revenge. In order to free oneself, one must stand upon a completely different level, upon which there is no place for any masters, instead there is room for dialogue partners—partners connected by a mutual care for the truth and regaining their dignity in this care.

3. Evil in the Dialogue of Temptation

We will attempt to put our problems in order. Let us look at temptation's relevant dimension. In temptation there are the one who tempts, the one whom he tempts, and that toward which temptation encourages. Therefore, tempter, tempted, and the object of temptation. In the garden of Eden there is a tree of knowledge and good and evil, upon that tree hangs the forbidden fruit. The fruit is the object of temptation. The temptation is in the dialogue between the serpent and Eve. Several problems arise from this basic situation.

The forbidden fruit, the topic and object of temptation, moves to the foreground. The fruit is beautiful and delicious. Why is it a forbidden fruit? What is the nature of its evil? Within this question another question is expressed—the question about the *temptation of the world*. In the pursuit of picking forbidden fruits, desiring forbidden things, the world's temptation lets itself be known. Reflection upon it leads us to bring to light a specific tie between man and his world— the world that is the stage of the human drama. I define this tie with the word *cultivating*. Cultivating constitutes the human world of the environment. Only from cultivating there emerges, as its pathology, the desire for the world awakened by the world's temptation.

The temptation of the world does not exhaust the whole matter, and does not even touch its core. The relation between the tempted and the tempter—the dialogical relation—turns out to be significant. The tempter persuades. The temptation is a form of a promise—it is a perverse promise in which the good is promised and evil is offered. The process of temptation requires its own separate description. I will take it up in a latter part of this examination. It is taken up there from the point of view of the one tempted. The one tempted falls for some illusion. He believes, or, at least assumes, that what he inclines toward is his good. One of the paradoxes of evil consists in this: evil, to draw toward itself, takes on a foreign countenance, the countenance of the good. It tempts not as an evil, but as its opposite.

Hence, a third question emerges from this: Why does the tempter tempt, why does he draw into evil? Through posing this question we change the point of view: we look at the phenomenon of evil from the side of the one who wants evil. After all, the one tempted does not want evil; he succumbs to evil as his good. The tempter is in a different situation, he knows what is going on. Why does he draw into evil? In describing this *why* we want to bring to light an attempt to rationalize evil by the malefactor himself. The thesis that evil is absurd is sometimes proclaimed—therefore it is not possible to reason about and understand evil. This does not seem quite right. Evil itself strives toward some rationalization, and this is proved by the persuasive character of fears and desires it awakens; above all, by the stance of the tempter toward what he does.

World: Promised Land

Man's world is the stage of his drama. Man comes into the world, searches for a home in the world, here he raises a temple to God, builds roads, has a workplace, here he finds the cemeteries of his forefathers, among whom he himself will at some point rest. What does it mean to say that the world is a stage of a drama? It means that one cannot separate ways of experiencing the world from ways of experiencing people, above all, from ways of living through the drama of man with other men. Man marks the earth with traces that witness to encounters, relations, and partings with others. The tie of man to the earth is also dramatic. Man carries within himself an archaic question: What is this earth, is the earth his promised land, or a denied land?

After the creation of the first people, God said, "Fill the earth and subdue it." These words are still within us. They define the basic outline of man's relation to the stage of the drama. First and foremost, they show the place of the earth in the hierarchy of values: man is *above* the earth, and the earth is *below* man. The earth is not God. The earth is not a man. It is the stage. However, the experience of the earth as a stage is not direct, but mediated through dialogue. It was dialogue that made of the earth a *promised land*. The archaic narrative reveals a fundamental philosophical truth: there are no direct experiences of the earth as a stage; all the experiences of the earth as a stage are mediated by some reciprocity with the other. This is expressed by the very idea of the promise itself. Touching the earth with one's legs, and striding across it to either encounter the other or to leave him, we touch the earth as a promise.

Man's relation to the earth cannot be passive. Man must, in order to stay alive, endure the initial harshness of the earth. We ought to distinguish the land of slavery from the land of self-willing. Man is capable of controlling the earth, therefore the earth is not a land of slavery. However, upon the earth-stage, trees with forbidden fruits also grow. Therefore, the earth is not the land of self-will. The earth has a specific nature. It has its own order, arrangement, and logic. One must not disregard the nature of the earth. The earth-stage must be understood in order to be controlled. Otherwise, the earth can rebel against man.

What word would render this special relation of man to the earth as the stage of his drama, given to him to understand and grace? Let us use the following word here: *cultivating*. For man, being upon the earth is cultivating. We are here as cultivators. We are upon the earth—neither as slaves nor as self-willed, but free and understanding the nature of the earth. We fulfill the archaic promise that lasts in us by cultivating.

Cultivating is based upon discerning the nature of the earth. For cultivating—this is extremely important—the earth has a specific nature. There is the nature of fire and the nature of water. There is the nature of woman and the nature of man. Whoever wants to cultivate must take into account the difference in natures. People build homes in which fires burn, where vessels with water stand, and suppers are prepared. One must deal with things—with the home, vessel, fire, food—according to their nature. Whoever disregards nature may cause the stage to rebel. The wisdom that permeates cultivating speaks about how to proceed with nature. It shows the cultivator what he ought to do in order to extract what is best out of nature, that is, what best serves life. The various forms of life arrange themselves in a hierarchy. This is why the wisdom of cultivating must think hierarchically. The life of man is more valuable than the life of grass, the life of trees, and the life of animals. This is because man is *upon* the world, while the world-stage is *below* man. The wisdom of cultivating is not so much the ability to choose the means to a goal as it is the ability to accurately discover the hierarchy of things, matters, and values. The wisdom of cultivation is a way of thinking that creatively links nature with the values of life.

Every cultivator attaches himself to his world—his cultivated world. What does this attachment depend upon? The words "I am from here" express it simply. Where are we from? We are from here. Here is my house, my homestead, my fatherland. We touch upon some paradox here: man comes *into* the world and at the same time is *from* the world. It follows from this that man is and is not upon the world, because he is simultaneously from the world. From a slightly different angle, this paradox reveals to us the sense of the word "my"—my world. The word "my" initially has a negative sense: I am not a part of the world—I and the world are not one and the same. This is accompanied by a positive sense: despite this, the world is not for me something foreign. What does this mean? What do both moments mean when they are joined together? They mean *for* me. The world is for me. The word "for" points to a promise—my world is the world of the promise given to me, simultaneously a promised land and a land promising. I attach myself to the world—me, the cultivator of the world—to the extent to which the archaic promise fulfills itself in my life in the world.

Let us take one more step toward explaining the mystery of cultivation. We spoke of the following: "the promise." This means that at the foundations of the relationship of man to the earth there hides some relation to the other man (God?). The core of the relation between man and man is the relation of reciprocity.

Reciprocity is an exchange of goods, which, as goods they would not have come into being if first there were not some encounter of man with man. When I encounter you, I feel that the good awakens in me, a good that is my good for you, and I know at the same time that you also bring me a good that my presence next to you has awakened. Something has brought us together, which we do not possess alone, nor can we possess it each alone. Reciprocity is our creativity directed toward each other. It creates our deepest *together*.

Cultivation is a manifestation of reciprocity. We are together in cultivating. We create ourselves through cultivation. We will also deepen our wisdom and ties to the earth together. The basic fruit of cultivating is the birth of *place*. "For here there is no place that does not see you," said Rainer Maria Rilke. The human environment is above all a world organized around places. Let us now look closer at these places. We have four chief places: home, workplace, temple, and cemetery. Reflections upon them will allow us to better understand our tie with the earth.

Human Lifeworld
Modern philosophy, especially since Husserl's times, devotes much attention to the study of the so-called lifeworld and analyses of the many varieties of consciousness of that world. The overwhelming majority of these analyses are various polemics concerning Husserl's views. One particular point of his theory evokes particular opposition. For Husserl, the lifeworld is the universal horizon of the intentional consciousness of the world. The core of this consciousness is the conviction about the real existence of the majority of the objects in this world and the existence of the world as their totality. It can be said that the main problem of the intentional consciousness of the world is the question of the existence and nonexistence of things. Consciousness of the world, according to Husserl, develops and transforms itself thanks to acts of recognition in existence and denial of recognition in existence, taken in all possible modalities, that is, recognition of reality, possibility, probability, and so forth. Furthermore, Husserl believes that the basic act of recognizing existence, or the denial of recognizing existence, is made in a lonely consciousness, totally individual and monadic, only the higher layers of the world's meaning are constitutively conditioned by dialogue with the other. The common world of many people is constituted upon a foundation of a conviction about reality maturing independently from the

dialogical relation. For Husserl, the basic meaning of the lifeworld is not the gift of the other. Jan Patočka worked out and showed the significant features of the Husserlian theory of the world upon the wider background of previous philosophies.[49] Gerd Brand also developed his theory of the world in the spirit of phenomenological philosophy.[50] The goal of the analyses, speaking generally, is the improvement of Husserl's descriptions. What interests us most here appears somewhat on the margins of these matters: grasping of the fundamental tie connecting man with his world.

Polemics against Husserl were undertaken by Heidegger and Levinas, among others. One and the other questioned the primacy of the intentional-objective relation in favor of, according to them, more originary relationships. For Heidegger, such a relation is the broadly conceived use of tools, resulting from care about being in the world. The originary world of man is not a world of objects recognized as real, or as this or that variant of reality, but the world of what is ready at hand, which, being near man, serves man for something in view of something. Levinas goes even further and also questions Heidegger's point of view. He draws attention to the bond constituted by *jouissance*—the bond of using the gifts of the world for *tasting* the delights and pains of life. Both the use of tools and the tasting of the world do not have an intentional character, meaning that the world is not given in them to man in an objective manner and does not constitute itself as a fruit of reality. Other questions about the world are more fundamental. Heidegger asks, Does something serve for something in view of something? Levinas asks, Does the world taste like a poison, medicine, or intoxication? And one more, very important matter: both of these ties of man to the world are dialogically conditioned. Both Heidegger and Levinas speak of this. Unfortunately, neither one shows the connections of this conditioning.

After writing *Sein und Zeit*, Heidegger will once again return to the issue of man's tie with the world. He will do this in connection with the question about technology. What is modern technology and what does the tie with the earth it proposes to man consist of? He will then distinguish two types of technology: Greek and modern. The concept of *truth* turns out to be key for the Greek understanding: technology is one of the ways of revealing the hidden truth about the world. The will to power is key for the modern understanding of technology: technology is the means to rule over the world. The fundamental relation of man to the world would therefore be located somewhere within the borders between revealing the truth and a stance of struggle and violence.

Let us consider several significant texts beginning with Levinas, who tries to reach layers more originary than the ones Heidegger pointed to.

As I mentioned, this relationship is, according to Levinas, constituted by a nonintentional *jouissance*, what I have translated as a "taste for life." Here, being in the world would mean to live in the world, to live through the world. We read in *Totality and Infinity*:

> We live from "good soup," air, light, spectacles, work, ideas, sleep, etc. . . . These are not objects of representations. We live from them. Nor is what we live from a "means of life," as the pen is a means with respect to the letter it permits us to write, nor a goal of life, as communication is the goal of the letter. The things we live from are not tools, nor even implements, in the Heideggerian sense of the term. Their existence is not exhausted by the utilitarian schematism that delineates them as having the existence of hammers, needles, or machines. They are always in a certain measure—and even the hammers, needles, and machines are—objects of enjoyment, presenting themselves to "taste," already adorned, embellished. Moreover, whereas the recourse to the instrument implies finality and indicates a dependence with regard to the other, living from . . . delineates independence itself, the independence of enjoyment and of its happiness, which is the original pattern of all independence.[51]

Levinas rightly indicates and accurately names the taste of things, the taste of life, the independence of utility and tasting, living from something—*jouissance*. But this is not the fundamental matter. The following problem is fundamental: a promised land or a denied land? From this comes what needs particular attention: the originary distance of man toward the earth. It is characterized by cultivation. Man is *upon* the earth. The cultivator lives from the earth, this is true, but in order for him to be able to live from the earth, he must find his place upon the earth. There is a significant difference between *living from* something and *living upon* something. Man must become aware that he is not supposed to serve the fruit of the trees, but the fruits are supposed to serve him. But to consume his fruit, man must preserve and ennoble the tree. In doing this he confirms his specific place among the things. Man lives in *distance*. This distance is nothing other than the originary basis of intentionality. Intentionality is a complex phenomenon. Husserl stressed in his descriptions of objectification that the act of intentionality objectivizes what it is directed at. But this is secondary. Distance is originary: me here and the world there, me above the world and the world under me; not me for the world, but the world for me. What does this mean? This means that the world is my promised land. But if it turns out that the elements of this world defeat me in a battle? Then I will say that the world is a denied land. Nonetheless, the distance itself will remain.

Let us also cite the so-called late Heidegger. Heidegger, while weaving his reflections upon the essence of technology, establishes the relations between the concept of *téchné* and the concepts of *poiesis* and *epistéme*. Man relates to the earth through *téchné*. But what is *téchné*? In the original Greek meaning, it is the bringing to light of some truth, above all, the truth about the world, but also truth about man. We read in *The Question Concerning Technology*:

> *Technikon* means that which belongs to *téchné*. We must observe two things with respect to the meaning of this word. One is that *téchné* is the name not only for the activities and skills of the craftsman, but also for the arts of the mind and the fine arts. *Téchné* belongs to bringing-forth, to *poiesis*; it is something *poietic*.
>
> The other point that we should observe with regard to *téchné* is even more important. From earliest times until Plato the word *téchné* is linked with the word *epistéme*. Both words are names for knowing in the widest sense. They mean to be entirely at home in something, to understand and be expert in it. Such knowing provides an opening up. As an opening up it is a revealing. Aristotle, in a discussion of special importance (*Nicomachean Ethics*, bk. 6, chaps. 3 and 4), distinguishes between *epistéme* and *téchné* and indeed with respect to what and how they reveal. *Téchné* is a mode of *alétheuein*. It reveals whatever does not bring itself forth and does not yet lie here before us, whatever can look

and turn out now one way and now another. Whoever builds a house or a ship or forges a sacrificial chalice reveals what is to be brought forth, according to the perspectives of the four modes of occasioning. This revealing gathers together in advance the aspect and the matter of ship or house, with a view to the finished thing envisioned as completed, and from this gathering determines the manner of its construction. Thus what is decisive in *téchné* does not lie at all in making and manipulating nor in the using of means, but rather in the aforementioned revealing. It is as revealing, and not as manufacturing, that *téchné* is a bringing-forth.

Thus the clue to what the word *téchné* means and to how the Greeks defined it leads us into the same context that opened itself to us when we pursued the question of what instrumentality as such in truth might be.

Technology is a mode of revealing. Technology comes to presence in the realm where revealing and unconcealment take place, where *álétheia*, truth happens.[52]

Heidegger is right when he writes that all *téchné*, and so also cultivating, develops in the domain of the project of the truth about the world—the truth of being. One cannot separate the way of being of man in the world from his convictions about the truth of the world. I must be convinced that the fruit is for me, in order to be able to discover that it is delicious to eat. The event of technology and cultivating is fulfilled in the domain of some truth project. But this project has its limitations. It is marked out by what is at stake in the world—life itself, the irrational instinct of life itself. But, after all, what matters is not exclusively one's life, but also, or, maybe above all, it is about the lives of those closest to oneself. The bond with those closest goes before the bond with the earth. I do not want fruits exclusively for myself. It is not the discovery of the earth's nature at the beginnings of technology that comes first, but the establishing of new interpersonal relations that leads to the revealing of earth's nature. What can be done with clay is not first, but *for whom* it is possible to make something with clay. To be on the earth means to touch it through the tears and smile of the other.

Let us now return to the positive thread of our reflections.

I said above that cultivating is an expression of reciprocity. The relation of reciprocity is a mystery. The sole path for shedding light on this mystery appears to be considering the fruits of reciprocity. The mystery of life is known by its fruits. The place is the fruit of reciprocity. We have, as I said, four fundamental places: home, workplace, temple, and cemetery. These places mark the main foundations of man's drama with man. There is a basic order in the world of man thanks to these places. There remains only wilderness where place disappears. Man loses the thread of his drama. In order to understand the human lifeworld, one must understand the meaning of the fundamental places. This discussion will bring us closer to our main task of understanding what is the temptation of the world—what is man's attachment to the world and what is its distortion.

Home
The home is the space closest to man. All the roads of man through the world are measured by his distance from home. The view from the home's windows is the first view of man upon the world. When man is asked where he comes from, he points to home. The home is the nest of man. Here the child comes into the world, here matures the feeling of responsibility for the order of the first community, here man comes to know the main mysteries of things—windows, doors, spoons—he has joys and suffers, he leaves here for his eternal rest. To have a home means to have around oneself a domain of originary homeliness. The walls of the home protect man against the severity of the elements and the hostility of people. It makes life and maturing possible. By living in a home, a man can feel like himself, at home. To be oneself at home is an experience of a sensible freedom. The home does not allow for self-will, but also does not mean slavery. The space of a home is the space of multiple meanings. To build a home means to *settle in*.

Man cannot settle down in loneliness. The lonely build cells, others erect hiding places. Settling in is the fruit of feminine and masculine reciprocity. It assumes gender as nature. A woman in solitude does not possess a home. The lonely man also does not possess a home. Nevertheless, a man offers a home to a woman and a woman offers a home to a man. The essence of reciprocity is man offering the other what only becomes possible thanks to the presence of the other beside him. The woman in the home is a mother and the man a father. The child is the natural fruit of reciprocity. The child crowns the meaning of a home. The home, above all, is for the child. This is why we say in Poland that homes without children are empty.

Man attaches himself to his home. Attachment to home is so deep and so extensive that it exceeds man's consciousness. When a man loses his home, when he distances himself from home, then he feels in the pain of loss the power of settling in. The fate of a home is part of his fate. Spouses who promise a home to each other are convinced that in their promise there is a meaning anterior to their promising; they believe that they were "created for each other." Their promises are only the echo of an archaic promise. When a child appears in a home the attachment to home reaches its peak. The child is the promise of all promises. In those who built a home there awakens the faith that here, in this home, in this garden, by this cradle, their promised land has come into being.

The attachment that permeates being settled is the response to the discovery that the bit of land given to man is *for* man. Man bends down to what is *for* man and ties himself to it. He draws the power to live from here. He can now say—I am from here, I come from this home.

However, the home is also a place of drama and even tragedy. Is there anything more fragile than a home? Lightning, earthquake, and flood threaten from the side of the stage. From the side of the other, the rejection of reciprocity threatens. But not only that. The logic of life itself—the flowing of time itself—makes homes decay. Children grow up, move away from home, leave, or build their own homes. People die—spouses die, as do fathers and mothers. Every home is condemned to be abandoned.

The essence of the human drama is expressed by the questions, What is a home, is it a reliable home, or only the promise of a home? Is man capable of building a reliable home? Is he capable of settling down here? Is his attachment to the home an attachment to something strong and lasting? Upon losing a home, a man enters into a limit situation in which a new meaning for a run-down home crystallizes: there comes about the conjecture that the home was only a promise of a home. Something began in this home, some echo sounded, some light shone, but this was not yet what really matters. Settling in seems to be measured with larger measures than the dimensions of the actual home. A run-down home opens up the horizon of transcendence. It leaves an indistinct trace upon the soul of a man—the idea of another home, untouched by fire, by betrayal—a home of truth. This idea will determine, in hiding, the drama of man with an actual home, even when he doubts it.

Workplace
This is a different fruit of cultivation, a different place. It can be a field, forest, smithy, school, factory, a steam locomotive, and so on. By overcoming the natural resistance of materials, work brings out the life-giving nature of raw materials, the earth, and also people. Thanks to work, the space surrounding the home changes into a space that serves the home and living in the home. Work has the ability to construct. It is an intermediary world between man and nature—a world adapted to satisfy both the stable and changing needs of man. Heidegger described the basic structure of this world with the words "that to which something else is indebted." The hammer is what serves the blacksmith to make horseshoes because of the need to fit a horse that will pull the wood for the home. . . . The intermediate world is the world of various workplaces that are variously tied to each other. This world by its very existence reveals and confirms the truth of cultivation: the earth and its treasures are *for* man.

To work in this world means to *become enrooted*.

The rooting of man in the world is also a fruit of reciprocity, which takes on the form of cooperation. Man works with someone and for someone. The essence of cooperation is realized by the relation "with someone." *With someone* does not simply mean *alongside*. It means on the basis of an agreement. Work is not only the overcoming of the material's resistance, but, above all, a form of agreement between man and man. The reciprocity of cooperation constitutes the concrete meaning, concrete role, of the man of work. Man is a teacher among teachers, a doctor among doctors, an artist among artists, and a farmer among farmers. His concrete meaning within the world of work is derived from the act of recognition by his co-workers.

Being-enrooted is the second, alongside settling in, form of attachment to the earth. Man attaches himself to the earth through his work. The main sources of the power of attachment are those *for* whom man works. The sick are this for the doctor, students for the teacher, readers for the writers, and so on. Where there is no direct contact with people for whom man works, the attachment to work becomes weaker. Then there remains the bond with co-workers, and also with the very place of work itself. Work makes its mark on man. This is indicated by the language that describes the phenomenon of work. The doctor does not say, "I deal with healing," but instead "I *am* a doctor." The man of work is from those for whom he works. They are for him the soil for becoming enrooted.

Attachment to the world and the earth, and the realization through work, is also, like settling in, an answer to experiences that confirm themselves daily, that the world surrounding man is for man. The earth is for man since it gives birth to bread. This is the meaning of working people's cares about what will happen when I die—with my field, with my school, with my hospital, with my factory—if I leave this world?

Thanks to work performed, man comes closer to knowing some truth about the earth—the stage of his drama. Man experiences the nature of the world as a promised land by extracting from the earth what is best. In tasting bread, man tastes the promise that has come true. He believes that he is not an intruder here. Work coming to fruition is the confirmation of an archaic promise. But work does not also come to fruition. There come years of crop failure, volcanoes erupt, and waters leave their riverbeds. A short earthquake turns the work of many generations to ruin. Furthermore, in dying, man dies defeated by his own work. The same work that served development and the supporting of life becomes the source of weaknesses and death. Work not only humanizes man, work can also kill a man. Man dies worn out by work.

Again, the question arises: Where are we—upon a promised land, or upon the promise of land?

Temple
This is also a fruit of cultivation. The temple is a place of encounters—of man with God and of man with man. "The ground you stand on is holy," says God to Moses during their encounter. The temple is a space of sanctification for man. What is holiness? Holiness is the form of the good's action—the good works in such a way that it sanctifies. The space of the temple is there to bring out from man his good

and in this way to open the horizon for encounters. The time of the temple has a similar sense. Man comes to the temple to sanctify himself. The order of the holy place, its light and shadows, its signs, symbols, and paintings are supposed to make man aware that "the Lord is near." The time of the temple reveals the deepest sense of time: time is the time of hope, the path of God returning toward man. The temple opens the horizon of an Other Reality. What surrounds us, as touchable and seeable, is only a metaphor for what really is.

To visit a temple means to *sanctify oneself*. Man is subject to the creative action of reciprocity in a temple. The meaning of this reciprocity is revealed by the idea of sacrifice—sanctification through devotion. Devotion means to sacrifice what one possesses in order to be what one really is. The sacrifice expresses the conviction that man is *for Someone*. We do not live for ourselves. For whom is a man? Man does not know this precisely; it comes to man through faith. He only knows that he is for.... He is a music that loses its meaning when nobody hears it. However, man does not lose himself in his *for*. He becomes himself thanks to being for. Music impresses all the more, the more it is music. However, reciprocity would not be reciprocity if it were one-sided. Faith is the answer to man's sacrifice, since in the temple, God is also *for* man—he is for man before man is for God. God offers himself on the altar as an offer to men. But he does not stop being God because of this. In the sacrificial reciprocity, both sides remain themselves. At the same time, something significant is being created: the fatherhood of God grows along with the sonhood of man, and vice versa.

In the temple's space, settling in and enrooting take on entirely new meanings. Here, in the temple, the ultimate truth about the earth—the stage of the human drama—appears. The earth is a metaphor for the earth. The home is a metaphor for the home, and the obedience, with which the earth greets the working man, is a metaphor for true obedience. One ought to read these metaphors as signs of hope. To read the signs of hope is to understand the promised land as the promise of the earth. This understanding involves having the courage to abandon the incomplete for the complete. This abandonment is the very essence of poverty. Poverty has at its basis the discovery of a new meaning of the earth. It is man's way of being upon the earth-stage of his drama, designated by the meaning of the earth as the true promised land, true home, true workplace. As I said above, cultivation has its own wisdom. The whole wisdom of cultivating concentrates itself in these words: to be able to be impoverished. The earth is a stage and the stage is for man, but only as a road sign standing by the road is. Does anyone attach themselves to road signs?

Cemetery
It belongs to man's world just as does a house, workplace, and temple. It is sometimes called (unjustly) a place of parting. The home is a place of parting, while the cemetery is a place of encountering the dead. Here the dead become our true ancestors—those who built for us our villages, cities, and worked in the fields. By going to a cemetery we return to those who once were. Everyone has his own grave here. Some graves are marked with crosses, others are unmarked. Some have plates with inscriptions speaking about the final requests of the deceased. Man encounters the mystery of death at the cemetery. The manner of building cemeteries summarizes what man knows about death.

To build a cemetery and grave means *to undertake a heritage*.

Man is a being that inherits. Inheriting is a form of reciprocity. We stand above a grave. Here lies a soldier who died for the fatherland. Here lies the father of a large family. Here is the grave of a teacher—the educator of many generations. This small, prematurely dead, child was the hope of its parents. The dead speak, they form more or less defined obligations. This binds. Sometimes the dead obligate more powerfully than the living. Man becomes aware at the grave of the dead that he is an heir. What does it mean to be an heir? Chiefly, it means partaking in the dignities of those who were before us. Through continuing, we continue, above all, dignity. We are heirs thanks to ancestors, and they are ancestors thanks to heirs.

However, we must not forget about tragedy. Despite all this, the cemetery is a tragic place. Here sorrow and despair touch a man after he loses loved ones. The cemetery proclaims the defeat of cultivation, settling in, rootedness, the fiasco of attachment to the earth. At the cemetery, the earth appears to us as a denied land. "Not here," says the cemetery. The home is not here, nor is rootedness here. The consciousness of the distance between man and earth grows at a cemetery. The cemetery land is the land of the promise not fulfilled. Signposts grow upon such a land. But are they legible enough to be as legible as the denied land of the cemetery is legible?

Denied Land

The philosophy of the lifeworld, which I alluded to at the beginning, concentrates primarily upon descriptions of functional structures of the world, and that is why it is incapable of demonstrating the contingency and fragility of that world clearly enough. It is true that man might feel "familiar" in this world, as a "functionary" adapted to his "functions," that he can have the impression of ruling this world, controlling its powers, and even of the nature that lies at its foundations. All of this is possible as long as the "functions function," and all the band is playing. But then "accidents" happen, such as a spring breaking, the axle of the car breaks, and the plane does not return to the airport. Something that seems irrational enters into a rationalized world. The functional type of truth gives way to the truth of nature. There was even a tree of forbidden fruit in the garden of Eden. It is as if the space of the prohibition seemed to increase after the banishment from paradise.

We have considered the issue of cultivating the earth as a promised land. Despite tragedy, cultivating develops within the domain of hope: we move from the promised land to the idea of the earth as a promise. The power of hope is such that it encompasses every rebellion of the earth, transforming the meaning of the promised land into the meaning of the earth as a promise. The capacity for poverty grows with hope. The human drama allows for the possibility that the strength of hope weakens and its momentum decreases. Then awakens the suspicion that we lived upon a land of exile, a hostile land, a rebellious land. I came into the world, so what? I walk upon alien soil, I move around upon a foreign stage, I pick someone else's fruit, I live in someone else's home, and I die someone else's death. Everything that is, is *denied* to me. Who am I? I am a usurper, intruder, and thief. I am full of guilt. My attitude toward the earth and my cultivation now have a different sense. Fear encroaches upon it. I am afraid of every step here, because I am walking upon someone else's road. I keep repeating: forgive me for being here. I am guilty. Even my love is full of sin, because it is love for someone who from the beginning is *alien*.

Fleeing is nature's answer to fear. And so fleeing from the earth. But, it is impossible to flee the earth, because there always must be some stage. What remains? *Fighting* remains. One must take up a fight against what is rebelled, one must negate negation. What will cultivating become now? What happens with the attachment stricken from within by fear? It becomes *desire*. Desire is striving to have and to rule—a striving that shows fear to the alleged rebellion. Whoever desires, fights for possession. He fights because he knows that he does not have and is afraid of it.

One should immediately, from the beginning, distinguish two directions for desire: toward the earth and toward the other human being. The turn toward man is more fundamental, but the one that turns toward the earth is clearer.

Desiring the earth is to want to *have* the earth as the fulfillment of a promise, to have it without remainder, to have it for oneself. But what does it mean to have? Desire has an axiological sense. It means not only ruling, but, above all, confirming the fact of ruling over the earth, that one has the right to the earth. I am free to do what I can. The boundaries of power are the boundaries of the law. And yet I have mastered what was denied to me! I picked the fruit! And if so, I apparently had the right to it. Cultivating takes on the meaning of fighting for the recognition of having that right. Fighting is the building of a home, fighting becomes an enrooting. And what is fighting? It is not only about the home, the fruits of labor, and whatever else? It is chiefly the fight for the right—the basic right to the earth. It expresses itself in the desire for wealth.

The ray turned upon man is even more fundamental. Cultivating was conditioned by the relation of reciprocity. Desire destroys reciprocity, not that in its place it introduces depersonalization, but so that it transforms reciprocity into revenge. Revenge means that you have to anticipate the blow. It is necessary to drive the other away before he drives me away. I must flog him with the same pain that I expect to get from him. Reciprocity ultimately grew out of the discovery of an archaic promise. Revenge grows out of what opposes the promise—from an archaic denial. Wherever there is a denial, there must be a perpetrator of denial. Who is the perpetrator of the archaic denial? Can he be reached? The perpetrator of the denial gets lost in the darkness of historical forgetting. But his place can be occupied by a concrete human being—a man who is approaching me. What does he want from me? He comes like some specter. What should I do with him? I must defend myself.

Let us look more closely at desire as a relation to the earth. The problem of revenge's reciprocity will require a separate discussion. What happens to cultivation when it is struck by fear? What happens to settling in, enrooting, sanctification, and tradition?

First, a few observations about desire in general.

We must modify the view that desire is the same as human eroticism. It is essentially a wider phenomenon. In the ascetical literature, desire is described as man's "blind striving." It is opposed to "reasonable striving," in which there is knowledge about the object of desire. Therefore, desire strives toward something, without really knowing toward what. St. John of the Cross, without giving any explicit definition of desire, writes about it as follows: "Desire blinds and darkens the soul; for desire, as such, is blind, since of itself it has no understanding in itself, the reason being to it always, as it were, a child leading a blind man. And hence it comes to pass that, whensoever the soul is guided by its desire, it becomes blind; for this is as if one that sees were guided by one that sees not, which is, as it were, for both to be blind.... Wherefore the darkness and rudeness of the soul will not be taken from it until the desires be quenched."[53] He compares the callings of desire to peevish children who, with no regard to the situation, yell "give, give." The author writes about desire as of something everyone knows; for moderns this understanding is no longer obvious.

Let us return to Levinas's *jouissance*, which I translate as "tasting" (the Polish translation of "utility" does not show the significant difference between using a tool and using a life—a difference the author is concerned with). Above we opposed *living off of something* to *living upon something*. *Jouissance* is primarily living *off of something*. *Living upon* goes in tandem with living *from something*. The words "upon" and "from" indicate distance. Whenever they are missing, there remains only the unmediated. "Living off of something" contains self-knowledge of a specific sensory experience. "Living upon something" and "living from something" assume knowledge about an object, which serves life. I know *how* something tastes and I know *what* tastes like that. I know that *this* is an apple, and I know *how* it tastes. Desire has knowledge of *how*, but it lacks knowledge about *what*. It is blind in this sense. But it is not blind in the same sense as a rock is blind to the one who places his foot upon it. Direct self-knowledge of experience is a self-knowledge of unpleasantness, pleasure, pain, thirst, hunger, satiety, and so on. Without it there would be no desires. Desire is primarily a manner of experiencing oneself, and secondarily is it a reference to an object.

Man lives off of something. I know how an apple tastes. Being alive, I know how life tastes. Life tastes of the tastes of all the blisses and pains that are given to man to live through. By tasting life man tastes himself. Desire is born from this taste. It remains when fear about something creeps into living off of something. Fear is expressed by the following question: What will happen tomorrow? Man no longer lives by the taste of the apple, but by the bitterness of the fear about the taste of the apple. This is where the power of desire originates—a power mined from the soul to overcome fear. In desire there is less about satisfying needs and more about relieving the fear that has been born in the womb of need. The one who fears no longer wants just an apple, but instead wants a whole apple tree.

Hegel says that desire is the rationale behind a certain realism in treating things of this world. Desire establishes the reality of an object in the measure that this object is able to satisfy a given desire. I believe in the existence of water according to the power of the desire that I feel. However, at the same time desire abolishes the reality of the object when desire is saturated. Desire confirms itself by destroying its object and confirms the object when it feels that it is being destroyed by the need of the object. But the Hegelian concept of desire does not coincide with ours: it is a synonym for living off of something, but not of that life itself (living off of something) affected by fear. Hegel does not include the moment of fear in his description. However, this fact does not change the essence of the realism of desires, and even sharpens this realism. It is commonly said that fear has big eyes. Desire—living off of something saturated with fear—establishes the reality of specters as its threats. Desire evokes a specter out of everything that it touches. The imagination projects images upon the objects of desire that frighten it. Man stares at what is not and is no longer able to notice what is.

This changes the meaning of cultivation. It changes being settled, enrooted, sanctified, and taking up a tradition. In every one of the manners of cultivating there now begins to speak the motif of revenge in relation to people and the motif of violence in relation to the earth. There are no longer *places* in the world surrounding man. Man stands helpless upon the earth like a homeless and uprooted creature. What happens to the place of reciprocity?

Home as Hideout
The home emerged, we know, as a place of reciprocity of the woman and man—reciprocity that results in new life. The space of the home is an intimately familiar space—within it man is himself at his own place. What happens with the space of the home when reciprocity transforms itself into revenge? Then the home changes its meaning— it becomes man's hideout. Then, what is the home for? The home is so that man can have a place to hide. The space around the home is a space of denial—it is a desert that gives birth to thistles and thorns, a desert exposed to the elements, bad animals, and bad people, it is a cemetery ground, full of frightening specters. Only a small part of the earth let itself be mastered. On it man builds his home. He closes the windows tight, bolts the door. He believes that he is safe here.

Let us consider the example of such an experience of space from Nietzsche's *The Gay Science*:

> Here I stand amidst the fire of the surf, whose white flames are licking at my feet: from all sides it is howling, threatening, screaming, shrieking at me, while the old earth-rattler sings his aria in the lowest of depths, deep as a roaring bull, while pounding such an earth-rattling beat that the hearts of even these weather-beaten monsters of the rocks are trembling in their bodies. Suddenly, as if born out of nothingness, there appears before the gate of this hellish labyrinth only a few fathoms away a large sailing ship, gliding along as silently as a ghost. Oh, this ghostly beauty! How magically it touches me! What? Has all the calm and silence of the world embarked here? Is my happiness itself sitting in this quiet place—my happier self, my second, immortalized self? Not yet to be dead, but also no longer alive? As a spiritlike, silent, watching, gliding, hovering intermediate being? As though

I were that ship that moves over the dark sea with its white sails like an enormous butterfly! Yes! To move over existence! That's it! That would be it!⁵⁴

And so we have the denied land, the land of rebellion, and upon it a small island of calm. There you see denial, but here the trace of some promise. Man erects the walls of a home. The walls become thicker, ever mightier, according to the measure of the fear growing in man. The house becomes a stronghold, castle, and a fortress. It no longer serves as a dwelling, but for dominating the surrounding land and the people who inhabit it. Arousing fear is the task of this building. It no longer is a home, but a warning and a threat.

Man lives inside the hideout. Outside the hideout are the enemies, while the allies are in the hideout. The boundary between an enemy and an ally is fluid. Every ally is a potential traitor. You must track the allies to be able to forestall their betrayal. Suspicion is the basic rule of conduct for people in hideouts.

Man turns out to be incapable of reciprocity. This is expressed in Nietzsche through a reference to women:

When a man stands in the midst of his own noise, in the midst of his own surf of projects and plans, he is also likely to see gliding past him silent, magical creatures whose happiness and seclusion he yearns for—women. He almost believes that his better self lives there amongst the women: in these quiet regions even the loudest surf turns into deathly silence and life itself into a dream about life. Yet! Yet! My noble enthusiast, even on the most beautiful sailing ship there is so much sound and noise, and unfortunately so much small, petty noise! The magic and the most powerful effect of women is, to speak the language of the philosophers, action at a distance, *actio in distans*: but that requires, first and foremost—distance!⁵⁵

The result of the rule of suspiciousness is keeping the other at a distance. The crisis of settling down and the phenomenon of homelessness come from this. Man goes through the world with the conviction that he has no place here for himself. He is an exile. He has been thrown onto somebody else's meadow. Everything here is foreign to him—people too. Whatever he touches awakens his anger. He fights until he has no strength left. But he has to succumb at some point. Even he himself has been denied to himself.

Workplace as Drudgery
Upon a foreign and rebellious earth, work is a form of fighting. The earth is an element that must be defeated. We must assume the following for the victory to be complete: the earth has no nature, it is pure material for the omnipotence of work. The assumption that a rebelled earth has no nature permeates those streams of technology that are expression of modern man's will to power. Heidegger turned his attention to this in his critique of the modern technological ideology. This technology is no longer concerned with revealing the natural truth of things, because things no longer have any natural truth in them, instead it is concerned with mastering fear before the misfortunes coming to man from the side of the earth and its elements, mastery through violence against the earth. We read:

> The revealing that rules in modern technology is a challenging [*Herausfordern*] which puts to nature the unreasonable demand that it supply energy that can be extracted and stored as such.... [A] tract of land is challenged into the putting out of coal and ore. The earth now reveals itself as a coal mining district, the soil as a mineral deposit. The field that the peasant formerly cultivated and set in order [*bestellte*] appears differently than it did when set in order still meant to take care of and to maintain. The work of the peasant does not challenge the soil of the field. In the sowing of the grain it places the seed in the keeping of the forces of growth and watches over its increase. But meanwhile even the cultivation of the field has come under the grip of another kind of setting-in-order, which sets upon [*stellt*] nature. It sets upon it in the sense of challenging it. Agriculture is now the mechanized food industry. Air is now set upon to yield nitrogen, the earth to yield ore, ore to yield uranium, for example; uranium is set upon to yield atomic energy, which can be released either for destruction or for peaceful use.[56]

Heidegger continues, "This setting-upon that challenges forth the energies of nature is an expediting [*Fordern*]."[57]

The earth is a denied land. From all the world's sides, man is threatened by a rebellion of the land. Man's task upon the earth is controlling the rebellion. Work is to be the means to this. Work is then the only form of fighting—fighting against the earth as an opponent. To work means to fight. Man gets into a test of strength with the earth. Who will emerge victorious? The tasks of work are controlling the storm, rains, heat, earthquake, protecting man from accidental misfortunes. The ultimate goal of labor is postponing the moment of death. I maintain myself above the earth so long as I fight. The questioning of death is the ultimate consequence of questioning nature. I fight to master; I work so that I do not die.

Work, understood as one of the varieties of fighting, establishes particular bonds between co-workers. They are essentially bonds of mastery and subjection. To fight it is necessary to unify all powers, and to unify all powers the powers must be subjected to a uniform command. I gain the right to command others by subjecting myself to a uniform command. From here, from this subjection, my nature emerges. Man is also, for the ideology of work, purely a material— only work makes man human. Man becomes himself by entering a uniform system of social work—as one of the units of power, as the most perfect productive power, as an activist whose one task is to act. The essence of man identifies itself then with the totality of social relations. Man is nothing outside of this totality.

Upon this road the radical ideology of work provides the rational justification to various forms of modern enslaved labor. Enslaved labor is labor that presents itself to the working man as work deprived of meaning. Man labors, but knows that his effort has no meaning. Working without meaning can take on various forms, beginning with work that has no meaning exclusively for the working man (i.e., badly paying work) and ending with work that has no meaning for anyone (i.e., work wasted from the start because of the ineffective functioning of co-workers together). Work without meaning is a torment. Man is convinced that he falls the victim of revenge in it. Revenge gives birth to the need for revenge. The world of work becomes a world of the curse.

Abandoned Temples
Sacred places as places of hidden revenge—is this possible?

Here is a man in whom the place of reciprocity has been occupied by the desire for revenge. He comes to the temple believing that he is holier than those who do not come, or even holier than those who are here next to him. He finds himself here to fight with the other and with the earth that has rebelled. He believes that the holy place is a source of supernatural powers that should be taken over and exploited in the fight. The grace God grants here is a variant of power. He builds his faith in God upon a deep lack of faith in the other human. He says, "I am not like them," when standing before the altar. Above all, he carries to the temple an awareness of pain and having been harmed. The peace and quiet of the temple allow him to once again concentrate his attention upon this pain. And he needs this. Thanks to the severity of the pain, his revenge appears to him as a work of justice. He begs God for strength in the fight. In the temple he draws power and justification for his advantage over the others.

Nietzsche described this type of faith as a "priestly vindictiveness." He writes,

> As we know, priests make the most evil of enemies—but why? Because they are the most powerless. Out of this powerlessness, their hate swells into something huge and uncanny to a most intellectual and poisonous level. The greatest haters in world history, and the most intelligent [*die geistreichsten Hasser*], have always been priests: nobody else's intelligence [*Geist*] stands a chance against the intelligence [*Geist*] of priestly revenge ... the Jews, that priestly people, which in the last resort was able to gain satisfaction from its enemies and conquerors only through a radical revaluation of their values, that is, through an act of the most deliberate revenge [*durch einen Akt der geistigsten Rache*]. Only this was fitting for a priestly people with the most entrenched priestly vengefulness.[58]

Condemnation is the expression of vengefulness. We throw the other human being into a situation of living without justification by condemning him, that is, into a justified nonexistence. The temple as a place of revenge becomes a tribunal of condemnations. Its altar is not a sacrificial altar where man offers himself to God, but a place where judgments against other people are realized. Here man gives birth to his own private "reprobates." There is no longer space for encounters. When modern man searches for God, he most likely seeks him outside the temple in a flight from the sight of man.

What happens to the stage of the human drama without sacred places? It becomes the earth of self-will. Here is a place where everything is permitted. "God is dead—everything is permitted to me." Man even threatens the earth with destruction. He does not feel guilt for destroying the earth, because he is convinced that he is destroying the land of exile.

Cemetery as a Seat of Specters
Is it possible to direct revenge against the dead? Yes, they can be denied a cemetery. The enemies who have fallen victim to revenge are denied a resting place. Their bodies are not put into graves, but instead are "thrown into pits," they are covered over, their traces erased, and forests are planted upon their graves. There is no trace of man anymore.

The renunciation of the dead as ancestors is another form of revenge. A luxurious tomb is built for the dead, but no heritage is taken over from them. This is usually connected to a specific ideology of progress. The achievements of the dead are what can be, and ought to be, disregarded in order to carry forward the history of the world. We leave it behind with contempt in our hearts. We find reasons to be proud of the achievements of modernity. We have no participation in any dignity of the ancestors . . .

What is the cemetery site now? It is a place of specters that frightens contemporaries. During dark suffocating nights, in dreams, in fevers—our killed ancestors return to us. They tell, in the voices of our consciences, about what we really are like. They repeat their truth that the "world is going to hell in a handbasket."

They arouse anxiety, increase fear, multiply desire, and stimulate the will to fight. Cemeteries become the seat of disturbing, historical specters. Here the specters, knowing the hearts of the living, accomplish the acts of their revenge. They do not kill, but they accuse and scoff. This forces the living to fight against cemeteries. The living, in their fight against cemeteries, believe that in this way they can liberate themselves from their own history.

Temptation of the World
The tree of the knowledge of good and evil found itself right in the middle of the paradisiacal garden, and upon it the forbidden fruit—the object of the first temptation. The whole of paradise was the promised land of man; only this tree and these fruits appeared as a denied land. Later, already after the Fall, the promised land distanced itself, and then the whole stage turned out to be foreign and hostile to man. It became a place of exile, a denied land. The metaphysical nostalgia after a paradise lost and looking for the ancient promised land will become the fate of man. This gives birth to the "temptation of the world."

The temptation of the world is an ur-word, whose meaning and power rest at the bottom of man's soul as his oldest heritage. The temptation of the world determines anew, as it were, the relationship of man to the earth: it changes the meaning of cultivating, putting it under the control of desire's logic. The desire for the earth is that power with whose help man attempts to overcome the fear emerging from the fact that he has found himself upon a denied land. The foundation for the temptation of the world is an archaic conviction about the refusal. Man experiences this situation of the world's temptation as the voice of the earth—the stage of his drama—a voice that encourages him to acknowledge what is forbidden as what is promised. Temptation is an attempt to promise to man what has been forbidden to him. Temptation as an act of promising is a moment—a blink of an eye. However, it is a moment that leaves a lasting trace in the form of a particular vision of the human lifeworld.

Temptation works by constructing through destruction—it awakens desire, it intensifies the pain of insatiability. The voice of temptation awakens desire. Desire is an action of questioning the inner truth of cultivation and its basic varieties—it is a quadruple *no*, as a consequence it changes the meanings of the human world's places. The fundamental *no* abolishes the idea of nature—from now on everything is a material for work, and work a way of saturating desires. Work changes its meaning and becomes a fight. In a world without nature there is no longer any place for a home, everywhere there are battlefields—past and future. The home changes into a hideout, into a castle, a smaller or larger fortress, serving to dominate others. There are also no workplaces that extract from nature what is best in it. Work becomes a form of enslavement and ruling, and workplaces slowly change into places of drudgery. Temples become deserted. The cemetery is the seat of ghosts of the past—evil spirits, which terrorize the living. The historical development of life becomes progress in the work of denigrating those who came before us. We climb upward by denigrating our ancestors. Slowly the difference between the stage and the man living upon the stage blurs. The earth has no nature and man has no nature. Animals do not have homes, cemeteries, and temples—man too. Man reaches the state in which he himself has not yet been created as a man in order to create everything anew.

The temptation of the world is built from this negation. Temptation through destruction constructs. The deeper the misery, the stronger becomes the voice of temptation, "You shall be as gods." Eve looks at the fruit and sees no evil in it. The fruit is as it is. It is beautiful and tasty. It is *for* man. Man becomes attached to what is upon this foreign land, even if it is only for a second *for* him. Temptation reaches out toward man through what is *for* man.

However, the essential source of evil does not lie upon the line of experiencing the world. The essence of temptation is who-with-whom-against-whom? The beginning of evil can be found upon the dialogical level. Its condition of possibility is the ability to reciprocate and take revenge. Faithfulness comes from reciprocity. The readiness to betray comes from revenge. All varieties of cultivating are the fruits of some faithfulness. The places of the world are also the fruits of faithfulness: home, workplace, temple, and cemetery. The destruction of these places is the result of reciprocity's end, that is, betrayal. In the most basic sense, evil—substantial evil, dialogical evil—manifests itself as betrayal.

What is betrayal?

A new horizon of reflection upon the mystery of evil opens up before us through this question. What is the meaning of betrayal? What is the temptation of betrayal? What is the logic of betrayal? The possibility for understanding betrayal seems to be a step toward the direction of a possibility for understanding the mystery of evil.

Around Devotion and Betrayal

Substantial evil does not come to man as violence, but as a possibility of choosing presented to man, based upon persuasion. Man must agree to evil, he has to choose evil himself. Only when he does this, can we say that evil has taken place. Certainly, the conditions of possibility of such a choice are important: man's freedom, the ability to make decisions, some degree of knowledge's imperfection, and sometimes weakness of the will. The totality of these conditions constitutes the ontological structure of man. This structure can be more or less perfect, but it is neither evil nor good. Seeing a lame man, short-sighted, invalid, we can say that misfortune has happened. However, we cannot say that evil has happened. Evil is not a reality of the ontological order, but the dialogical order. The beginnings of evil appear when somebody tempts someone else to evil, persuades him that evil is his good, where someone promises something to someone, and, through tempting guarantees his promise in some way. In short: evil as evil appears in the horizon of faithfulness and betrayal.

Besides the threat, temptation is the manner of evil's appearance. It has two semantic dimensions (I will remain silent about other dimensions, which are less important to us): the dimension of "toward what one is being tempted" and the dimension of "who tempts" (I pass over "whom it tempts" for now). That toward which temptation tempts is to be found somewhere in the world; temptation intertwines with powers that tie man to his world—with cultivating of the world, with striving toward becoming settled, enrooting, sanctification, and undertaking a tradition. The power of temptation becomes the power of a desire awakened in cultivating. The one who tempts is a different dimension of temptation. Who is the one who tempts? Who is the tempter? But let us first ask, What is at stake in this question? Certainly it is not about giving a sketch of the tempter's ontology, but about the question, Is he somebody worthy of faith or not? The tempter demands to be trusted. But, is it possible to have certainty at the beginning of the tempting that the tempter is wrong? Unfortunately, it is not possible to have this certainty. Everything takes place upon the plane of trust. Certainty comes only after the fall. Therefore, uncertainty is an element of temptation.

One thing seems to be beyond doubt: the experience of temptation is tied in a necessary manner with the experience of the problem of truth. The man touched by temptation poses a radical question: How is it really? The question touches several planes. Is the fruit that I see a forbidden fruit? Can it be evil since it is tasty and beautiful? If I pick it, will I be punished? The above questions are concerned with the stage of the world. Other questions are concerned with the dialogue partners: What does God promise, and what does the tempter promise? Who is trustworthy? Who is God and who is the tempter? If man knew the answers to these questions (or, at least to one of them), then there would be no temptation. Temptation makes a problem of the truth. The matter of the truth starts to be something important to man.

Let us still pause at the one who tempts. Whatever one might say, the act of tempting emerges from the horizon of some reciprocity. Temptation is not a command: do this or that. Somebody commanded something and ... washed their hands. There does not have to be any personal relationship between the one giving the command and the one executing it. Things are different between the one tempted and the tempter. Here, the matter of who-with-whom-against-whom emerges. Temptation brings out the question of reciprocity. Reciprocity is what tempts in the temptation. Man's temptation is the other man—possibly some other creature capable of reciprocity. Reciprocity expresses itself through dialogue. The main question of dialogue is this: Is the tempter credible? The question, "Is the fruit good or evil?" has a subordinate meaning.

After these preliminary remarks, let us turn to the phenomenological analysis of the phenomenon of temptation. Temptation is a dialogue, therefore it is a process. It has certain fixed elements and certain variables. Above all, the general horizon of the problem is stable: What is the truth and who-with-whom-against-whom? The persuading arguments are variable, and, above all, the picture of the tempter. I will once again use the famous scene from Shakespeare's *Richard III*, where the murderer Gloucester seduces the victimized Anne, in order to make all the moments of the described content as clear as possible. This scene is interesting, among other things, because the tempter appears before Anne at the beginning of the temptation as the embodiment of evil—he is a liar and murderer. Anne changes her initial judgment about him in the process of the temptation. The evil of the murderer becomes a problem for her. The end of the scene brings something like an acquittal of the criminal in Anne's eyes.

Let us turn our attention to the speech of temptation. The speech of temptation is a speech of flattery, of accusing the accusers, a call to verify whether evil is truly evil. Since it is a dialogue, temptation is always an invitation to deepen reciprocity—reciprocity in flattering, in accusing the accusers, in examining.

Flattery
Temptation is first a form of flattery. To flatter means to awaken the conviction that man is worthy of greater recognition and respect than the recognition and respect offered to him by those close to him. Flattery aims at transforming axiological convictions associated with the one being tempted, associated with his existing system of recognitions. He begins with "they are not right—they do not appreciate you." He adds, "You are more valuable than you think." Finally, "I only really appreciate you." So, at the very beginning of the temptation, there appears a new space of possible entrusting—a new who-with-whom-against-whom? But this change occurs stealthily, quietly, in the background of the conversation. The focus of attention is the underestimated value of the other. Gloucester says to Anne, "[You are a] sweet saint," you are an "angel" when you are "so angry." And adds, "divine perfection of a woman." This beauty leads to madness. Did anyone tell Anne this? Did Gloucester prove that it is so through his acts? And finally, what counts, "He lives that loves thee better than he could," he says, pointing to himself. A new space of possible entrusting opens up.

Flattery achieves its aims when it awakens some form of reciprocity. However, it must penetrate through the convictions of the one being tempted. To be convinced means to give a meaningful name to what remains unspecified on the margins of expression. Thanks to a meaningful name, the indeterminacy becomes specified. Conviction becomes specified and becomes perpetuated. The giving of a name strengthens the contents. Now the meaningful content can become the reasons for behaviors. But I did not reach my convictions by myself—the other strengthened and defined me. Whoever this other was, I must admit that at least in this instance he did not miss the mark. I must call him "my discoverer." And this is how reciprocity begins. I know thanks to him who I am, and he knows thanks to me that he is the discoverer of my truth. Just as I am not a random person, so he in the same measure is not a random person.

Ascetical literature says that *pride* is the source of evil in man. Pride is an axiological conviction that previous acts that recognize the individual value of man do not refer to the highest values that determine a man. All of these evaluations of his dignity are essentially a humiliation. Hence, the expectation of flattery. Pride is a source of evil because it is an opening up onto illusion regarding one's own value and connected to the lowering of the value of others. Pride also contains an expectation for adoration. To adore means to make an absolute value out of the other.

Accusing the Accusers
It is the fulfillment of the horizons outlined in flattery. But it contains something more: its own "philosophy of evil." Based upon this philosophy, the guilty become innocent and the innocent become guilty. The principle of interpretation is the thesis that evil is not evil but misfortune. Accusing the accusers can take various forms and has various reach. It does not always have to express itself in an unambiguous way. In the case of Gloucester and Anne's conversation, it took on an overt form, because it was tied to Gloucester's need for self-defense.

Who is the accused? The one tempted is the accused. The others, if there are any, play only subordinate roles. One must therefore deal with the tempted himself who sees the devil in the tempter. To accuse the accusers, one must use persuasion, appeal to the truth. The second and third moments of temptation go together hand in hand.

Let us look at verification and then come back to the accusation.

Eve looks at the fruit in the biblical paradise and does not see the prohibition in it. The fruit is tasty and beautiful. The fruit itself encourages consumption. But, effectively it is the same as any other fruit in paradise. Gloucester killed. He killed a noble man. A noble man left the vale of tears and went to heaven. Here you also *cannot see* any evil. What follows from that? It at least follows that on the basis of previous experience it is impossible to determine who is right. There is a need for further experience. But further experience means to succumb to temptation. Verification is also reciprocity. You see a tasty fruit and I see it. You see beauty and I see it. Therefore, we have a common point of view on the matter.

Let us return to the accusing of the accusers. Here it is said, "The evil I have done in the world is not my, but rather your, fault." Anne herself is the cause of Gloucester's crime:

> Your beauty was the cause of that effect;
> Your beauty: which did haunt me in my sleep

Gloucester hands Anne a sword and encourages her to execute the sentence that she issued against him at the moment where the dramatic tension of the dialogue reaches its peak:

> Nay, do not pause; for I did kill King Henry,
> But 'twas thy beauty that provoked me.
> Nay, now dispatch; 'twas I that stabb'd young Edward,
> But 'twas thy heavenly face that set me on.

However, Anne is not up to the task of delivering the blow.

What does the interpretation of evil contained in this accusation consist in? As I already said, upon transforming evil into misfortune. The damages done by evil are similar to the damages caused by flood, lightning, and earthquakes. Anne's beauty leads to madness. Gloucester went mad because of her beauty. Anne is his absolute. He wants to be by her, he wants to be possessed by her, and so to possess her in this manner. An obstacle appeared on the way to this goal—Anne's husband. Is it any wonder that a flooded river breaks this obstacle? Who is at fault? If Gloucester is at fault, then Anne is also at fault. Her fault lies in her very existence. However, it would be absurd to say that Anne is guilty because she does not want the crime. In that case Gloucester would also be without fault. The moment when they met is unfortunate. Evil is a misfortune.

However, accusing the accusers can have a different meaning. It is not about substituting the concept of evil with the concept of misfortune, but about showing that there is no difference between the axiological level of the one tempted and the tempter. Deep down we are all the same. All virtue is the semblance of virtue. When man succumbs to temptation, he reveals what he really is. To succumb to temptation means to vindicate oneself. Shakespeare's text does not exclude such an interpretation of the dialogue, but it also does not impose it. Therefore, it is better to reach for an example somewhere else—in the texts of Nietzsche in which he deals with Christian morality. His discourse is an example of accusing the accusers.

Nietzsche believes that the Christian idea of a heroic love of enemies is a symptom of the desire for vengeance against those who once were victors over Israel. Unable to overcome their enemies upon the battlefield, they strive to overcome them upon the field of ethical convictions. He writes:

> But *that* is what happened: from the trunk of the tree of revenge and hatred, Jewish hatred—the deepest and most sublime, indeed a hatred which created ideals and changed values, the like of which has never been seen on earth—there grew something just as incomparable, a *new love*, the deepest and most sublime kind of love: and what other trunk could it have grown out of? ... But don't make the mistake of thinking that it had grown forth as a denial of the thirst for revenge, as the opposite of Jewish hatred! No, the reverse is true! This love grew out of the hatred, as its crown, as the triumphant crown expanding ever wider in the purest brightness and radiance of the sun, the crown which, as it were, in the realm of light and height, was pursuing the aims of that hatred, victory, spoils, seduction with the same urgency with which the roots of that hatred were burrowing ever more thoroughly and greedily into everything that was deep and evil.[59]

Love of enemies appears here as a substitute for revenge. Revenge is not about killing but about humiliating—depriving of respect and a sense of dignity. However, it means that there is no significant difference between a Christian and a pagan. And if there is one, then it is to the pagan's advantage. At least the pagan does not lie.

However, I said above that the proper goal of temptation is not making changes upon the world's stage, for example, picking the forbidden fruit, but a radical change in the area of entrustments. In picking the fruit, we betray someone and entrust ourselves to someone else. The subject of temptation emerges from temptation—a mysterious *somebody* who promises something new. Who is this somebody?

Such a question is accurately answered by the scene from Shakespeare cited above. At first the perpetrator of the temptation is the embodiment of all evil—Gloucester, almost a demon. Then the experience of the demonic dissipates somewhere in the fog and there remains only a man—a man who is deeply unhappy. The significant role in this process of "dissipating" is played by the very truthfulness of Gloucester. Because Gloucester begins by professing the truth, Anne is amazed and exclaims, "O wonderful, when devils tell the truth!" We encounter something here that is crucial for the theory of evil. In the initial experience, evil has a substantial character: he (the other) *is* evil. Evil exists through the existence of a man, it directly defines his substance. In the final experience, evil reveals itself as an illusion rooted in the imperfection of human existence—the human substance is good, and the evil that results from it is only the confluence of unfortunate circumstances. Between these extreme experiences we find another one: evil is a specter that tempts, calls to cooperation, argues, suggests decisions, and sets the course of action. Who then is this mysterious tempter? He is first given as an "evil substance," later as the perpetrator of specters, until he finally appears as an ordinary unfortunate wretch.

The paradox is that these three experiences do not exclude each other. The tempter has a changing visage. He is evil and good, happy and unhappy, faithful and treacherous—all at the same time. He is indeterminate. But not only this. At some point in the drama his experience of destitution starts to dominate. The tempter suffers. He is alone in his suffering. Everybody has condemned him, cursed him. The tempter tempts because he desires reciprocity. Nobody has ever gotten up the courage for engaging in reciprocity with the tempter. In this way the tempter calls to bravery, to love, to the ability for sacrifice, to compassion. The act of reciprocity for which he pleads appears in this context as an act that can tear him away from his volatility, strengthen him in the good, and constitute his authentic I. The essential force of temptation is the promise that thanks to an act of sacrifice he, the tempter, will let himself be saved. Succumbing to temptation becomes a saving action in the eyes of the tempted, saving a poor being from its misery.

Only now comes the key moment-verification. Previously, it was not known whether the temptation was a temptation, or the promise of some good, "You shall be like God, knowing good and evil." Gloucester also promises—promises himself, his love, and indirectly assuagement of the storm that is in him. The tempter, in promising, guarantees with himself what he promises. His guarantee is the road toward a new future. The system of entrustments will change in the new future. The tempted will rely on the tempter, and vice versa. They will be together in sickness and in health. Eve believes in the guarantee given. So does Anne. At this moment the evil reaches its fullness. The moment of verification comes in a moment. Will the tempter uphold what he promised? The tempter does not grab the outstretched hand. The tempter betrays. He urged betrayal and now, when he has achieved it, he himself betrays. The final sense of the whole drama is unveiled. What appeared to be a promise of the good now turns out to be temptation. The essence of the human drama becomes apparent: to sacrifice yourself in vain. The goal of temptation is to lead to a meaningless sacrifice. A meaningless sacrifice is the high point of the drama—a drama beginning from some betrayal and ending with betrayal. The betrayers, while searching for reciprocity, have been betrayed themselves.

What happens now? Now fate runs in two directions. The night of evil comes. Somewhere toward the end of the night you can hear the weeping of an angel—a symbol of the renewal of the promise.

The night of evil is a night in which everything is engulfed by mockery. Mockery does not have an aesthetic character here, but a metaphysical one. The true principle of being is to be shown through mockery: being is based upon meaninglessness. The meaninglessness of existence is based upon the good having to perish in its clash with evil. Even more: the good exists only to be the victim of evil. Naïve people succumb to temptations thinking that they can remedy something through their sacrifices. Gloucester says after Anne leaves:

Was ever woman in this humour woo'd?
Was ever woman in this humour won?

And further on:

> Having God, her conscience, and these bars against me,
> And I nothing to back my suit at all,
> But the plain devil and dissembling looks,
> And yet to win her, all the world to nothing!
> Ha! . . .
> . . . And will she yet debase her eyes on me,
> That cropp'd the golden prime of this sweet prince,
> And made her widow to a woful bed?
> On me, whose all not equals Edward's moiety?
> On me, that halt and am unshapen thus?

How little is needed for a man to betray—that is the meaning of mockery. Is it really not much? All of this looks different from Anne's side, who followed the path of the promise of the good. The murder of her husband deprived her of hope. To a person deprived of hope there comes a promise of reciprocity and the possibility of taming a monster. Anne knows not what she does. What she knows is not what she truly does. Maybe she is not concerned with salvation? Maybe she also succumbs to desire? In that case, she all the more exposes herself to mockery.

The "weeping of an angel" is a metaphor describing sorrow over the crisis of the good whose fate in this world was determined by freedom. This weeping is, above all, a witness to the existence of the good. What does it say? It says that whoever succumbs to temptation is not fundamentally evil. A flame of good desires burns in his heart. But it is not enough. The flame is too weak. The tragedy is that freedom turns itself against the good. How little is needed for so much to undergo destruction! But the weeping of the angel is something more than only weeping. This weeping is an expression of an order that is different than the order of betrayal and evil. It does not have common ground with evil. It is *wholly other*. This is why it is untouchable for evil. It exists as light, as glory, as a pure space of hope. From the bosom of this order there once came, after the expulsion from paradise, a new Promise. The New Promise is the opposite of the first temptation. It is addressed to the traitors who have been betrayed. Thanks to it the traitor who has been betrayed regains some hope.

Neighboring the Demonic
But have the analyses carried out so far led us to more fundamental experiences of evil? Let us consider this. Temptation reveals evil as something external in relation to man. Man must come out of himself, must reach for evil, assimilate it, and only then does he become evil. We similarly experience evil as a source of fear. It also is external to man. The external situation of evil is stressed by some symbols of evil—the symbol of a stain, symbol of a burden, the symbol of enslavement in a foreign land. The externality of evil means that man is fundamentally good, that evil can indeed be in him, but is not from him. But these are not the only symbols of evil. It is sometimes said that hate is the symbol of evil, or even evil itself. Hatred is not external to man, it is in him. Evil given as hatred is not the source of temptation, nor a source of fear. Hatred does not tempt and it does not frighten. Hatred pulls in. Why do I hate? Because I must hate. Hatred expresses itself with a stance of revenge. Why revenge? Because it must be so. Hatred pulls in, generating a kind of joy, consent, and recognition. Thus, we have before us one additional type of experience of evil—evil in the power to pull in.

The hatred that pulls in proclaims that in the beginning was hatred. Everything that has come into being, came into being from hatred. Even love exists exclusively in order to serve hatred.

Evil pulls in. These words point to something that is in us a point of accepting evil. The call of evil echoes in our soul. There is a space within us that makes possible such an echoing. In every moment we can join the procession of those who hate for no reason.

What does evil pull us into? Evil pulls into betrayal. Betrayal is the fruit of hatred. It is hatred placed upon the dialogical plane. Only the one who knows what faithfulness is can betray. Why does a being that knows what faithfulness is betray? But is the question, "Why?" appropriate here? It assumes that evil has a logical structure. Do they who betray, betray for betrayal itself? Possibly. Nonetheless, they justify their betrayal somehow. They rationalize it. As if they wanted to reveal its meaning. When we ask, "Why?" we have precisely this in mind: to grasp a way of justifying betrayal through betrayal itself, hatred through hatred itself, evil through evil itself.

What does it mean to betray?

It means something more than just not being faithful. It means to first promise faithfulness and then to betray. Faithfulness demands reciprocity. It possesses a dialogical structure, like a question and answer. Betrayal also has a dialogical structure—it is like a false answer to an honest question. It is not betrayal to not answer a question, or to answer a question that was not posed. We speak of misunderstanding in such instances. Gloucester promises Anne a love greater than all her previous loves. He promises a greater faithfulness with the same. He ends his promising with betrayal. Anne also betrays, above all, the memory of her murdered husband. The evil she prepared for others falls upon Anne. Why did Anne betray? We know this: she was tempted by an illusion of the good. But why did Gloucester betray?

Two directions for exploration are drawing themselves out. One can consider the relation of evil to evil and say that man always commits the sort of evil that seems lesser—fleeing from the greater evil. This explanation is based upon the logic of emotions: the lesser fear must give way to the greater one. Another explanation points to specifically axiological relations. Betrayal is the refusal to justify the existence of another man, undertaken in the name of the conviction that I myself exist in an existence that is not justified. I betray because I was betrayed. Let us consider both of these directions for reflection.

Deafening Pain
The following text of Nietzsche's contains an explanation based upon the emotional side of experiencing evil:

> For every sufferer instinctively looks for a cause of his distress; more exactly, for a culprit, even more precisely for a *guilty* culprit who is receptive to distress,—in short, for a living being upon whom he can release his emotions, actually or in effigy, on some pretext or other: because the release of emotions is the greatest attempt at relief, or should I say, at *anaesthetizing* on the part of the sufferer, his involuntarily longed-for narcotic against pain of any kind. In my judgment, we find here the actual physiological causation of *ressentiment*, revenge and their ilk, in a yearning, then, to *anaesthetize pain through emotion*—for this, one needs an emotion, the wildest possible emotion and, in order to arouse it, the first available pretext . . . the attempt is made to

anaesthetize a tormenting, secret pain that is becoming unbearable with a more violent emotion of any sort, and at least rid the consciousness of it for the moment.... The sufferers, one and all, are frighteningly willing and inventive in their pretexts for painful emotions; they even enjoy being mistrustful and dwelling on wrongs and imagined slights: they rummage through the bowels of their past and present for obscure, questionable stories that will allow them to wallow in tortured suspicion, and intoxicate themselves with their own poisonous wickedness—they rip open the oldest wounds and make themselves bleed to death from scars long-since healed, they make evil-doers out of friend, wife, child and anyone else near to them. "I suffer: someone or other must be guilty"—and every sick sheep thinks the same.[60]

To put it more precisely, this text is concerned with two matters: the silencing of one pain with the help of another pain and about a particular justification of pain with the suspicion that "someone or other must be guilty." However, the need for silence is stronger here. The justification is something secondary, not developed to the end and most likely incapable of being developed, because the falsity inherent in it becomes too apparent at the moment of articulation. Is it really the case that someone must be guilty? Should I really, a bypasser met by chance, be at fault? It is a different matter altogether with silencing. We introduce into ourselves a great deal of noise thanks to which it is impossible to hear another noise. From a small evil, from a small suffering and pain we make a great evil, great pain, and great suffering, so that we put the truly great evil beyond the scope of our attention. The man who is threatened with dying concentrates his attention upon a headache. It is not about attention itself, but about a whole way of being a man. The Polish colloquial language knows the word "tragicizing" well. Man tragicizes his small drama in order to run away from his real tragedy in this way.

The need for silencing indicates that in the depths of man there lies some evil. It is not a stain, nor a weight, nor exile—it is a word that means something. A word that means something speaks within man. Only speech is something that can be silenced. The word of evil is an evil word living in man. It has some meaning. However, silencing does not connect with the meaning of that word, but exclusively with its sound. The noise does not permit the sound, but it leaves the meaning untouched. This is why silencing is not the appropriate response to evil.

Evil Pulls In

The evil word in man is a word that is *badly spoken* and at the same time *speaks evil*. The word that speaks acts. It brings to the surface what is bad in man, what is bad in what surrounds man, and strives to make man a specter, placing him among specters. To be a specter means to exist in an exiled land, not having the right to exist. The meaning of this experience is summed up in the words "he exists in a betrayed existence." I am a betrayed being. Everything that I experience here confirms the truth about betrayal. The serpent put me to the test in paradise, therefore I was not trusted. The land grows thistles and thorns, therefore I live in a denied land. A home is impossible upon a denied land, as is a temple. My brother threatens me with death in order to enslave me. Life hurts me: cold, hot, tiredness, misunderstandings with others. I am *condemned* to life like a traitor. The condemnation took place before the betrayal. I would not be a traitor if not for the condemnation.

In the bosom of the consciousness of the "I am betrayed," there lies a hidden valuation, "It would have been better had I not been born." It is better not to exist, than exist in a betrayed existence. This conviction contains a general meaning, which concerns not only me, but all existing in a betrayed existence. My individual truth has a general meaning. This obliges that it be proclaimed to the four winds. All the betrayed should hear it, that is, all people. But how to proclaim the truth about betrayal so that it might become convincing? There is one way: to commit betrayal oneself. I tempt someone to betrayal, because I have been betrayed; I am betrayed, therefore I betray. In this way, evil itself takes place along with the truth about evil. It is not enough to proclaim evil, it must be realized.

Here we come across the peculiar logic of evil. Evil pulls in more than it tempts. It pulls in by provoking.

It would be an absurdity if evil would destroy something that is already destroyed. The beautiful, good, and true are a provocation for evil. Anne is beautiful and faithful. Anne exists in a justified existence. Her very beauty and her faithfulness justify her. Whoever faces beauty does not ask, Why does beauty exist? Beauty itself is the reason for beauty's existence. Gloucester is the opposite of what is in Anne—he is a murderer and monster. Looking at him we ask, Why does he exist? Existence is not self-explanatory; the existence of evil is incomprehensible. Anne's beauty and faithfulness are a provocation for Gloucester. The battle between Anne and Gloucester is a battle between the one who thinks existence a curse and the one who thinks it a blessing. Gloucester takes revenge as his fate. Anne believes in herself. She trusts in the power of the beauty and goodness that she incarnates. Gloucester must question this faith. This is why he pulls her into betrayal and then betrays her.

The voice of mockery resounds. Mockery is the laughter that goes through the world proclaiming the failure of the good. Here is what has happened: he betrayed and was betrayed. There are no longer any saints upon the land of exile. The saints also betray. Nobody regrets anyone. Anne deserved her fate. The demons breathe a sigh of relief. Finally things are like they really are. Let us betray! Let us betray because we were betrayed. The gift of existence is a betrayal.

My intention was and remains the explanation of the mystery of the encounter—more precisely, the impossibility of the encounter upon the plane of evil. The rationale of this impossibility is clear: the encounter is impossible because the plane of evil is a plane of betrayal. The encounter and betrayal are not compatible. There is nothing revealing in this explanation. I am only repeating a truth that everybody knows. Nevertheless, the path of explaining this truth turned out to be immeasurably interesting and fruitful. What we have managed to see along it puts the ontological philosophy of evil in a wholly new light. This philosophy, as we know, considers evil through the prism of the category of being. That which is good is—insofar as it exists. When some lack appears in being—something that should be there as a property or quality—evil will also occur. Here evil is essentially identified with an illusion. This falsifies the whole problem from the very beginning.

Evil is neither a being, nor a nonbeing—it is a phenomenon; more precisely, it is a *specter*, which frightens and tempts. We count evil in the general category of phenomena. This does not mean that we trivialize it in this manner. It is not important how evil exists, but what it wants. When we say it is a specter, we do not push the matter too far.

In fact, we still stand with one leg in ontology. We must abandon ontology in order to touch the essence without regard for the paradoxes that will result from it. Our key ascertainment is that evil is beyond being and nonbeing—it is transcendent in a radical sense. There is no sense in asking whether evil exists. There is no sense in asking whether there is no evil. Evil is given as a meaning. Also, the good is given as a meaning. Being and nonbeing are derivative of meaning. When we describe good and evil with categories that emerge from the concept of being or nonbeing, we do not hit the essence of its sense.

We have considered evil here on two planes: in relation to the world-stage and in relation to the other (man).

In some not entirely strict sense, it is possible to say that, on the level of the relation to the world, evil is similar to nonbeing. It appears as destruction. Evil destroys. What does it destroy? It destroys places—homes, workplaces, temples—and profanes cemeteries. The beginning of the destruction lies in a change of the stance toward cultivation: cultivation transforms itself into desire. The striving toward riches, toward having, is a symptom of desire. But not every destruction is an evil. The analogy between evil and destruction limps. Man eats bread and destroys it in this way, but there is nothing evil in this. Evil that appears as the destruction of *places* is an evil because it is turned against someone. Destruction is an act of revenge. Therefore, evil is determined by the invisible sense of action, not only by the visible results. This sense points toward dialogue. Therefore, we must take a step back and search deeper for evil, at the very sources of destruction—at the source of the stance of revenge.

Revenge is the opposite of reciprocity. Both revenge and reciprocity are projects of dialogical living together with the other. Above all, they characterize the project of that living together, therefore they are directed toward the future. This does not exclude a reference to the past, thus to man's ancestors. By reaching into the past, this project takes up reciprocity or denies reciprocity for the future. The project of living together is a project of meaning. Reciprocity constitutes meaning and revenge constitutes meaning. In order to explain the genesis of meaning, one must pose the question about the conditions of its possibility. Thanks to such a question we also touch upon the conditions for the possibility of evil. We are not taking Kant's road, because our concern is still the dialogical sense.

We must once again stress what has been already highlighted: evil does not want to present itself as an absurdity. The drive toward rationalization comes from the very essence of evil. Evil wants to be rational, justified, and grounded. Only misfortunes are accidents, while evil wants to present itself as a logical chain. This can be seen both in the threat and in the temptation. Evil frightens, there revealing fear's rationale. Evil tempts, revealing the rationale of the promise. It is not a precise judgment to say that evil—in order to tempt—must always reveal itself under the guise of the good. Only in temptation does evil don a mask of the good. On the other hand, in every instance, therefore both in the threat and in pulling in—and obviously also in tempting—evil reveals itself as the truth. "That's the truth," proclaims the mocker, pointing toward the just one, who has betrayed and was betrayed. The striving toward rationalizing evil—its justification—obviously cannot reveal itself in a place other than in the consciousness of the tempter. The evil that justifies itself no longer presents itself as an illusion, but as a type of phenomenon—as a frightening and tempting specter.

The logic of evil's self-justification has a particular character. It is based upon the axiology of revenge. Its starting point is an existential-axiological experience: I am—I am betrayed. The sign of betrayal can be my fallibility, my illness, my ugliness, the hatred of those surrounding me, and so on. Betrayal has an archaic sense. It is more radical than the circumstances that call it up from forgetfulness. They bring a wound into the open in which there rests the pain that appears in all other pains. I was given existence on a trial basis. But to give something to someone on a trial basis means that I do not trust them. Therefore, my existence is the fruit of a lack of trust, a fruit of betrayal. I am here upon a denied land. I have the right to revenge. "But what is this revenge for?" someone might ask. So that the truth is let out into the open.

The meaning of the following words is cleared up along the way: this person is evil. Why the word "is"? Does such a deep tie occur between man and evil for us to be able to say "*is* evil"? We make a mistake imagining that evil is similar to paint, which colors the figure of a man from the outside. It is not the case that evil comes to man. Rather, it is that man emerges from the horizon of evil—man comes from the interior of evil as some emissary of a specter. We say, "An evil man is an emissary of hell." This is profound. Hell is a power whose executors are people. The evil *is* in the executors. The barbarian carries the fire that destroys homes. The murderer destroys lives. The one who desires limitless riches destroys nature. Revenge causes the emptying out of churches and profanes cemeteries. The betrayer destroys every love directed toward him. There is evil in all of them. Not as a lack, but as a positive force—the force of revenge for an archaic betrayal. But, at the same time, their destruction carries something that boasts for itself a pretense to a metaphysical truth: everybody is betrayed, all are condemned, everybody has the right to kill and betray all.

The recourse to the truth, to logic, to some reason, at the same time marks out some boundaries for evil. The classical theory of evil tied evil to a lack in being. We do not hold this theory here, but it is not totally meaningless. It means that for the negative meaning to appear, the positive sense must come forth. More precisely: evil, in order to act, must have recourse to some good. The threat is only a threat where there appears the possibility of losing some values—goods. Evil took on a mask of truth in temptation. The most direct experience of evil, expressed in the need for betrayal, is based upon the acknowledged value of the truth. Thus, evil reveals itself as a shadow, the good as the light. If not for the light there would be no shadows. Mockery can never really be truly radical. It wants, at the very least, that someone hear it. It is directed toward someone who is open to the truth from the beginning. In this manner, the one who does evil still seeks reciprocity, that is, the possibility of an encounter.

CHAPTER 4

Space for Being-with the Other

The theory of knowledge of another human being continually finds itself in the situation of a certain impasse. We are witnesses to a growing interest in the question of experiencing and knowing the other human being. The source of this increase is both a social-civilizational threat to human existence and the need to find the basis for the theory and practice of communication. The growth in interest pulls in its wake not only the multiplication of particular results, but also a sharpening of the awareness about their limitations. Sociology, psychology, but especially psychiatry provide many detailed results regarding interpersonal relations. At the same time, these discoveries lack the ordering that science usually owes to philosophy. Drowning in a flood of particulars, we do not know the road that leads from the knowledge of particulars to understanding the whole.

The dominant need for synthesis flows from this. The following question arises: Where should we search for the basis of the synthesis? A synthesis cannot be the result of an arbitrary decision, but instead should emerge from within the phenomenon under investigation, that is, the very essence of the phenomenon of coming to know and understanding a human being. What is the leading factor that synthesizes all the possible cognitions of others?

When searching for the answer to this question, we first direct ourselves toward the phenomenon of language. Our choice is not dictated by anything more than the supposition that if in coming to know (more precisely: in a cognitive being-with) the other there is some internal logic, if we are not condemned to chance here, if this knowledge emerges from something and strives toward something, then this should be reflected upon the plane of the language that we use, describing in a prescientific manner the results of these cognitive being-withs with the other. Whatever language might be, and whatever the relations between it and experience might be, we ought not pass over the givens of language. After all, one of the basic, if not to say "banal," phenomena of language tied to the knowledge of man by man is the fact of "introducing oneself" to the other. To "introduce oneself" to the other means to speak directly about who one is.

The act of introducing oneself is not a typical result of the growth of interpersonal experiences, it is not a generalization of them. Admittedly, it cannot occur without some experience, but it is a decisive ascension *above* experience. Furthermore, it is supposed to reveal the *true sense* of experience, and mark out for the other the further direction of its interpretation. When I say, "I am a teacher," not only do I lead the other beyond the previous repertoire of his experiences about me, but I also turn his attention toward those experiences that in the future will be decisive for recognizing who I am. The act of introducing oneself is an act of a true objectification of oneself; I make myself into an *object* and I am showing myself as an *object*. But every object is an object in some world, in some space. What kind of world and what kind of space is the condition for an act of introducing oneself? What structure must this space have for such an introduction to be meaningful?

Therefore, our interests are focusing upon elementary language phenomena connected with the idea of knowing the other. The first task we pose for ourselves is the semantic analysis of meanings. (Only at a few points, when it becomes necessary, will we attempt to point to their experiential bases. Basically, we will leave them for another study, a study of the phenomenological bases of the semantics of being-with the other.) As a result of studying language, we will attempt to gain an insight into the phenomenon that in our need for a synthesis will prove to be crucial, something that we will call "the space of cognitive being-with the other." The *a priori* organization of this space is the basis of all possible judgments of *what man is*. But the space of cognitions and being-withs does not owe this organization to itself. The organization is the result, as will become apparent, of an experience that is more fundamental than the experience of space—it comes from the experience of *values*. Thus, our need for a synthesis will lead us through linguistic phenomena and through experience of space toward elementary axiological data. Without considering the axiological dimension of human existence, the understanding of this existence is not, it seems, possible. At the same time as values sculpt interpersonal space, they also open and close man before the other man.

I will say a few words about the starting point of the research before we undertake our problem.

By following the example of Daniel Christoff's indispensable simplification, we can divide all the best-known conceptions of the cognitive being-with the other into two groups, depending on what they consider to be the appropriate starting point for research.[1] Some, for example Husserl, judge that the proper starting point for research is the subjective activity of the knowing subject, in particular the consciousness of the transcendental ego, worldless, constituting the meaning of the world and the meaning of the other as a being similar to me, which exists in this world. Such a starting point for research guarantees the apodicticity, that is, indubitability of the results. With this type of decision the theory of knowledge is paired to a specific concept of the other. The other man appears here as another-I, in the sense of *alter ego*: at first we have being-with ourselves, with our I, and then, following the knowledge about the I contained in this being-with, we recognize the other as a Thou (I-other). I know that the other is the *other*, because I know that *I am*. But others, for example Max Scheler, Martin Buber, Gabriel Marcel, hold the opposite opinion. The Thou is not other-I, but rather my-I is an other-Thou. At the origins of the consciousness of the I lies the presence of the Thou, or maybe even the presence of a more general We. Only in dialogue, in dispute, in opposition, and also in the pursuit of a new community there comes about consciousness of my I as an independent being, separate from the other. I know that *I am* because I know that the *other is*. The starting point of the research should mirror the direction of egotic genesis.

How is it possible to step beyond the sketched-out opposition?

We proposed here, as a theme, the analysis of the act of introducing oneself along with the whole context that makes this act possible. It is thanks to it that we can go beyond the opposition of both starting points. At the same time, with it we give expression to a fundamental truth, to the truth learned, which is the condition of the possibility for this going beyond and is concerned with the difference between cognitive being-with the other and cognitive being-with an object, with a thing. What kind of truth is at stake? In what way does it make possible the overcoming of the sketched out oppositions?

The difference between man's relation to things, to an object, and a cognitive being-with of man with man is based upon—without going into further details—the fact that the known object (thing) does not have consciousness of being known, whereas the known man can have such a consciousness. For objects, the truth of their existence is not a problem, meanwhile for a man it is the basic question of his life. Hence, the knowing of objects and things is tied with specific forms of dominating things: in order to come to know a thing, one must use power to manipulate the thing, experiment, disassemble it, and then again put it back together, often destroying it. The manipulation of things is not incidental to knowing them, but is the result of the very essence of the knowing stance toward things. Meanwhile, the knowing of a man must run its course differently from the very beginning. Even when it is conducted on the basis of objectified models, as in, for example, experimental psychology, it must acknowledge the existence of a boundary for the applicability of these models. The other is himself conscious that he is being studied, watched, observed, being known, he is one who can adjust himself to this watching and being known, who being subject to the demands of truth can open up or close up before the knower, who can also confront the knowledge gained about him with his own internal experience. A characteristic trait of the cognitive being-with the other should be, according to Marcel, the stance expressed by the words "let the other be." This stance is free from the pursuit of dominance and manipulation. It is characterized by striving toward dialogue "on equal terms" (Kępiński). This excludes the uncritical transference of objective and thing-oriented models onto the field of cognitive being-with the other.

Therefore, the starting point occupied by us repeats the route of neither the "transcendental I" (from I to Thou) nor the "genetic objectivism" (from Thou to I). We propose here an intermediate route, which is expressed by the formula "I know that you understand me, therefore we are." In this way we respect the rationales of the first and second stance, while at the same time avoiding their extremes. Taking into account the experience "I know that . . . ," we come from the apodictic givens of reflection (Husserl). However, we do not lose the opposite stance. The consciousness of "we are" awakens in dialogue with the other, in a confrontation of gazes and in dispute, but at the same time in pursuing agreement in which initiative and insight frequently comes from the other.

This question requires further analysis. Here we will only say what is indispensable.

"I know that you understand me . . ." In the final analysis, consciousness (knowledge) that I was understood is within me, is my knowledge about myself and about the relation of the other to me. I find within myself the criterion of whether I have been, or not been, understood. The understood proposition comes from the other, but the act of recognizing it as the truth comes from me. Things cannot be otherwise, since it concerns me. The act of recognition makes it so that it gains the value of a truth obligating me and everyone else. However, the role of the other cannot be completely eliminated. It is not just that the other poses questions, directs my attention, or maybe even proposes a word of understanding. It is more important that the other *confirms* within me my reason and my truth. He acknowledges in this way that what was within me, as my personal value, also possesses a universal character and participates in a more general intelligibility. The result of such being-with the other is not only a particular "cognitive result" but an "existential event" that creates a unique interpersonal tie, which is a permanent acquisition of the self-consciousness of a man.

The act of introducing oneself, if it is carried out freely and without mendacity (and this is what we are concerned with here), is an integral ingredient of dialogue, and that is how it should be treated theoretically. It emerges from me as a proposition addressed directly to the other. This proposition has the character of a reasonable proposition: I tell the other how I understand myself and expect that the other will understand me in the same way. I assume that I know who I am. I assume that the other does not know about this, but desires to know it. In introducing myself I respond to his expectation. With this goal in mind, I give him my name and add on who I am, "I am a teacher," "I am a doctor," "I am a student." Who I am creates a distinct plane of being-withs between the other and me: I am a teacher, doctor, student *for* the other and toward the other. I did not make myself into who I am, instead it was accomplished because of the presence of the other. By introducing myself I expect that the other will recognize in me who I am, and will believe that I am also ready to recognize in him who he is. The relation of the mutual recognition creates the possibility of a mutual understanding.

Function of the Name

By introducing myself to the other, I tell him what my name is, or my first and last name. The basic function of the name is indicating that a man is an individual. The Polish language achieves this result thanks to the combination of a first and last name. Let us skip over considering all the aspects of this combination, and let us remain by the indicating alone. The name most frequently does not have any meaning, and, in any case, meaning is not important here. Its essence is an intentional directional factor,[2] thanks to which it points toward a concrete man and so makes possible his identification within time and space.

The view that nothing substantial can be known from and about a man through his name has become generally established.[3] And so knowing the name of a man does not at all mean knowing a man. When I give someone my name, I am not aware whether I unveil before the other what (who) I am. Nonetheless, giving one's name fulfills a momentous and irrefutable role in the process of revealing oneself. "When suffering comes," writes Thomas Merton somewhere, "and asks what your name is, one has to be able to give one's name." To capture the role of the name in being-with the other, it is enough to focus upon cases where we either give someone a "false name" or even wholly refrain from giving him our name. We usually do this to "not be recognized." The other will maybe have the opportunity to come to know our appearance, character, or temperament, but it seems to us that he will not truly know us without knowing our name.

What meaning hides within the act of giving one's name to the other?

Basically, only man possesses a name (here we disregard the names of God). Animals or things do not have names. The names of animals are names similar to the names of cities, countries, or things. Only the one who can recognize himself in his name can possess a name. Man possesses a name because he knows himself in his name and identifies himself through his name. This is why he can give his name to the other and introduce himself in this way.

What does the intentional directional factor of the name point toward? We said that it points toward the human individual. But if it only pointed toward that, then the name would not at all differ from individual names. The directional factor of the name brings to light a particular axiological moment that determines human existence, which I have called the *axiological-I*.[4] The axiological-I does not possess any general content, but possesses its own *dignity*, it is a *value*. The name that brings to light the presence in man of the axiological-I also gains some value through this function. In a certain sense it stands in the place of the man it describes. We feel touched whenever somebody overuses our name. We speak to each other by our names only when our acquaintance has reached a certain degree of intimacy. The man who utters for the first time the name of the person he loves experiences something like an initiation.

The cognitive function of the name does not depend only upon it making identification possible. The name brings to light the presence of an individual human value and—being a kind of beginning of an initiation—accomplishes the opening before men of a particular horizon of meaning in the frames of which there can develop a further cognitive communion of man with man. In communing with the other through his name, we free ourselves from the pressure of reifying models and we enter into the rich world of uniquely human values. The opening up of a horizon does not yet constitute knowledge. But without it, knowledge would not be possible. Just as the first sounds of music "open the horizon" of listening to a piece, as the first observations of the appearance of trees "open the horizon" for further observation, so does the giving of the name open up a particular horizon of meaning for the further communion with the other. The encounter with the name is the encounter with some *promise*. Only man can make a promise.

This horizon of meaning opened up by the name (or its substitute) we will call here the name "horizon of meaning." It outlines the totality of all possible knowing communions of man with man from the side of sense, meaning. This horizon contains all possible determinations thanks to which the relations of man with man are possible to express within a given level of language development. Every human gesture, every step leading from man and to man, every sign conveyed to man, and every word about man owes its meaning to belonging to a whole constituted by the general name "horizon of meaning." This horizon marks out the direction of our communion with the other even before we encounter him. Communions beyond the name horizon are actually possible, and even very frequent, but they are not "human communions." While listening to a concert, we can, beyond the horizon of the piece being performed, hear the murmur of the street, just as here beyond the name horizon we can "be aware" of the existence of people without communing with them cognitively and in a human way.

In the field of the name horizon of meaning we ought to distinguish two types of meanings for names. Some define generally who man is and what he is capable of. The others define the possible relations of man with man. The first are part of the concept of man in the abstract, while the second define the structure of interpersonal space of communion.

We will call "abstract man" the ideal subject of all possible name-related judgments and other possible combinations, representing the entirety of our prescientific and scientific knowledge about man, that is, about what man is and what he is capable of. Abstract man is not only the man of our everyday experience but also the man of contemporary science, the man of sociology, economics, literature, medicine, psychology, and psychiatry. The presence of abstract man in our communion with a concrete man is pointed out by utterances such as these: "it is impossible that man should act that way," "such an act required superhuman powers," "this does not fit within what I imagine of man," "man sounds proud," "man is the most important," and so on. Each time the "abstract man" is an instance of reference, that is indispensable in every attempt to understand a concrete man. Understanding is the capturing of human facticity in light of its abstract possibility. It remains to establish what relations hold between what is factual and what is abstract.

The name "horizon of meaning" and the abstract man living within its space depend upon various factors: upon the cultural development of a given society, upon religion, upon the reigning ethics, upon the richness of language and history, and also—as Marx indicated—upon the material modes of production. Abstract man constitutes himself in social time and social space. He also depends upon the situation of a concrete man who is the carrier of this concept. There are people with a rich picture of man and a differentiated vision of interpersonal relations, but there are people with an impoverished image, frequently one-sidedly skewed. The individual differences between name-horizons are the root of many interpersonal misunderstandings and conflicts.

Despite these differences, the basic structures of the name horizon of meaning seem to be stable. For example, the difference between abstract man and the space of interpersonal communion is stable. Some basic structural frameworks of this space are also stable. We will attempt to bring these foundations to light in the further course of our analyses. This is a very important task, because the structure of the name horizon of meaning determines, so to say, the *a priori* direction of our possible relations with others.

Place of the Name

When introducing myself to the other, I answer the question, Who am I? I say, "I am a teacher," "I am a doctor," or "I am a student." I define myself in a holistic, global way; I do not talk about how I am currently living, what my moods are, or my current intentions, instead I am pointing to something that, to a great degree, is independent from actual intentions and moods. I become an object to myself, determine myself with a word that is comprehensible to the other, and in this way "I expose myself to his gaze." It is with this goal that I "make use" of the name horizon of meaning, common to myself and the other. It is obvious that one must be in a common name horizon of meaning with the other in order to intelligibly answer the question posed, one must submit one's opacity to the *a priori* transparency of this sense.

But a problem emerges here.

The question, "Who am I?" has the form of an essential question. This is the way we ask about the essence, about the nature, about the internal truth of the object and the man. Meanwhile, in the answer, we do not at all receive this essence or nature. It would be difficult to assume that the fulfillment of this or that social role constitutes the essence of what I am. Man is instead aware that he could be himself, yet fulfilling a different social role in a different society. Perhaps man is not even able to indicate his essence or nature, maybe he does not know it, maybe he cannot put it into words. In any case, his answer is not essential. To what then does it point?

By carefully considering the formulas of introducing oneself, we discover that every time we indicate with them a *place* that man occupies in the name-space of meaning: man by speaking about who he is reveals *where* he is. The transparency of man for the other man is the result of spatialization. Thus, the act of introducing oneself to the other is an act of exteriorization; it is a going outside of oneself, it is the showing of oneself as a being connected with space, with place. The other, seeing the *place*, sees *me* at the same time. It is the use made of space, which makes possible showing the other who I am. My transparency for the other is the result of my participating in the transparency that marks the space spreading out around us.

What is this space?

Let us leave a more detailed analysis of the idea of space to the side. In particular, we will not address the question whether this space exists in an absolute or relative manner, but we will limit ourselves to capturing those of its aspects that condition the meaningfulness of the act of introducing oneself. When I say, "I am a teacher," I point toward my place in space, a place that is not the place of things. The space where I am a teacher, doctor, student is not an extended space. Extension is a property of things, my place in space is neither my property nor a property of things. We will proceed most appropriately by saying that the place to which we point is a place in the nonextended space of meaning. The concept of this type of space is not foreign to the language of science. Psychology and psychiatry speak of open and closed space, about the space of thought, space of freedom, and the space of hope. In semantics, we encounter the concept of a semantic field, which is a space of the meaning of particular formations of language. In sociology the concept of a social space has been accepted, a space within which man can develop his social activity. These concepts do not seem to be empty metaphors. A nonextended space of meaning is even something more fundamental than the thing-oriented space of extension.

Leibniz conceived of space as a "relation, the ordering not only of existing things, but also the possible, as if they existed."[5] Elsewhere he wrote that "space and time are only ideal things, just as all relative beings."[6] Here space is the opposite of chaos, the primordial principle of order and harmony of coexistence, is "an immeasurability, which also gives parts and order to the unmediated acts of God."[7] Thanks to space, things can coexist together without mutually canceling each other out. Space marks out not only the moral order but also the possible order, that is, the possible coexistence of beings. Referring to Leibniz, we will define the primordial space of meaning as the "order of possible coexistence." This definition can be secondarily referred to as the "extended space of things."

"I am a teacher," "I am a doctor," and "I am a student" means every time that I am in a specific place of the space of meaning where alongside my existence there also exist places of other people.

Here a key question emerges: Where does it come from that the idea of place becomes the key to understanding who someone is? By pointing to my place in the space of meaning, I not only point to what permanently distinguishes me from other, but at the same time to what remains in close and direct relation to my existence—with what I identify or at least strive to identify with. What is this place in the space of meaning that I can enter into such direct and profound relationships?

In saying, "I am a teacher," "I am a doctor," and "I am a student," I point toward a place as the field of my possibilities, which is a field of possibility among and for others. The field of possibilities remains in relationship with the field of impossibilities. The field of my impossibilities is, at least in part, the field of possibilities for others. Whoever is a teacher, and is capable of what a teacher is capable of, usually is not a doctor and is not capable of what a doctor is capable of. Whatever a man is capable of he is capable of within the field of his possibilities. The field of possibility is equivalent to the field of freedom. Thus, space, at its core, is the field of man's sensible freedom standing before him. The place of man in space is the field of freedom, which belongs to him more or less lastingly.

The place of the space of meaning in common with others is not something external in relation to man, but it is (or in any case can be) the true reflection of his face. Man can be a good or bad teacher, a good or bad doctor, despite this his relation with the place occupied by him in the space of meaning will remain for him the basic factor shaping his way of being among others. Thanks to this place, man can serve others and be served by them, he can—even without comprehension of his own fate—be somebody understandable to others. When man's name lacks such a place in the world, man is ready to say about himself, "I am nothing."

Let us now ask, What relations with the other men are *a priori* dictated by the place of man in the common space of meaning? In what direction do these relations mark out the course of communing with the other?

Structure of the Horizon of Communing

The idea of space as the order of coexistence among possible beings includes, necessarily, the conjunction "and." In the space of meaning, the word "and" connects and divides, it introduces ordering and primordial order. For Leibniz, the conjunction expresses the fittingness of all spatiality, thus not only the extended spatiality of the existing world, but also the spatiality of the possible world. The conjunction is also the law that introduces order into the name horizon of meaning. We say, "teacher *and* student," "doctor *and* patient," "student *and* professor." But is the word "and" enough? Is it, in a number of instances, a bit too impoverished? The place of man in the space of communion is not a point alongside a point, rather it is a field of definite possibilities and impossibilities, closely related to man's own freedom and the freedom of the other. The concept of the field conceals the concept of a road, a road that is closed or open, leading from somewhere to somewhere. The place of man is joined with the place of another man by a structure more complex than the one indicated by the word "and."

In order to advance the matter of this structure, we will turn our attention to the meaning of conjunction words that serve to describe the basic reference of man to man. What are these words? Well, if our current analyses are right, these will be, above all, prepositions pointing toward various ways of a place adhering to a place. We will eliminate "volumetric" words, concerned with the spatial placing of things. Let us stay with those that, above all, or even exclusively, refer to people. Such words are *"toward* someone," *"with* someone—*without* someone," "*for* someone—*against* someone," "on behalf of someone—in place of someone." The first of these words appears to be the most basic: "toward." Any "toward" is an answer to a name and, at the same time, an opening of the name horizon. Further words seem to emphasize the internal organization of this horizon.

The word "toward" is the basic term for the relationship of man to man, more broadly speaking, of the relationship of conscious beings to each other. "To be toward" does not mean "to be alongside" or "to be near." A tree grows alongside a tree, but is not *toward* a tree. The meaning of the word "toward" demands reciprocity: I look and I am seen, I care and I am the object of care, I think about someone and someone thinks of me. These do not have to be acts of seeing, caring, and thinking fully. In order to be *toward*, it is enough to have some form of *consciousness*. I am "conscious" that the other is, even though at the present moment I am occupied by something else. The word "toward" indicates simultaneously toward some space: *being toward* means to be sufficiently close so as not to lose the other from one's field of vision, but at the same time to be sufficiently far to not lose him in direct use (the *jouissance* of Levinas). This introduces a temporal dimension: "being toward" means to be present in the present, which, however, can stretch out into eternity.

The analysis of the word "toward" demands to be supplemented by a phenomenological analysis, which is uniquely able to show the experiential conditions for the application of this concept to a concrete example of encounter. It requires a discussion of the question of "empathy" (Stein), the constitution of the sense of the other (Husserl), the gaze (Sartre), "the revelation of the face" (Levinas), and so on. We do not want to anticipate these investigations here. We will say only one thing: where the situation demands the application of the word "toward," the initiative comes not from me but from the other. The other looks at me, sees me, and speaks to me. The other "talks me down," I am "penetrated" by his "eloquent gaze," offended by the "unintentional word," and drawn in by the "call." The other is a true transcendent. The originary transcending is *making present*.

The meaning of the word "toward" lies at the foundation of meanings of further words describing the relation of man to man. "Being with" is anchored in "being toward" as is "being without," "being for" and "being against," "being above" and "being under."

Every "toward" is "toward" someone who possesses a name. The moment of the constitution of the relation "toward" is the moment of opening up of the name horizon of meaning. This horizon is organized in the manner indicated by the abovementioned pairs of words.

We mentioned in the first place the pair "with/without." "John is waiting *with* me for the train"; "today I wait for the train *without* John." Or, "the violinist performed his composition together *with* an orchestra"; "the violinist performed his composition *without* an orchestra." Being *with* someone and being *without* someone means to be connected with someone through a third factor that is binding. This factor can be an approaching train, and it can be a musical composition. Participation is the principle of binding here. The forms of participation vary: permanent or temporary, accidental or necessary, more or less superficial. Thanks to participating in the same, reciprocity is formed, which the word *with* indicates. The teacher is *with* the student, the doctor is *with* the patient, and the writer is *with* the reader. The structure of reciprocity does not disappear even when the word *with* is replaced with the word *without*. I wait for the train *without* John, perform my composition *without* an orchestra. When being a teacher *without* students, a doctor *without* patients, and a writer *without* readers, one all the more experiences the call of reciprocity. It seems that the most fundamental form of participation and the condition of all possible reciprocity is participation in being—the Heideggerian *Mit-sein*. I participate in being and the other participates in being. We both similarly understand what being is. Understanding in what we ultimately participate is the basis for our reciprocity.

The place of man in the space of meaning is the field of his possibilities. The structure of reciprocity points to the fact that human fields of possibility are not isolated from each other, but, rather, one adheres to the other. It is known *a priori* that by making my own the field of possibility of the teacher, I enter into a specific relation with the field of possibility of the student. Fields of possibility mutually condition each other, one cannot exist without the other. The conductor cannot exist without an orchestra. Of course, it cannot exist in the sense that there is no meaning of being a conductor without the meaning of being an orchestra. The space in which fields of possibility condition each other on the principle of reciprocity we will call here the "semantic area of reciprocity."

The structure of reciprocity provides the basis of meaning for further concepts, which more closely specify the type of this reciprocity. The pursuit of precision goes in two directions: in the direction of concretization and in the direction of indicating a lack. Examples of concretization are the meanings of the following words: co-worker, partner, and so on. Examples of indicating a lack are the following words: unreliable, bungler, corner-cutter, off-tune in the orchestra, and so on.

We mentioned in the second place the pair "for/against." "I am *for* John receiving thanks, I am *for* John." Or, "I am *against* forgetting John's merits; I am *against* those who want to omit John." Between myself and the other there comes about the tie of "being for" or "being against." The one cannot be separated from the other. Whoever is *for* someone is at the same time *against* something or someone. Particular concepts arrange themselves in pairs and are ordered by the structure of opposition. The opposite of the concept of police officer is the concept of the criminal, the opposite of the exploited is the concept of the exploiter, the opposite of the concept of political right is the concept of the left. Where the idea of opposition appears, the idea of reciprocity ends, it ends because actual participation in one and the same ends. Particular fields of possibility are impossible to reconcile: if the criminal "can do anything," then the police officer "cannot do anything." Here the logic of concepts calls for a life-and-death struggle, even though everyday human practice does not always mirror this call. Nonetheless, we always sense situations of this type as some lack or pathology. The space of meaning in which particular fields of meaning exclude each other in such a manner that they oppose each other we call "semantic fields of opposition."

The structure of opposition also finds its definitions in concepts specifying the type, reach, and category of that opposition. Here too the pursuit of precision goes in two directions: in the direction of concretization and of indicating lack. An example of concretization is an intransigent and consistent hero, and so on. An example of indicating a lack is the one reticent, cowardly in battle, full of compromise, undecided, and so on.

Finally, the horizon of meaning was mentioned in the third place. We will call it here the "area of ruling." We usually define it with the words "over/under." Although these words refer to extended space directly, here they have a different application. "To be under" means to "be under someone's rule"; to "be above" means to rule someone. The relation of ruling is the same as the relation of opposition: in the case of opposition, the fields of possibility cancel each other out; in the case of ruling, the higher pole of possibility is the foundation of the lower one. What is higher defends what is lower and weaker. What is weaker acts and lives through the power of the higher. The minister rules "in the name of the king," the military commander "in the name of the minister," and so on. Here the logic of concepts points to extending care and to submitting to the one who rules. Again, where life does keep up with the logic of concepts, we sense such a situation as some kind of lack. Let us repeat: the semantic space in which particular fields of possibility condition each other, in such a manner that one is the foundation of the other, we call the "semantic field of ruling."

The structure of ruling finds its specifications, which are also concretizing and indicating a lack. An example of the first is the multitude of nouns and adjectives defining power: king, general, minister, subject, citizen, slave, and so on. An example of the others is anarchist, brawler, rebel, and so on.

As a result, we discover three fundamental semantic fields within which the presence of man to man develops and concretizes itself: *field of reciprocity*, *field of opposition*, and *field of ruling*. Introducing oneself, and by this indicating the field of my possibilities, I simultaneously locate myself within one of these fields. I reveal myself in this manner pointing simultaneously to what is adjacent to my field of possibilities: the other as a participant with me in some third thing; as my opponent; as my ruler or my subject. My proper place is found somewhere at the intersection of these lines.

I said above that all three "structural lines" of the space of communing are concretizations of the fundamental concept of presence. Somebody is present for me in such a manner that he is ..., and so on. Now we can say that depending on the place we occupy in the name horizon of meaning, eventually in dependence upon what place the other occupies in this space, the concepts of presence related to me or the other will vary. Living with someone in a region of reciprocity, I feel *foreign* toward those who come from within some other regions: for example, I do not know my opponent. Living in a region of opposition, everyone who is not with me or against me becomes *foreign to me.* This will be similar in the region of ruling. We ought to add a fourth concept of presence to these three: absolute foreignness, which is never mediated by any form of presence.

Research Perspectives

The structure of interpersonal space outlined above draws out the fundamental types and manners of everyday communion of man with man. In this space we first distinguish the *field of presence* of man for man, which we will call a *place*, and *fields of communion*, in which we meet with the other as our co-worker, opponent, ruling over us, and subject to us. There are substantial differences between the place and particular fields of communion that entail far-reaching differentiations in the sphere of interpersonal attitudes, nonetheless these are not differences of the type that *in concreto* one stance excludes the other. Man is a "multilayered" existence, and from this comes the possibility of him occupying several fields of communion simultaneously. Somebody can be my opponent in some regard, but in another regard my subject or ruler. Essentially, all the main forms of possible communion of man with man are marked out *a priori* by the outlined structure of the name space of meaning. The transparency specific to this space and its structure gives something of its shine to human existence and makes what exists comprehensible to others. When I reveal my name before the other, I introduce the other into my field of presence—into a place. By further speaking about who I am, I reveal alongside whom, against whom, and under what rule I live. In this way, I make myself understood to the other. Spatialization is the condition of intelligibility.

The space of interpersonal communions is a category that cannot be removed by any reduction. By reducing, one can only mutilate space, for example, replacing interpersonal space with the space of things. Even the religious sphere of man's communing with God bears upon itself the structural mark of an interpersonal name space—a naming one. It can also be reduced to the level of objective space.

The space of things has its ontic foundation in the extension of things. In extended space, particular extended objects exist next to one another, in lesser or greater distance from each other. The space of things does not know any fields of reciprocity, any fields of opposition, or any fields of ruling. Various powers function in objective space, frequently turned in opposite directions, then overlapping, enhancing, or revealing their actions. These various configurations of powers are not the same as reciprocity, opposition, and ruling. The differences between reciprocity, opposition, and ruling in the name space of communion are differences of quality, whereas the arrangements of powers in the space of things have a quantitative character. We will come back to this matter later, especially since man, through his body, also participates in extended space, specific to things. Here it comes in contact with objects, acts upon them and is acted upon; similarly it comes in contact with other people. The space of things is the kingdom of causal relationships, while nonextended space is the kingdom of intentional relations. The boundary between one and the other is not obvious. In either case, it can be said in a simplified way that the space of things is a field of only preconscious action of man upon man, and at the same time it can become the object of *knowledge* (I know where the heart lies in the other man, how far a man in a room is from another), the space of human *understanding* (I understand why the other suffers, where he is going, what he is running away from). The transition from understanding to knowledge about man is a descent from the level of intentionality to the level of reality. The space of things opens the door to reified cognitions of man.

Religious space, which is the place and the field of communion of man with God, also seems to carry the structural mark of interpersonal space. Thus, God appears as the One who is *present*—"in him we live and move and have our being"; the one who, though he is everywhere, nonetheless has "his own places," for example, the place of the temple or the "place" in the form of bread and wine. At the same time he is the One, "apart from whom you can do nothing" (field of reciprocity). For those who have rebelled, God is an "opponent" (field of opposition). Simultaneously he is the One who "rules over the nations" and who "did not come to be served, but to serve" (field of ruling). Ricoeur points out that man's feeling of guilt toward God expresses itself in symbolism whose core is a space, a path, going off path. But religious space can also be subject to a reductive impoverishment to the level of the space of things. Space then becomes a field of causal relationships through which God, as *suum esse*, upholds man in existence. The Thomistic way of proving God presupposes such space. This entails a difficulty in passing from the *suum esse* to a God who "has a Face," or more broadly from the man who has been conceived through space as a *res* to a man conceived as a "being with a face," from knowledge to understanding, from the space of actions to the space of being-withs.

Therefore space is irreducible. To be understood by another is to show oneself in the name space of meaning. The transparency of space is a principle of understanding. But is it the originary principle? Does space owe its organization to itself, or to "extraspatial" factors?

Space opens up the horizon of coexistence. But in itself it does not decide about the fundamental lines of that coexistence. The organization of the space of being-withs comes from extraspatial factors. Values are these factors. The structure of interpersonal space refers to axiology. Values are the causes of this. The structure of interpersonal space refers to axiology. This key thesis marks out the direction for our further research. However, before we take it up, there is one point referring not so much to being-with of man with man, but to the ways of coming to know man. This point should sharpen our vision of the axiological aspect of interpersonal being-withs.

Let us ask, What situations in everyday life awaken in us the need to know the other person? Well, this need most frequently arises when "normal being-with" is subject to disturbances of some sort. Then we ask, "How is it really with this man?" But what does it mean to say that "normal being-with" is subject to disturbances of some sort? It means that someone present until now has become absent, that my co-worker stops working with me, that my opponent becomes my ally, that my guardian becomes my opponent, and my subject becomes my enemy. Then in every instance we ask, "Why?" Why did the other behave differently than indicated by the place in the space of meaning occupied by him? Being-with without disturbances does not provide motivations for asking questions about the truth. This problem appears only as a result of some "jarring."

This fact affects the manner of knowing the other person. It makes it so that the typical manner of coming to know the other is, to use St. Augustine's terminology, "knowing through reproaching." We come to know the other, while "reproaching" him, by saying to him, "You are out of place," "you are outside of your truth."

What is the truth of the other in this context? It is faithfulness to the place that a man occupies in the space of meaning. All of this requires further refinement. Knowing "through reproaching" is marked by a particular form: the other appears *a priori* in the field of influence of negative values as the opposite of what or who he should be. Knowing through reproaching exists thanks to the form of the axiological opposition. Man's truth appears here through the falsehood of man. The falsehood of the sinner's existence shows the truth of the saint, the falsehood of a betrayed presence shows the truth of faithfulness, the falsehood of enmity shows the truth of friendship. "Tell me who your enemy is and I will tell you who you are."

This way of coming to know the other, through a form of opposition, also finds its philosophical articulations. Marxism is one of them. The man of Marxism is a man of a social class. There is a relation of opposition between individual social classes. A relation of opposition allows man to discover his truth as a component of the historical truth of the proletariat or the bourgeoisie. Reciprocity (the idea of a "comrade in arms") and ruling (the idea of a worker's party) are made possible by taking into account the structure of opposition. And so the transparency of a concrete man is the result of the transparency of the field that man occupies in the general social space. However, this idea is not only present in Marxism. In Nietzsche, man's full truth reveals itself thanks to man's opposition to God. Nietzsche's idea is continued by Sartre. In early Heidegger, the dialectic of opposition emerges from the experience of death: the "truth of decisiveness" is the response to the death that permeates man. In Claude Lévi-Strauss, the "oppositional function of consciousness" constitutes social space, thanks to which human truths are revealed. And Karl Jaspers is no different: only "boundary situations," in which the human "to be or not to be" is weighed, show what man really is. Antoni Kępiński appears to be one of the few exceptions: man's truth is revealed where his "place of presence" is. In the "place of presence" man is neither our co-worker, nor opponent, nor ruler, nor subject, but the one whom we first, and above all, simply "let be."

CHAPTER 5

The Last Word of the Drama

We assume in the philosophy of drama developed here that evil belongs to the category of phenomena, which distinguish themselves from the rest of objective phenomena in that they are possible exclusively between the persons of the drama. Evil presents itself to us as either a tempting or frightening *specter* invoked by the presence of others alongside us. It is as if a third someone—someone who, while being among us, can speak to us. Does something more hide behind this specter? We will not settle this. The phenomenological method we adopted for our research does not permit this. But let us not bemoan this limitation. The position occupied remains in harmony with the classical philosophy of evil, which proclaims that evil is a lack of being; for what is the phenomenon if not a lack of being—claiming to be being? Yet, we also do not fall into the contradiction with the Manichean conception of evil, according to which evil exists as an independent being. Maybe it really exists; however, we stop at researching phenomena themselves. In this way we take up a neutral stance from the start, not opting for any of the feuding parties.

We ought to say something similar about the good. It also emerges as a phenomenon from interpersonal space. It speaks to us as a *third someone*, from us and not from us, from others and not from others. But is it something more besides this? Is it an independent being? Or, only an illusion of an independent being? We will not settle this. We will also maintain neutrality about the issue of the good. We desire to study the good according to how it is given to us. We can know nothing about a good that is in no way given to us. We have not experienced it, so how can we understand it?

The biblical story about the fall of Adam and Eve still remains the horizon of the philosophy of drama. The philosophy of drama does not run away from metaphors, because it knows that metaphorization belongs to the nature of thinking. Hence, its philosophizing is decidedly a "thinking from within the metaphor." In the story of the Fall, the voice of the good that resounds between Adam and Eve is the voice of God. The voice of evil is the voice of the tempter (in this instance the serpent). This third one (and maybe also this fourth) appears between the two persons of the drama. Does *this third* really exist? This question is the eternal torment of ontology, which believes that only what is real can act. In his acting, man equally succumbs to what is and what is not. In philosophy, the possibly existing demon plays the same role as the demon who really exists. According to Kant, God played a similar role in classical ontology. So, instead of asking, "What is?" we asked, "Whom and what are we listening to?"

We are speaking about a voice. This is significant: the main metaphors with the help of which the Bible (and not only it) attempts to describe the experience of good and evil are connected with the experience of hearing. Good and evil let themselves be known through the voice. In distinction from this, things are given to us through sight and touch. We ought to say that the good does not let itself be seen, but it does let itself be heard. Similarly evil: evil cannot be seen, but it can be heard. Good and evil come to us most frequently through prohibitions and injunctions in which the objective content is less important than the tone with which they are given. The picking of the fruit from the tree became something more than an object changing place, since it was the violation of a previous prohibition. The fruit upon the tree does not call for picking, nor do things call out to not be touched—*a third one* calls, who has come *between us*. Levinas's philosophy of the face also witnesses to the primacy of speech in the experience of the good. The face, contrary to what might be suggested by the literal understanding of this word, is not what is visible, but what is heard. The face says, "You will not commit a murder." The speech of the face emerges from the horizon of the good and awakens a desire for the good in those who hear it.

Usually, studies about the mystery of good and evil consider in the first place the question about the nature of the good, and only later the question about the nature of evil. In this introduction to the philosophy of drama, we took a different path: we began with evil in order to, through evil, come slowly to an understanding of the good. This is the result of the conviction that the good is admittedly closer to our hopes, but evil is closer to our experiences. The philosophy that adheres to applying the phenomenological method is, in a way, predestined to admit the primacy of the study of evil before the study of the good.

Let us try to capture what is fundamental in speech about good and evil as we conclude these analyses. Let us ask about the last word — the last word of evil and the last word of the good, uttered over a man.

Condemnation

We already said that evil leads to *condemnation*. Its goal is to hear, "You are condemned." The one who is condemned is evil. He, and his existence, is evil. Scheler wrote, "The existence of a negative value is itself a negative value." The existence of an evil man is an evil existence.

We know that evil speaks to man either as a temptation or as a threat. The ultimate goal of evil is to lead man to the state in which these words become the truth: "He is evil." Whoever is evil should be condemned, because there is nothing that could justify his existence.

What does it mean to say "I am evil"? We know that these words can take on various meanings. The analyses conducted so far drew attention to several possibilities. Thus, I am evil because I am ugly. Moreover, I am evil because I am rebellious. Also, I am evil because I am a liar. And also, I am evil because I am a betrayer. Ugliness, lying, the ability to rebel, and to betray are manifestations of my existential evil.

But before I can say — because of ugliness, lying, the ability to rebel and betray — "I am evil," the word "I" must take on a particular meaning. One should first identify me with a certain value (namely, beauty, truthfulness, obedience, and faithfulness) that I lack but would like to possess. The man who, because of ugliness, comes to the conviction that he is evil has identified the whole of his good with beauty, and that is precisely what he lacks. The same applies in the other cases. Now that he sees that he is not like what he thinks he is, he falls into despair, like someone worthy of condemnation.

The identification of the I with a certain value—an "axial value"—we call the "process of egotic solidarization." The process going in the opposite direction is a process of desolidarization.[1]

What is the purpose of evil speech then? It strives to arouse in the consciousness of the drama's person a process of constituting axiological meaning whose final result will become the identification of the I with evil. The beginning of this process is dialogue with evil—evil that threatens or tempts.

Good speech, dialogue with the good, is parallel to evil speech. Good speech leads to the binding of the I's consciousness to values that can lend a helping hand in the dispute with evil. So what if I am ugly since I am truthful? And if I have been caught lying, this is nothing, because I am obedient to my master. And if I am not obedient to the master, then I am faithful to my neighbor. Thus, in the dispute with evil, the I inspired by good speech changes the planes of its proper existence—withdrawing from one in order to be itself in another. And it will never be convinced that it is evil. It will always find some good, some value, under whose roof it will search for shelter.

All these changes of consciousness are an internal reflection of the external drama of man. The particular chapters of the drama leave behind ever-new layers in the souls of those persons participating in it. The external dramatic thread changes into the internal thread. Interpersonal good and evil become the good and evil of a man—evil that destroys him, and good that builds him up.

Aesthetic Condemnation

We spoke earlier about going astray in the element of beauty. We turned our attention more toward the positive side of beauty, taking into consideration the beauty of the other. The beautiful person grabs, changes, justifies us—like some work of art. But in the beauty that reveals itself to us there is also a hidden germ of contempt. Beauty can, in any moment, turn to the artist delighted with it with the words,

"You are not worthy of me." These words sound like a condemnation. Beauty lets it be understood that only the beautiful can stand in its retinue. Whoever is not beautiful falls victim to contempt. They can admire, but they will not be admired.

Aesthetic condemnation, whose basis is the experience of beauty, differs essentially from condemnations that are, let us call them, "ethico-religious." The voice of condemnation does not fall here from interpersonal space, from *some third*, but directly from the work of art itself. It mocks and it has contempt. However, precisely because of this it is not a voice that speaks good and evil. Here we hit upon an essential difference between aesthetic experience and ethico-religious experience. Aesthetic experience is the intrigue of two, whereas ethico-religious experience requires *some third*. Anyone who has become the victim of contempt from the side of the work of art—and to become the victim of contempt is to acknowledge that the contempt is deserved—knows that he is ugly. His ugliness has an existential character. This means that he *is* ugliness itself. This cannot be changed. You can hide existential ugliness, but it cannot be changed. Changing it would mean committing suicide. Indeed, aesthetic condemnation sometimes leads to suicide.

Yet, a dispute with aesthetic condemnation is possible. There are two possibilities: either give the condemnation the lie, and show that it is wrong, or change the axial value of egotic solidarization. In this second case, beauty stops being an integral component of the I. Another value takes its place.

Man says the following in changing the axis of egotic solidarization: "Oh, well, I am not beautiful since, for example, I am diligent." Beauty stops being what one is and becomes something one possesses. What you have can be lost without you ceasing to be what you are. This is the manner in which aesthetic condemnation misses the mark. It does not evoke despair, at most only a shrug of the shoulders.

Political Condemnation

Absolute power accuses and condemns with words that simultaneously contain its justification: "You are a rebel." Absolute power sees man as a subject through the prism of a never completely extinguished rebellion. Man is an indomitable anarchist. Opposition is his will's principle of action. Freed from the control of power, man immediately becomes an arsonist who wants to set the world on fire. He replies with recalcitrance to every call to obedience. This is why he needs the authority he does not want over him. Authority, to control a human being, must use fear or deceit. Fear and deception are intertwined into one in the formula of accusation and condemnation: "You are a rebel."

Political condemnation resembles aesthetic condemnation in certain respects. Here *some third* is also not necessary. The more absolute the power, the greater independence it displays in condemnation. Truly absolute power always speaks in its own name. It does not permit any instance above itself—an instance the subjected could have recourse to. A relatively absolute power allows such an instance and even strives to establish it. Only then *some third* enters between it and the subjected—God, the Law of History, Progress, or Humanity. The negative side of *some third* is then some fourth—a demon, a misunderstanding of the historical moment, backwardness, or inhumanity.

Therefore, you are a rebel because you do not listen to God, but a demon because you do not understand the laws of History, because you are not following Progress, you go in reverse because you are not acting in the interest of Humanity. Power, making itself the representative of these and similar values stops being a pure absolute power. This does not mean that it is limited in its potency, because it tries to exploit *some third* for those of its goals that appear in interpersonal space.

Therefore, I am a rebel. I must go into exile if I agree to this condemnation. However, exile will not change my essence. I will also be a rebel in exile. Thus, it is better for me to perish. Is this necessary? Could I not change? No, this is impossible. After all, *I am* a rebel. If my rebellion were only an event, everything could be fixed. But I am a rebel. The only way out in this situation is for me to not exist.

I have to deny the accusation to save my life. My denial is, "I am not." I am not a rebel because I am obedient to someone and something else. This obedience expresses itself through my faithfulness. I am faithful—this is an answer and a rescue.

Denial of the accusation entails an opening onto *some third* to whom, or to what, I am faithful when I rebel against power. Power wanted to exploit this against me, but now I exploit it against power. The *third*: maybe it is God, maybe my neighbors, maybe my own conscience. Each one of them is a concrete incarnation of the ideas of good and evil. In this way the fields of ethics, law, morality, custom, and religion begin to spread widely before the subjects and authorities. There is now no space for the absolute command of absolute power and absolute obedience to this power. But there is also no place for self-will, anarchy, and the terror of unbridled individuality. Ruling and subjection begin to depend upon what happens between people.

Religious Condemnation

"Go cursed into the eternal fire" is what the verdict upon the condemned sounds like. The tragism of this verdict is that God pronounces it—the Eternal Heart. If somebody else were in the place of God, it would be possible to argue with the verdict, but in the case of God, it is not possible. Absolute Truth does not make mistakes. The Absolute Good is not unjust. The Eternal Heart is not cruel. Nonetheless, the verdict is what it is.

Incomprehensible Wisdom can suffer from the verdict, but can it change it?

I am condemned. Why? Because I am evil. What does this mean? Let us first look at the path that led to the condemnation. Then we will attempt to grasp the state of condemnation.

Betrayal is the beginning of the path to condemnation. This is how it looks in a nutshell: I was chosen by the Good, and the act of this election awakened in me the good will of choosing the one who chose me. I chose it. But the time of trial came. I betrayed. The one who chose me repeated the act of election. But then rebellion came into me. I betrayed. The act of the repeated election did not awaken in me the good will of choosing the Good that chose me. Rather, it awakened the opposite—the will to oppose, ill will. This is how I became evil. Does a rescue exist for me? If it exists, then, above all, it exists in me. I can only become good myself. However, I have just become evil. I have locked myself up in this anger. I have hardened. I can be destroyed, but I cannot be changed without myself. The condemnation that comes from God is a judgment about who I am.

Condemnation is the consequence of a specific dialogical situation that comes into being when the call of the Good does not awaken in man a response of choosing the good, but causes an all the more resolute choice of evil. This is how the road of the second fall goes: the higher the good calling, the higher the resistance and the deeper the anger grows. To deny a small good, a small anger is enough. To reject the Eternal Heart, a vast anger is needed.

Looking at the perspective of the path to condemnation, we see the outlines of the state of condemnation. This state is reminiscent of despair, about which Kierkegaard wrote that it is a "sickness unto death." The state of despair is a chosen state. It does not befall man without his consent. However, man does not choose despair for himself as despair. Despair comes when man chooses evil and does this against the Good that has elected him. In choosing an increasingly great evil against an increasingly great good, man chooses his own curse. Living through his curse, man agrees to be in despair—despair is his very breath. This should bring him to death. But death is impossible. The spirit cannot be killed. The condemned exists but he exists in a cursed existence—an existence whose expression is the cursing of existence. The condemned curse. Those that curse become the cursed. This is how the closed circle of evil comes into being, which is no longer reached to by the voice of the Eternal Heart.

Justification

The path to salvation leads in the direction opposite that of the road of condemnation. The path of salvation is the path of a continually renewed faithfulness to the Good that calls. It is incarnated in me thanks to my choice, it also goes through a trial situation. However, man is a weak creature, so every trial ends with his greater or lesser defeat. Even victories are crises of some sort. After the crisis, one hears a new call and this complements the new repetition of the choice. And so, step after step, in flights and falls, fidelity is born—an absolute fidelity, that is, fidelity without regard for circumstances. This is what opens the road to salvation. Salvation is expressed with the words "Go and be blessed."

The state of salvation can be thought of as a state of justification, which is the opposite of the state of condemnation. Condemnation means despair. Happiness is the opposite of despair. If despair is a "sickness onto death," then happiness will be something approaching a "vigor for life." Man is wholly healthy—he has a healthy soul and body, reason and will, healthy senses, and healthy feelings. Health continually brings and multiplies life. Such life is a mark of blessedness. Happiness is the expression of a continually growing life.

But happiness is only an approximation of the state of salvation. To push this approximation further we must say that the state of blessed happiness is a state of election. It does not come by man without his will. In this choice, happiness is not the theme of the choice. The Good is the theme of the choice. Happiness comes when man chooses the Good against the evil that is pulling him in. By choosing the Good that is giving itself to man, man becomes happy. The higher the good he chooses, the stronger is his life. Continually choosing life according to the Good, man rises toward something that is above time. He is convinced that it is as if the Eternal Heart pulls him toward itself. Man has put his fragile fate under the roof of the Good, which blesses him.

The question, "Who are you?" is born at the outset of the drama. There appear two opposing possibilities in the end: cursed or blessed. Man's drama takes place among these possibilities. What do they mean? We do not precisely know. This ignorance does not prevent us from living among them, thinking according to them, judging others and ourselves according to them. If someday they would disappear from our eyes and ears, then we would stand helpless upon the stage of the world, like words that have forgotten the grammatical rules that make them into speech.

NOTES

Chapter 1

1. Emmanuel Levinas, *Ethics and Infinity: Conversations with Philippe Nemo*, trans. Richard A. Cohen (Pittsburgh: Duquesne University Press, 1995), 85, 86, 89.
2. Levinas, *Ethics and Infinity*, 85–86.
3. Stéphane Mosès, *System and Revelation: The Philosophy of Franz Rosenzweig* (Detroit: Wayne State University Press, 1992), 285.
4. Emmanuel Levinas, *Totality and Infinity: An Essay on Exteriority* (Pittsburgh: Duquesne University Press, 1969), 198, 199.
5. Emmanuel Levinas, *En découvrant l'existence avec Husserl et Heidegger* (Paris: Vrin, 1967), 225, as translated by Edith Wyschogrod, *Emmanuel Levinas: The Problem of Ethical Metaphysics* (The Hague: Martinus Nijhoff, 1974), 136.
6. Levinas, *Ethics and Infinity*, 91, 92.
7. Levinas, *Totality and Infinity*, 33, 34.
8. Levinas, *Totality and Infinity*, 34, 35.
9. Levinas, *Totality and Infinity*, 102–3.
10. Emmanuel Levinas, *Collected Philosophical Papers* (Pittsburgh: Duquesne University Press, 1998), 56.
11. Levinas, *Collected Philosophical Papers*, 56.
12. Levinas, *Totality and Infinity*, 61.
13. Levinas, *Totality and Infinity*, 62.
14. Levinas, *Collected Philosophical Papers*, 57–58.
15. Levinas, *Collected Philosophical Papers*, 59.
16. Levinas, *Collected Philosophical Papers*, 97.
17. Levinas, *Collected Philosophical Papers*, 97.
18. Levinas, *Collected Philosophical Papers*, 98.
19. Levinas, *Totality and Infinity*, 50.
20. Stephan Strasser, *Jenseits von Sein und Zeit: Eine Einführung in Emmanuel Levinas' Philosophie* (Den Haag: Martinus Nijhoff, 1978), 221–22.
21. Levinas, *Collected Philosophical Papers*, 104–5.
22. Levinas, *Collected Philosophical Papers*, 106–7.

23. Levinas, *Totality and Infinity*, 75.
24. Levinas, *Totality and Infinity*, 196.
25. Levinas, *Totality and Infinity*, 196–97.
26. Strasser, *Jenseits von Sein und Zeit*, 225.
27. Emmanuel Levinas, *Otherwise Than Being* (Pittsburgh: Duquesne University Press, 1998), 9.
28. Levinas, *Otherwise Than Being*, 9.
29. Levinas, *Otherwise Than Being*, 18.
30. Martin Heidegger, "Letter on Humanism," in *Basic Writings* (New York: Basic, 2008), 213–66.
31. Max Scheler, "On the Tragic," in *The Question of Tragedy*, ed. Arthur B. Coffin (Lewiston, NY: Edwin Mellen, 1991), 108.
32. Scheler, "On the Tragic," 109–10.
33. G. W. F. Hegel, *Aesthetics: Lectures on Fine Art*, Vol. 2, trans. T. M. Knox (Oxford: Clarendon, 1975), 1208.
34. Max Scheler, *Formalism in Ethics and Non-Formal Ethics of Values: A New Attempt toward the Foundation of an Ethical Personalism*, trans. Manfred Frings and Roger Funk (Evanston, IL: Northwestern University Press, 1973), 26.
35. Levinas, *Totality and Infinity*, 43.
36. Henryk Elzenberg, *Wartość i człowiek* (Toruń: PWN, 1966), 49 [my translation.—Rosman].
37. Jean-Paul Sartre, *Being and Nothingness* (New York: Washington Square, 1993), 369.
38. See Peter Kampits, *Sartre und die Frage nach dem Anderen* (Munich: Oldenbourg, 1975).
39. Józef Tischner, *Świat ludzkiej nadziei* (Kraków: Znak 1975), 162–82.
40. Sartre, *Being and Nothingness*, 362.
41. Antoni Kępiński, *Schizofrenia* (Warszawa: Wydawnictwo Literackie, 1972), 154.
42. G. W. F. Hegel, *Phenomenology of Spirit*, trans. J. N. Findlay (Oxford: Oxford University Press, 1977), 317.
43. Antoni Kępiński, *Poznanie chorego* (Warszawa: PZWL, 1978), 56.
44. See Józef Tischner, "Ludzie z kryjówek," in *Myślenie według wartości* (Kraków: Znak, 1982).
45. Gilles Deleuze, *Difference and Repetition* (New York: Columbia University Press, 1995), 118–19.

Chapter 2

1. Levinas, *Totality and Infinity*, 78.
2. Levinas, *Totality and Infinity*, 75.
3. Ferdinand Ebner, *Das Wort und die geistigen Realitäten: Pneumatologische Fragmente* (Frankfurt am Main: Suhrkamp, 1980), 18.
4. Mosès, *System and Revelation*, 108.

5. Franz Rosenzweig, *The Star of Redemption* (Madison: University of Wisconsin Press, 2005), 189.

Chapter 3

1. Leo Tolstoy, *Anna Karenina*, trans. Richard Pevear and Larissa Volokhonsky (New York: Penguin Classics, 2004), 30, 31.
2. Plato, *Phaedrus*, trans. Robin Waterfield (Oxford: Oxford University Press, 2009), 34 (250c-d).
3. Tolstoy, *Anna Karenina*, 30.
4. Søren Kierkegaard, *Either/Or*, Vol. 1, trans. Howard Vincent Hong and Edna Hatlestad Hong (Princeton, NJ: Princeton University Press, 1987), 379.
5. Immanuel Kant, *Critique of the Power of Judgment* (Cambridge: Cambridge University Press, 2000), 151.
6. Kierkegaard, *Either/Or*, 1:65.
7. Kant, *Critique of the Power of Judgment*, 90.
8. Raymond Polin, *Du laid, du mal, du faux* (Paris: PUF, 1949), 93.
9. Kierkegaard, *Either/Or*, 1:71.
10. Kierkegaard, *Either/Or*, 1:71. [There appears to be no correlate for "Prawdziwa wzniosłość jest wartością wszystkich" in the Polish translation of Søren Kierkegaard, *Albo-albo* (*Either/Or*) (Warsaw: PWN, 2010), 1:78. Adam Workowski, in his adroit editing of the early versions of this manuscript, suggested that Tischner probably misquoted Kierkegaard.—Rosman]
11. Kierkegaard, *Either/Or*, 1:75.
12. Kierkegaard, *Either/Or*, 1:75–76.
13. Kierkegaard, *Either/Or*, 1:77.
14. Kierkegaard, *Either/Or*, 1:80.
15. Plato, *Symposium*, trans. M. C. Howatson (Cambridge: Cambridge University Press, 2008), 48 (210a-b).
16. Kant, *Critique of the Power of Judgment*, 227.
17. Charles Baudelaire, *The Flowers of Evil*, trans. James McGowan (Oxford: Oxford University Press, 2008), 201.
18. Kierkegaard, *Either/Or*, 1:100–101. [Either Tischner, or the translation he is working from, erroneously cites Kierkegaard as saying "Don Juan."—Rosman]
19. Kierkegaard, *Either/Or*, 1:332.
20. Kierkegaard, *Either/Or*, 1:360–61.
21. Kierkegaard, *Either/Or*, 1:312.
22. Kierkegaard, *Either/Or*, 1:309.
23. Friedrich Nietzsche, *Beyond Good and Evil: Prelude to a Philosophy of the Future*, trans. Judith Norman (Cambridge: Cambridge University Press, 2002), 7.
24. Nietzsche, *Beyond Good and Evil*, 9.
25. Nietzsche, *Beyond Good and Evil*, 39.

26. Fyodor Dostoevsky, *Crime and Punishment*, trans. Richard Pevear and Larissa Volokhonsky (New York: Vintage, 1993), 269.
27. Dostoevsky, *Crime and Punishment*, 270–71.
28. Dostoevsky, *Crime and Punishment*, 333.
29. Dostoevsky, *Crime and Punishment*, 272–73.
30. Dostoevsky, *Crime and Punishment*, 269.
31. Dostoevsky, *Crime and Punishment*, 343.
32. Dostoevsky, *Crime and Punishment*, 332.
33. Dostoevsky, *Crime and Punishment*, 332.
34. Dostoevsky, *Crime and Punishment*, 266–67.
35. Dostoevsky, *Crime and Punishment*, 336.
36. William Shakespeare, *Richard III*, 1.2.49–50, 64–66.
37. Augustine, *Concerning the Nature of the Good, Against the Manicheans*, in *Nicene and Post-Nicene Fathers*, First Series, Vol. 4, *St. Augustine: The Writings "Against the Manichaeans" and "Against the Donatists,"* trans. Philip Schaff (London: T&T Clark, 1887), 352.
38. G. W. F. Hegel, *Phenomenology of Spirit*, trans. A. V. Miller (Oxford: Oxford University Press, 1977), 117.
39. Hegel, *Phenomenology of Spirit*, 115.
40. Alexandre Kojève, *Introduction to the Reading of Hegel: Lectures on the Phenomenology of Spirit*, trans. James H. Nichols Jr. (Ithaca, NY: Cornell University Press, 1980), 7.
41. See Hans Friedrich Fulda, ed., *Materialen zu Hegels "Phänomenologie des Geistes"* (Frankfurt am Main: Suhrkamp, 1979).
42. Fyodor Dostoevsky, *The Brothers Karamazov*, trans. Richard Pevear and Larissa Volokhonsky (New York: Farrar, Straus and Giroux, 2002), 254.
43. Dostoevsky, *Brothers Karamazov*, 258–59.
44. Dostoevsky, *Brothers Karamazov*, 254.
45. Dostoevsky, *Brothers Karamazov*, 257.
46. Dostoevsky, *Brothers Karamazov*, 259.
47. Soren Kierkegaard, *The Sickness unto Death*, trans. Howard V. Hong (Princeton, NJ: Princeton University Press, 1983), 17–18.
48. See Józef Tischner, *Świat ludzkiej nadziei* (Krakow: Znak, 1992), esp. the chapter titled "Impresje aksjologiczne."
49. Jan Patočka, *The Natural World as a Philosophical Problem*, trans. Erika Abrams (Evanston, IL: Northwestern University Press, 2016).
50. See Gerd Brand, *Die Lebenswelt: Eine Philosophie des konkreten Apriori* (Berlin: De Gruyter, 1971).
51. Levinas, *Totality and Infinity*, 110.
52. Martin Heidegger, *"The Question concerning Technology" and Other Essays*, trans. William Lovitt (New York: Harper & Row, 1977), 12–13.
53. St. John of the Cross, *Ascent of Mt. Carmel*, trans. E. Allison Peers (Mineola, NY: Dover, 2008), 42–43.
54. Friedrich Nietzsche, *The Gay Science*, trans. Josefine Nauckhoff (Cambridge: Cambridge University Press, 2001), 60.
55. Nietzsche, *Gay Science*, 71.

56. Heidegger, *Question concerning Technology*, 14–15.
57. Heidegger, *Question concerning Technology*, 15.
58. Friedrich Nietzsche, *On the Genealogy of Morals*, trans. Carol Diethe (Cambridge: Cambridge University Press, 2006), 17
59. Nietzsche, *On the Genealogy of Morals*, 18.
60. Nietzsche, *On the Genealogy of Morals*, 93–94.

Chapter 4

1. Daniel Christoff, "La temporalité et la conscience d'autrui," *Studia Philosophica* 25, no. 14 (1965): 199–203.
2. The concept of an "intentional direction factor" comes from Roman Ingarden, *The Literary Work of Art*, trans. George Grabowicz (Chicago: Northwestern University Press, 1979), 85.
3. See Izydora Dąmbska, *Znaki i myśli* (Warsaw: PWN, 1976), 34–48.
4. Józef Tischner, *Świat ludzkiej nadziei* (Kraków: ZNAK, 1976), 162ff.
5. Gottfried Wilhelm Leibniz, *New Essays in Human Understanding* (Cambridge: Cambridge University Press, 1996); Leibniz, *Nowe rozważania dotyczące rozumu ludzkiego*, trans. I. Dąmbska (Warszawa, 1955), 355.
6. Gottfried Wilhelm Leibniz, *Philosopher's Confession*; Leibniz, *Wyznanie wiary filozofa*, trans. S. Cichowicz, J. Domański, H. Krzeczkowski, and H. Moese (Warszawa, 1969), 355.
7. Yvon Belaval, "La théorie Leibnizien e de l'espace," transcript of lecture at Entretiens de Berne, 1967.

Chapter 5

1. See Józef Tischner, "Solidaryzacja i problem ewolucji świadomości," in *Studia z teorii poznania i filozofii wartości*, ed. Władysław Stróżewski (Warsaw: PAN, 1978).

NAME INDEX

A
Abel, 8–9, 18
Abraham, 2, 10, 18–20, 25–26, 32
Aristotle, 154–55
Augustine of Hippo, 121–22

B
Baudelaire, Charles, 75
Buber, Martin, 118

C
Cain, 8–9, 18

D
Deleuze, Gilles, 41
Descartes, René, xxix, 10, 16, 22–23, 102, 145–46
Dostoevsky, Fyodor, 84–88, 89–92, 104–9, 136–42, 145–46

E
Ebner, Ferdinand, 56–57
Elzenberg, Henryk, 33

F
Freud, Sigmund, 8, 41

G
Gyges, 49–50

H
Hegel, Georg Wilhelm Friedrich, 19–20, 23, 39, 129–37, 140–43, 145, 165

Heidegger, Martin, 2, 19–20, 152–55, 158, 168–69, 204, 210
Husserl, Edmund, xxii–xxiv, 24, 42, 49–50, 53, 92, 109, 118, 151–52, 154, 193

I
Ingarden, Roman, 68

J
Jesus Christ, 28–29, 37, 31, 44–45
Judas, 30–31

K
Kant, Immanuel, 23, 67–68, 74–75, 212
Kępiński, Antoni, 38–40, 194, 210
Kierkegaard, Søren, 65–67, 70–73, 77–79, 142–43, 218
Kojève, Alexandre, 132

L
La Rochefoucauld, François de, 83
Leibniz, Gottfried Wilhelm, 46, 201–2
Levinas, Emmanuel, 2–27, 31–32, 42–45, 48–49, 52–54, 152–53, 164, 212
Lévi-Strauss, Claude, 210
Locke, John, 71

M
Marcel, Gabriel, 214

Marx, Karl, 41, 133, 199, 210
Moses, 159
Mosès, Stéphane, 5–6, 43, 58
Mozart, Wolfgang Amadeus, 72

N
Nietzsche, Friedrich Wilhelm, 80–81, 99, 166–68, 170–71, 179, 184–85

O
Odysseus, 2, 11
Oedipus, 27–31

P
Pascal, Blaise, 30
Patočka, Jan, 152
Plato, xxviii, 12–13, 48, 64–66, 73, 154

Prometheus, 27–31, 37

R
Ricoeur, Paul, 30, 208
Rosenzweig, Franz, 2, 5–6, 19–20, 58–59

S
Sartre, Jean-Paul, xxvi, 33–34, 36, 133
Scheler, Max, 28, 31, 124, 213
Shakespeare, William, 113–14, 121, 175, 179, 180
Socrates, 54, 79, 81
Strasser, Stephan, 19, 24

T
Tolstoy, Leo, 63, 64

EXTENDED TABLE OF CONTENTS

Table of Contents	v
Foreword, by Cyril O'Regan	vii
Translator's Preface	xv
Introduction	xix
Consciousness of the Stage	xxii
Consciousness of the Other	xxvi
The God Question	xxix
CHAPTER 1 The Event of the Encounter	1
The Face of the Other	3
Face-to-Face	5
Homicide	7
Desire	10
The Trace of the Infinite	18
Levinas and Others	22
The Good	25
Agathology	27
Veil	32
Mask	37
Face	42
CHAPTER 2 The Answer to the Question, That Is, Reciprocity	46
Question	48
Philosopher, Inquisitor, God	49
Presence	53
Questioner	53
Answerer	54
Reciprocity	55
I–Thou	56
Bridge over an Abyss	59
To Carry a Burden and to Be a Burden	60

CHAPTER 3 Going Astray — 62

A. Going Astray in the Element of Beauty — 63
 Beauty as Light and Justification — 64
 Justification — 68
 Tragic Nature of Beauty — 73
 Crossroads — 74
 Mystery of the Face — 76

B. Going Astray in the Element of Truth — 79
 Value of Lying — 82
 Two Conceptions of the Truth — 84
 Common Sense — 85
 Game upon a Double Stage — 85
 Double Dialogue — 87
 Experience of Existence — 89
 Common World — 92
 Emotions of the Liar — 94
 Trap — 96
 Political Reason — 99
 Evil Demon — 102
 Victory — 104
 Victor's Demon — 106

C. Going Astray in the Element of the Good — 109
 1. Evil in the Domain of Dialogue — 113
  The Flight of Man from Man — 114
  Evil and Misfortune — 119
  Dialogical Evil — 121
  Summary — 125
 2. Enslavement to Fear — 126
  The Basic Meaning of Threatening with Death — 127
  Enslavement through Suffering — 136
  Threat of Condemnation — 142
  Limits of the Threat and Possibilities of Liberation — 144
 3. Evil in the Dialogue of Temptation — 147
  World: Promised Land — 148
   Human Lifeworld — 151
   Home — 156
   Workplace — 158
   Temple — 159
   Cemetery — 161
  Denied Land — 162
   Home as Hideout — 166
   Workplace as Drudgery — 168
   Abandoned Temples — 170
   Cemetery as a Seat of Specters — 171
   Temptation of the World — 172

Around Devotion and Betrayal	174
Flattery	176
Accusing the Accusers	177
Neighboring the Demonic	183
Deafening Pain	184
Evil Pulls In	186
CHAPTER 4 Space for Being-with the Other	191
Function of the Name	196
Place of the Name	199
Structure of the Horizon of Communing	202
Research Perspectives	207
CHAPTER 5 The Last Word of the Drama	211
Condemnation	213
Aesthetic Condemnation	214
Political Condemnation	215
Religious Condemnation	217
Justification	218
Notes	221
Name Index	227
Extended Table of Contents	229

JÓZEF TISCHNER (1931–2000) was one of the most influential Polish philosophers of the twentieth century and the semi-official chaplain of Solidarność. He was a Roman Catholic priest, served as professor at the Pontifical Theological Academy in Krakow, and was a cofounder of the Institut für die Wissenschaften vom Menschen in Vienna.

ARTUR ROSMAN is an associate research professor at the University of Notre Dame and the editor-in-chief of *Church Life Journal*.